Classics of Western Thought

Classics of Western Thought

UNDER THE GENERAL EDITORSHIP OF
Thomas H. Greer
MICHIGAN STATE UNIVERSITY

I. The Ancient World

EDITED BY *Stebelton H. Nulle*
MICHIGAN STATE UNIVERSITY

II. Middle Ages, Renaissance, and Reformation

EDITED BY *Karl F. Thompson*
MICHIGAN STATE UNIVERSITY

III. The Modern World

EDITED BY *Charles Hirschfeld*
RICHMOND COLLEGE, CITY
UNIVERSITY OF NEW YORK

EDITED BY

Karl F. Thompson

MICHIGAN STATE UNIVERSITY

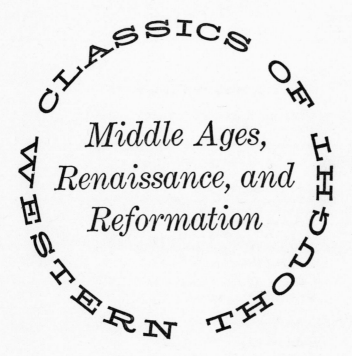

CLASSICS OF WESTERN THOUGHT

*Middle Ages,
Renaissance, and
Reformation*

Harcourt, Brace & World, Inc.

New York / Chicago / San Francisco / Atlanta

General Introduction

The editors of this three-volume series strongly believe that the best means of introducing students to their humanistic heritage is through a selection of original writings by the great minds of the Western tradition. It is for this purpose that we have brought together what we regard as classics of the Western tradition—of Western *thought,* in the broad sense. This collection of primary documents is intended for use in college-level courses in humanities or in the history of civilization, normally in company with a brief narrative text. One such text designed especially for use with these volumes is Thomas H. Greer's *A Brief History of Western Man* (Harcourt, Brace & World, 1968).

The volume and range of documents in Western civilization are, of course, enormous, and good reasons can always be advanced for making one selection over another. We have decided to restrict our own choice to what is truly *classic,* that is to say, valuable both for its intrinsic merit and for having exerted a paramount influence on its own and later times. We have, therefore, selected writings that reveal judgment applied to observation and that display creative thought and literary skill. In deciding upon the length and quantity of selections, we have aimed to keep in balance two purposes: to make each document *long enough* to give a substantial view of the author's ideas and to offer, at the same time, a substantial *number* of the foremost writers. (In a few instances we have omitted a familiar classic because the full text is readily available in satisfactory and inexpensive paperback editions, as for example, Homer's *Iliad*.)

The documents appear for the most part in chronological order and are arranged in three manageable volumes: *The Ancient World* (Volume One); *Middle Ages, Renaissance, and Reformation* (Volume Two); and *The Modern World* (Volume Three). Each document is introduced by a brief account of the author's life, of his role in the shaping of the Western tradition, and of the significance of the particular work. As in the selection of the writings themselves, we have kept student and teacher continually in mind.

We believe that the chief merit of these volumes is that they are guided by our aggregate experience of many years in the classroom— teaching college and university courses in humanities and in the history of civilization.

THOMAS H. GREER

January, 1964

Preface

This volume of *Classics of Western Thought* presents some of the more significant achievements of Western culture during the period following the decline of classical civilization and extending into the beginning of the modern era, that is, the period from 500 to 1600 A.D. The readings are arranged in chronological order, save for occasional rearrangements that respect the traditional divisions of Western history into Middle Ages, Renaissance, and Reformation.

During the early Middle Ages, Europe struggled to evolve its own distinctive civilization, and, by the year 1000, it had succeeded in developing a culture with certain marked characteristics. Men of the Middle Ages saw their world as a marvelously intricate but orderly arrangement, by which everyone was assigned a place and function in society in accordance with God's will. We remember this era as the Age of Faith, envy its spiritual stability, and admire the subtlety of its philosophy which, under the tutelage of Aristotle, deduced from the revealed truths of Christianity the harmonious interplay of cause and effect everywhere in God's creation. The noble aspirations of chivalry we can still admire, and we honor the medieval conception, inspired by the dual heritage of Rome and Christianity, of a universal Christian empire. The harsh actualities of medieval life contrasted with the ideals of the age, and these, too, were graphically depicted by contemporary writers. Sure that the world was a place of trial and testing, medieval man was equally certain that, to use the words of Dante, the greatest of medieval poets, "In His will is our peace."

By the fifteenth century, the form and content of Western culture were again being reshaped, and the medieval world and its ideals began to give place to the modern. This period of transition, known as the Renaissance, was an age of discovery, in which, paradoxically, changes often resulted from a diligent, scholarly examination of the literature and philosophy of the ancient world. Writers, scholars, and artists, with an increased sense of individualism, rejected medieval habits of mind and strove to emulate the cultural achievements of Greece and Rome. (In connection with the Renaissance selections, we suggest that students also read a Shakespearean tragedy, readily available in inexpensive editions.)

The sixteenth century brought the Reformation and, with it, the dissolution of the Christian unity of the Middle Ages. During this period the foundations of modern Protestantism were laid, while the Roman Church corrected abuses but reasserted the truth of its dogma and the soundness of its organization. Many of the salient points of the religious controversy are set forth in the selections from Calvin, Luther, and St. Ignatius of Loyola.

By 1600, the end of the period covered by this volume, the changes wrought by the Renaissance and Reformation had been pretty well assimilated into Western art, thought, and life.

KARL F. THOMPSON

January, 1964

Contents

Classics of Western Thought

St. Benedict of Nursia

1

Rule of St. Benedict

Western Christian monasticism, as a movement, had as its ideal the preparation of the soul for the hereafter. This was accomplished by establishing a community life for the monks in accordance with Christ's precepts; thus they withdrew from the world in order to pray for it. The leading figure in the origin and growth of this movement was St. Benedict of Nursia (*ca.* 480–*ca.* 543). As a young man, St. Benedict fled from the immorality of Rome and for three years led a life of solitary contemplation, prayer, and strict austerity in a lonely hillside cave. Impressed by his devoutness and sincerity, the members of an ascetic religious community persuaded him to become their governor. They proved undependable and ungovernable, however; and St. Benedict, with a few chosen disciples, established a monastery on Monte Cassino, midway between Rome and Naples. This foundation has been associated ever since with his name and has been one of the chief centers of the religious life of western Europe. The monastery (in the Western sense of a community of work and prayer) found a model here, and the Rule, reflecting St. Benedict's mature spiritual wisdom, became a guide for monasticism as it developed into a major institution of medieval Europe.

Judged by the standards of its day, the Rule did not prescribe a life of excessive austerity. This wise discretion, recognizing both the strength of men's idealism and the limits of their physical capacities, colors the Rule and accounts in no small measure for its success. St. Benedict believed in a communal discipline that would help the individual monk live according to his vows of poverty, chastity, and obedience; and that would also permit him time to work in the fields and shops of the monastery, and to read and study. St. Benedict's precepts were binding on the abbot

St. Benedict of Nursia, *The Rule of St. Benedict,* in *Select Historical Documents of the Middle Ages,* trans. and ed. Ernest F. Henderson (London: Bell, 1896), 274–77, 279–81, 283, 289, 294, 297–99, 302–05.

as well as on the monks. The monastery thus became, under the Rule of St. Benedict, a self-sufficient community whose primary aim was service to God through work and prayer.

We are about to found, therefore, a school for the Lord's service; in the organization of which we trust that we shall ordain nothing severe and nothing burdensome. But even if, the demands of justice dictating it, something a little irksome shall be the result, for the purpose of amending vices or preserving charity; thou shalt not therefore, struck by fear, flee the way of salvation which can not be entered upon except through a narrow entrance. But as one's way of life and one's faith progresses, the heart becomes broadened, and, with the unutterable sweetness of love, the way of the mandates of the Lord is traversed. Thus, never departing from His guidance, continuing in the monastery in His teaching until death, through patience we are made partakers in Christ's passion in order that we may merit to be companions in His kingdom.

. . .

WHAT THE ABBOT SHOULD BE LIKE

An abbot who is worthy to preside over a monastery ought always to remember what he is called, and carry out with his deeds the name of a Superior. For he is believed to be Christ's representative, since he is called by His name, the apostle saying: "Ye have received the spirit of adoption of sons, whereby we call Abba, Father." And so the abbot should not—grant that he may not—teach, or decree, or order, anything apart from the precept of the Lord; but his order or teaching should be sprinkled with the ferment of divine justice in the minds of his disciples. Let the abbot always be mindful that, at the tremendous judgment of God, both things will be weighed in the balance: his teaching and the obedience of his disciples. And let the abbot know that whatever the father of the family finds of less utility among the sheep is laid to the fault of the shepherd. Only in a case where the whole diligence of their pastor shall have been bestowed on an unruly and disobedient flock, and his whole care given to their morbid actions, shall that pastor, absolved in the judgment of the Lord, be free to say to the Lord with the prophet: "I have not hid Thy righteousness within my heart, I have declared Thy faithfulness and Thy salvation, but they despising have scorned me." And then at length let the punishment for the disobedient sheep under his care be death itself prevailing against them. Therefore when any one receives the name of abbot, he ought to rule over his disciples with a double teaching; that is, let him show forth all good and holy things by deeds more than by words. So that to ready disciples he may propound the mandates of God in words; but, to the hard-hearted and the more simple-minded, he may show forth the divine precepts by his deeds. . . . He shall make no distinction of persons in the monastery. One shall not be more cherished than another, unless it be the one whom he finds excelling in good works or in obedience. A freeborn man shall not be preferred to one coming from servitude, unless there be some other reasonable cause. But if, justice demanding that it should be thus, it seems good to the abbot, he shall do this no matter what the rank shall be. But otherwise they shall keep their own places; for whether we be bond or free we are all one in Christ; and, under one God, we perform an equal service of subjection; for God is no respecter of persons. Only in this way is a distinction made by Him concerning us: if we are found humble and surpassing others in good works. Therefore let him (the abbot) have equal charity for all: let the same discipline be administered in all cases according to merit. In his teaching indeed the abbot ought always to observe that form laid down by the apostle when he says: "reprove, rebuke, exhort." That is, mixing seasons with seasons, blandishments with terrors, let him display the feeling of a severe yet devoted master. He should, namely, rebuke more severely the unruly and the turbulent. The obedient, moreover, and the gentle and the patient, he should exhort, that they may progress to higher things. But the negligent and scorners, we warn him to admonish and reprove. Nor let him conceal the sins of the erring: but, in order that he may prevail, let him pluck them out by the roots as soon as they begin to spring up; being mindful of the danger of Eli the priest of Shiloh. And the more honest and intelligent minds, indeed, let him rebuke with words, with a first or second admonition; but the wicked and the hard-hearted and the proud, or the disobedient, let him restrain at the very beginning of their sin by castigation of the body, as it were, with whips: knowing that it is written: "A fool is not bettered by words." And again: "Strike thy son with the rod and thou shalt deliver his soul from death." The abbot ought always to remember what he is, to remember what he is called, and to know that from him to whom more is committed, the more is demanded.

. . .

CONCERNING OBEDIENCE

The first grade of humility is obedience without delay. This becomes those who, on account of the holy service which they have professed, or on account of the fear of hell or the glory of eternal life consider nothing dearer to them than Christ: so that, so soon as anything is commanded by their superior, they may not know how to suffer delay in doing it, even as if it were a divine command. Concerning whom the Lord said: "As soon as he heard of me he obeyed me." And again he said to the learned men: "He who heareth you heareth me." Therefore let all such, straightway leaving their own affairs and giving up their own will, with unoccupied hands and leaving incomplete what they were doing—the foot of obedience being foremost,—follow with their deeds the voice of him who orders. And, as it were, in the same moment, let the aforesaid command of the master and the perfected work of the disciple—both together in the swiftness of the fear of God,—be called into being by those who are possessed with a desire of advancing to eternal life. And therefore let them seize the narrow way of which the Lord says: "Narrow is the way which leadeth unto life." Thus, not living according to their own judgment nor obeying their own desires and pleasures, but walking under another's judgment and command, passing their time in monasteries, let them desire an abbot to rule over them. Without doubt all such live up to that precept of the Lord in which he says: "I am not come to do my own will but the will of him that sent me." . . .

CONCERNING SILENCE

Let us do as the prophet says: "I said, I will take heed to my ways that I sin not with my tongue, I have kept my mouth with a bridle: I was dumb with silence, I held my peace even from good; and my sorrow was stirred." Here the prophet shows that if one ought at times, for the sake of silence, to refrain from good sayings; how much more, as a punishment for sin, ought one to cease from evil words. . . . And therefore, if anything is to be asked of the prior, let it be asked with all humility and subjection of reverence; lest one seem to speak more than is fitting. Scurrilities, however, or idle words and those exciting laughter, we condemn in all places with a lasting prohibition: nor do we permit a disciple to open his mouth for such sayings.

CONCERNING HUMILITY

. . . The sixth grade of humility is that a monk be contented with all lowliness or extremity, and consider himself, with regard to everything which is enjoined on him, as a poor and unworthy workman; saying to himself with the prophet: "I was reduced to nothing and was ignorant; I was made as the cattle before thee, and I am always with thee." The seventh grade of humility is not only that he, with his tongue, pronounce himself viler and more worthless than all; but that he also believe it in the innermost workings of his heart; humbling himself and saying with the prophet, etc. . . . The eighth degree of humility is that a monk do nothing except what the common rule of the monastery, or the example of his elders, urges him to do. The ninth degree of humility is that a monk restrain his tongue from speaking; and, keeping silence, do not speak until he is spoken to. The tenth grade of humility is that he be not ready, and easily inclined, to laugh. . . . The eleventh grade of humility is that a monk, when he speaks, speak slowly and without laughter, humbly with gravity, using few and reasonable words; and that he be not loud of voice. . . . The twelfth grade of humility is that a monk, shall not only with his heart but also with his body, always show humility to all who see him: that is, when at work, in the oratory, in the monastery, in the garden, on the road, in the fields. And everywhere, sitting or walking or standing, let him always be with head inclined, his looks fixed upon the ground; remembering every hour that he is guilty of his sins. Let him think that he is already being presented before the tremendous judgment of God, saying always to himself in his heart what that publican of the gospel, fixing his eyes on the earth, said, "Lord I am not worthy, I a sinner, so much as to lift up mine eyes unto Heaven."

· · ·

HOW DIVINE SERVICE SHALL BE HELD THROUGH THE DAY

As the prophet says: "Seven times in the day do I praise Thee." Which sacred number of seven will thus be fulfilled by us if, at matins, at the first, third, sixth, ninth hours, at vesper time and at "completorium" we perform the duties of our service; for it is of these hours of the day that he said: "Seven times in the day do I praise Thee." For, concerning nocturnal vigils, the same prophet says: "At midnight I arose to confess unto thee." Therefore, at these times, let us give thanks to our Creator concerning the judgments of his righteousness; that is, at matins, etc. . . . , and at night we will rise and confess to him.

· · ·

WHETHER THE MONKS SHOULD HAVE ANYTHING OF THEIR OWN

More than anything else is this special vice to be cut off root and branch from the monastery, that one should presume to give or receive anything without the order of the abbot, or should have anything of his own. He should have absolutely not anything: neither a book, nor tablets, nor a pen—nothing at all.—For indeed it is not allowed to the monks to have their own bodies or wills in their own power. But all things necessary they must expect from the Father of the monastery; nor is it allowable to have anything which the abbot did not give or permit. All things shall be common to all, as it is written: "Let not any man presume or call anything his own." But if anyone shall have been discovered delighting in this most evil vice: being warned once and again, if he do not amend, let him be subjected to punishment.

WHETHER ALL OUGHT TO RECEIVE NECESSARIES EQUALLY

As it is written: "It was divided among them singly, according as each had need": whereby we do not say—far from it—that there should be an excepting of persons, but a consideration for infirmities. Wherefore he who needs less, let him thank God and not be dismayed; but he who needs more, let him be humiliated on account of his infirmity, and not exalted on account of the mercy that is shown him. And thus all members will be in peace. Above all, let not the evil of murmuring appear, for any cause, through any word or sign whatever. But, if such a murmurer is discovered, he shall be subjected to stricter discipline.

. . .

THAT AFTER "COMPLETORIUM" NO ONE SHALL SPEAK

At all times the monks ought to practise silence, but most of all in the nocturnal hours. And thus at all times, whether of fasting or of eating: if it be meal-time, as soon as they have risen from the table, all shall sit together and one shall read selections or lives of the Fathers, or indeed anything which will edify the hearers. But not the Pentateuch or Kings; for, to weak intellects, it will be of no use at that hour to hear this part of Scripture; but they shall be read at other times. But if the days are fast days, when Vespers have been said, after a short interval they shall come to the reading of the selections as we have said; and four or five pages, or as much as the hour permits having been read, they shall all congregate, upon the cessation of the reading. If, by chance, anyone is occupied in a task assigned to him, he shall nevertheless approach. All therefore being gathered together, they shall say the completing prayer; and, going out from the "completorium," there shall be no further opportunity for anyone to say anything. But if anyone be found acting contrary to this rule of silence, he shall be subjected to a very severe punishment. Unless a necessity in the shape of guests should arise, or the abbot, by chance, should give some order. But even this, indeed, he shall do most seriously, with all gravity and moderation.

. . .

CONCERNING THE DAILY MANUAL LABOUR

Idleness is the enemy of the soul. And therefore, at fixed times, the brothers ought to be occupied in manual labour; and again, at fixed times, in sacred reading. Therefore we believe that, according to this disposition, both seasons ought to be arranged; so that, from Easter until the Calends of October, going out early, from the first until the fourth hour they shall do what labour may be necessary. Moreover, from the fourth hour until about the sixth, they shall be free for reading. After the meal of the sixth hour, moreover, rising from table, they shall rest in their beds with all silence; or, perchance, he that wishes to read may so read to himself that he do not disturb another. And the nona (the second meal) shall be gone through with more moderately about the middle of the eighth hour; and again they shall work at what is to be done until Vespers. But, if the exigency or poverty of the place demands that they be occupied by themselves in picking fruits, they shall not be dismayed: for then they are truly monks if they live by the labours of their hands; as did also our fathers and the apostles. Let all things be done with moderation, however, on account of the faint-hearted. From the Calends of October, moreover, until the beginning of Lent they shall be free for reading until the second full hour. At the second hour the tertia (morning service) shall be held, and all shall labour at the task which is enjoined upon them until the ninth. The first signal, moreover, of the ninth hour having been given, they shall each one leave off his work; and be ready when the second signal strikes. Moreover after the refection they shall be free for their readings or for psalms. But in the days of Lent, from dawn until the third full hour, they shall be free for their readings; and, until the tenth full hour, they shall do the labour that is enjoined on them. In which days of Lent they shall all receive separate books from the library; which they shall read entirely through in order. These books are to be given out on the first day of Lent. Above all there shall certainly be appointed one or two elders, who shall go round the monastery at the hours in which the brothers are engaged in reading, and see to it that no troublesome brother chance to be found who is open to idleness and trifling, and is not intent on his reading; being not only of no use to himself, but also stirring up others. If such a one—may it not happen—be found, he shall be admonished once and a second time. If he do not amend, he shall be subject under the Rule to such punishment that the others may have fear. Nor shall brother join brother at unsuitable hours. Moreover on Sunday all shall engage in reading; excepting those who are deputed to various duties. But if anyone be so negligent and lazy that he will not or can not read, some task shall be imposed upon him which he can do; so that he be not idle. On feeble or delicate brothers such a labour or art is to be imposed, that they shall neither be idle, nor shall they be so oppressed by the violence of labour as to be driven to take flight. Their weakness is to be taken into consideration by the abbot.

Although at all times the life of the monk should be such as though Lent were being observed: nevertheless, since few have that virtue, we urge that, on those said days of Lent, he shall keep his life in all purity; and likewise wipe out, in those holy days, the negligencies of other times. This is then worthily done if we refrain from all vices, if we devote ourselves to prayer with weeping, to reading and compunction of heart, and to abstinence. Therefore, on these days, let us add of ourselves something to the ordinary amount of our service: special prayers, abstinence from food and drink;—so that each one, over and above the amount allotted to him, shall offer of his own will something to God with rejoicing of the Holy Spirit. That is, he shall restrict his body in food, drink, sleep, talkativeness, and merry-making; and, with the joy of a spiritual desire, shall await the holy Easter. The offering, moreover, that each one makes, he shall announce to his abbot; that it may be done with his prayers and by his will. For what is done without the permission of the spiritual Father, shall be put down to presumption and vain glory, and not to a monk's credit. Therefore all things are to be done according to the will of the abbot.

· · ·

CONCERNING THE TABLE OF THE ABBOT

The table of the abbot shall always be with the guests and pilgrims. As often, however, as guests are lacking, it shall be in his power to summon those of the brothers whom he wishes. He shall see, nevertheless, that one or two elders are always left with the brothers, for the sake of discipline.

CONCERNING THE ARTIFICERS OF THE MONASTERY

Artificers, if there are any in the monastery, shall practise with all humility their special arts, if the abbot permit it. But if any one of them becomes inflated with pride on account of knowledge of his art, to the extent that he seems to be conferring something on the monastery: such a one shall be plucked away from that art; and he shall not again return to it unless the abbot perchance again orders him to, he being humiliated. But, if anything from the works of the artificers is to be sold, they themselves shall take care through whose hands they (the works) are to pass, lest they (the intermediaries) presume to commit some fraud upon the monastery. They shall always remember Ananias and Sapphira; lest, perchance, the death that they suffered with regard to the body, these, or all those who have committed any fraud as to the property of the monastery, may suffer with regard to the soul. In the prices themselves, moreover, let not the evil of avarice crop out: but let the object always be given a little cheaper than it is given by other and secular persons; so that, in all things, God shall be glorified.

CONCERNING THE MANNER OF RECEIVING BROTHERS

When any new comer applies for conversion, an easy entrance shall not be granted him: but, as the apostle says, "Try the spirits if they be of God." Therefore, if he who comes perseveres in knocking, and is seen after four or five days to patiently endure the insults inflicted upon him, and the difficulty of ingress, and to persist in his demand: entrance shall be allowed him, and he shall remain for a few days in the cell of the guests. After this, moreover, he shall be in the cell of the novices, where he shall meditate and eat and sleep. And an elder shall be detailed off for him who shall be capable of saving souls, who shall altogether intently watch over him, and make it a care to see if he reverently seek God, if he be zealous in the service of God, in obedience, in suffering shame. And all the harshness and roughness of the means through which God is approached shall be told him in advance. If he promise perseverance in his steadfastness, after the lapse of two months this Rule shall be read to him in order, and it shall be said to him: Behold the law under which thou dost wish to serve; if thou canst observe it, enter; but if thou canst not, depart freely. If he have stood firm thus far, then he shall be led into the aforesaid cell of the novices; and again he shall be proven with all patience. And, after the lapse of six months, the Rule shall be read to him; that he may know upon what he is entering. And, if he stand firm thus far, after four months the same Rule shall again be re-read to him. And if, having deliberated with himself, he shall promise to keep everything, and to obey all the commands that are laid upon him: then he shall be received in the congregation; knowing that it is decreed, by the law of the Rule, that from that day he shall not be allowed to depart from the monastery, nor to shake free his neck from the yoke of the Rule, which, after such tardy deliberation, he was at liberty either to refuse or receive. He who is to be received, moreover, shall, in the oratory, in the presence of all, make promise concerning his steadfastness and the change in his manner of life and his obedience to God and to His saints; so that if, at any time, he act contrary, he shall know that he shall be condemned by Him whom he mocks. Concerning which promise he shall make a petition in the name of the saints whose relics are there, and of the abbot who is present. Which petition he shall write with his own hand. Or, if he really be not learned in letters, another, being asked by him, shall write it. And that novice shall make his sign; and with his own hand shall place it (the petition) above the altar. And when he has placed it there, the novice shall straightway commence this verse: "Receive me oh Lord according to thy promise and I shall live, and do not cast me down from my hope." Which verse the whole congregation shall repeat three times, adding: "Glory be to the Father." Then that brother novice shall prostrate himself at the feet of each one, that they may pray for him. And, already, from that day, he shall be considered as in the congregation. If he have any property, he shall either first present it to the poor, or, making a solemn donation, shall confer it on the monastery, keeping nothing at all for himself: as one, forsooth, who from that day, shall know that he shall not have power even over his own body. Straightway, therefore in the oratory, he shall take off his own garments in which he was clad, and shall put on the garments of the monastery. Moreover those garments which he has taken off shall be placed in the vestiary to be preserved; so that if, at any time, the devil persuading him, he shall consent to go forth from the monastery—may it not happen,—

then, taking off the garments of the monastery, he may be cast out. That petition of his, nevertheless, which the abbot took from above the altar, he shall not receive again; but it shall be preserved in the monastery.

CONCERNING THE SONS OF NOBLES OR OF POOR MEN WHO ARE PRESENTED

If by chance any one of the nobles offers his son to God in the monastery: if the boy himself is a minor in age, his parents shall make the petition which we spoke of above. And, with an oblation, they shall enwrap that petition and the hand of the boy in the linen cloth of the altar; and thus they shall offer him. Concerning their property, moreover, either they shall promise in the present petition, under an oath, that they will never, either through some chosen person, or in any way whatever, give him anything at any time, or furnish him with the means of possessing it. Or, indeed, if they be not willing to do this, and wish to offer something as alms to the monastery for their salvation, they shall make a donation of the things which they wish to give to the monastery; retaining for themselves, if they wish, the usufruct. And let all things be so observed that no suspicion may remain with the boy; by which being deceived he might perish—which God forbid,—as we have learned by experience. The poorer ones shall also do likewise. Those, however, who have nothing at all shall simply make their petition; and, with an oblation, shall offer their son before witnesses.

2

The Song of Roland

The Song of Roland is probably the best example of the *chanson de geste,* or tale of exploits and adventure, popular in the Middle Ages. Written down some three hundred years after the events it purports to describe, *The Song of Roland* was probably composed and recited by the professional entertainers, or jongleurs, operating along the pilgrim route to the shrine of St. James at Compostella in northwestern Spain. Its connection with history is tenuous, although Charlemagne did campaign in northern Spain in 778 and, on his return to France, suffered the loss of the rear guard of his army, ambushed at Roncesvalles in the Pyrenees. The poem tells of the deeds of Roland, Charlemagne's vassal, who commands the rear guard on this campaign. Roland was put in command at the suggestion of Guenelun, a jealous traitor in league with the Saracen king Marsile, whose forces carry out the ambush. Oliver, Roland's companion-in-arms, thrice urges Roland to sound the horn Oliphant for aid, but Roland's pride forbids him to do so until it is too late. Summoned at last by Roland's horn, Charlemagne returns and destroys the Saracen army (after God, in response to Charlemagne's prayer, has ordered the sun to stand still to allow the emperor sufficient daylight). Guenelun afterward offers the specious defense that he wanted revenge on Roland but did not intend treachery against the emperor. However, his guilt is proved in trial by combat, and he is duly executed. The poem closes with Charlemagne's dream, in which God commands him to prepare for further battles against the forces of Islam.

The excerpt presented here is the climax of the poem—the death of Roland. Inevitably, the epic evokes comparisons with the *Iliad:* like Achilles, Roland embodies the ideals of his age, and his stubborn rashness and pride cause the death of his friend and disaster for many others. Al-

From the book *The Song of Roland,* translated by C. K. Scott Moncrieff. Published by E. P. Dutton & Co., Inc. [New York, 1931] and reprinted with their permission. [Pp. 56–78.]

13

though *The Song of Roland,* unlike the *Iliad,* is oversimple in characterization, its color and symbolism and its vigorous language (which the
present translation admirably recaptures) convey the qualities that gave
feudalism its vitality: a sense of religious mission in the war against evil,
high regard for personal honor, and mutual loyalty of vassal and overlord.

CXXIX

Then says Rollanz: "I'll wind this olifant,
If Charlès hear, where in the pass he stands,
I pledge you now they will return, the Franks."
Says Oliver: "Great shame would come of that;
And a reproach on every one, your clan,
That shall endure while each lives in the land,
When I implored, you would not do this act;
Doing it now, no praise from me you'll have:
So wind your horn, but not by courage rash,
Seeing that both your arms with blood are splashed."
Answers that count: "Fine blows I've struck them back."

CXXX

Then says Rollant: "Strong is it now, our battle;
I'll wind my horn, so the King hears it, Charlès."
Says Oliver: "That act were not a vassal's.
When I implored you, comrade, you were wrathful.
Were the King here, we had not borne such damage.
Nor should we blame those with him there, his army."
Says Oliver: "Now by my beard, hereafter
If I may see my gentle sister Alde,
She in her arms, I swear, shall never clasp you."

CXXXI

Then says Rollanz: "Wherefore so wroth with me?"
He answers him: "Comrade, it was your deed:
Vassalage comes by sense, and not by folly;
Prudence more worth is than stupidity.

Here are Franks dead, all for your trickery;
No service more to Carlun may we yield.
My lord were here now, had you trusted me,
And fought and won this battle then had we,
Taken or slain were the king Marsilie.
In your prowess, Rollanz, no good we've seen!
Charlès the great in vain your aid will seek—
None such as he till God His Judgement speak;—
Here must you die, and France in shame be steeped;
Here perishes our loyal company,
Before this night great severance and grief."

CXXXII

That Archbishop has heard them, how they spoke,
His horse he pricks with his fine spurs of gold,
Coming to them he takes up his reproach:
"Sir Oliver, and you, Sir Rollant, both,
For God I pray, do not each other scold!
No help it were to us, the horn to blow,
But, none the less, it may be better so;
The King will come, with vengeance that he owes;
These Spanish men never away shall go.
Our Franks here, each descending from his horse,
Will find us dead, and limb from body torn;
They'll take us hence, on biers and litters borne;
With pity and with grief for us they'll mourn;
They'll bury each in some old minster-close;
No wolf nor swine nor dog shall gnaw our bones."
Answers Rollant: "Sir, very well you spoke."

CXXXIII

Rollant hath set the olifant to his mouth,
He grasps it well, and with great virtue sounds.
High are those peaks, afar it rings and loud,
Thirty great leagues they hear its echoes mount.
So Charlès heard, and all his comrades round;
Then said that King: "Battle they do, our counts."
And Guenelun answered, contrarious:
"That were a lie, in any other mouth."

CXXXIV

The Count Rollanz, with sorrow and with pangs,
And with great pain sounded his olifant:
Out of his mouth the clear blood leaped and ran,
About his brain the very temples cracked.
Loud is its voice, that horn he holds in hand;
Charlès hath heard, where in the pass he stands,
And Neimès hears, and listen all the Franks.
Then says the King: "I hear his horn, Rollant's;
He'ld never sound, but he were in combat."
Answers him Guenes: "It is no battle, that.
Now are you old, blossoming white and blanched,
Yet by such words you still appear infant.
You know full well the great pride of Rollant;
Marvel it is, God stays so tolerant.
Noples he took, not waiting your command;
Thence issued forth the Sarrazins, a band
With vassalage had fought against Rollant;
He slew them first, with Durendal his brand,
Then washed their blood with water from the land;
So what he'd done might not be seen of man.
He for a hare goes all day, horn in hand;
Before his peers in foolish jest he brags.
No race neath heav'n in field him dare attack.
So canter on! Nay, wherefore hold we back?
Terra Major is far away, our land."

CXXXV

The count Rollanz, though blood his mouth doth stain,
And burst are both the temples of his brain,
His olifant he sounds with grief and pain;
Charlès hath heard, listen the Franks again.
"That horn," the King says, "hath a mighty strain!"
Answers Duke Niemes: "A baron blows with pain!
Battle is there, indeed I see it plain,
He is betrayed, by one that still doth feign.
Equip you, sir, cry out your old refrain,
That noble band, go succour them amain!
Enough you've heard how Rollant doth complain."

CXXXVI

That Emperour hath bid them sound their horns.
The Franks dismount, and dress themselves for war,
Put hauberks on, helmets and golden swords;
Fine shields they have, and spears of length and force;
Scarlat and blue and white their ensigns float.
His charger mounts each baron of the host;
They spur with haste as through the pass they go.
Nor was there one but thus to 's neighbour spoke:
"Now, ere he die, may we see Rollant, so
Ranged by his side we'll give some goodly blows."
But what avail? They've stayed too long below.

CXXXVII

That even-tide is light as was the day;
Their armour shines beneath the sun's clear ray,
Hauberks and helms throw off a dazzling flame,
And blazoned shields, flowered in bright array,
Also their spears, with golden ensigns gay.
That Emperour, he canters on with rage,
And all the Franks with wonder and dismay;
There is not one can bitter tears restrain,
And for Rollant they're very sore afraid.
The King has bid them seize that county Guene,
And charged with him the scullions of his train;
The master-cook he's called, Besgun by name:
"Guard me him well, his felony is plain,
Who in my house vile treachery has made."
He holds him, and a hundred others takes
From the kitchen, both good and evil knaves;
Then Guenè's beard and both his cheeks they shaved,
And four blows each with their closed fists they gave,
They trounced him well with cudgels and with staves,
And on his neck they clasped an iron chain;
So like a bear enchained they held him safe,
On a pack-mule they set him in his shame:
Kept him till Charles should call for him again.

CXXXVIII

High were the peaks and shadowy and grand,
The valleys deep, the rivers swiftly ran.
Trumpets they blew in rear and in the van,
Till all again answered that olifant.
That Emperour canters with fury mad,
And all the Franks dismay and wonder have;
There is not one but weeps and waxes sad
And all pray God that He will guard Rollant
Till in the field together they may stand;
There by his side they'll strike as well they can.
But what avail? No good there is in that;
They're not in time; too long have they held back.

CXXXIX

In his great rage on canters Charlemagne;
Over his sark his beard is flowing plain.
Barons of France, in haste they spur and strain;
There is not one that can his wrath contain
That they are not with Rollant the Captain,
Whereas he fights the Sarrazins of Spain.
If he be struck, will not one soul remain.
—God! Sixty men are all now in his train!
Never a king had better Capitains.

CXLIII

But what avail? Though fled be Marsilies,
He's left behind his uncle, the alcaliph
Who holds Alferne, Kartagene, Garmalie,
And Ethiope, a cursèd land indeed;
The blackamoors from there are in his keep,
Broad in the nose they are and flat in the ear,
Fifty thousand and more in company.
These canter forth with arrogance and heat,
Then they cry out the pagans' rallying-cheer;
And Rollant says: "Martyrdom we'll receive;
Not long to live, I know it well, have we;

Felon he's named that sells his body cheap!
Strike on, my lords, with burnished swords and keen;
Contest each inch your life and death between,
That ne'er by us Douce France in shame be steeped.
When Charles my lord shall come into this field,
Such discipline of Sarrazins he'll see,
For one of ours he'll find them dead fifteen;
He will not fail, but bless us all in peace."

CXLIV

When Rollant sees those misbegotten men,
Who are more black than ink is on the pen
With no part white, only their teeth except,
Then says that count: "I know now very well
That here to die we're bound, as I can tell.
Strike on, the Franks! For so I recommend."
Says Oliver: "Who holds back, is condemned!"
Upon those words, the Franks to strike again.

CXLV

Franks are but few; which, when the pagans know,
Among themselves comfort and pride they shew;
Says each to each: "Wrong was that Emperor."
Their alcaliph upon a sorrel rode,
And pricked it well with both his spurs of gold;
Struck Oliver, behind, on the back-bone,
His hauberk white into his body broke,
Clean through his breast the thrusting spear he drove;
After he said: "You've borne a mighty blow.
Charlès the great should not have left you so;
He's done us wrong, small thanks to him we owe;
I've well avenged all ours on you alone."

CXLVI

Oliver feels that he to die is bound,
Holds Halteclere, whose steel is rough and brown,
Strikes the alcaliph on his helm's golden mount;

Flowers and stones fall clattering to the ground,
Slices his head, to th'small teeth in his mouth;
So brandishes his blade and flings him down;
After he says: "Pagan, accurst be thou!
Thou'lt never say that Charles forsakes me now;
Nor to thy wife, nor any dame thou'st found,
Thou'lt never boast, in lands where thou wast crowned,
One pennyworth from me thou'st taken out,
Nor damage wrought on me nor any around."
After, for aid, "Rollant!" he cries aloud.

CXLVII

Oliver feels that death is drawing nigh;
To avenge himself he hath no longer time;
Through the great press most gallantly he strikes,
He breaks their spears, their buckled shields doth slice,
Their feet, their fists, their shoulders and their sides,
Dismembers them: whoso had seen that sight,
Dead in the field one on another piled,
Remember well a vassal brave he might.
Charlè's ensign he'll not forget it quite;
Aloud and clear "Monjoie" again he cries.
To call Rollanz, his friend and peer, he tries:
"My companion, come hither to my side.
With bitter grief we must us now divide."

CXLVIII

Then Rollant looked upon Olivier's face;
Which was all wan and colourless and pale,
While the clear blood, out of his body sprayed,
Upon the ground gushed forth and ran away.
"God!" said that count, "What shall I do or say?
My companion, gallant for such ill fate!
Ne'er shall man be, against thee could prevail.
Ah! France the Douce, henceforth art thou made waste
Of vassals brave, confounded and disgraced!
Our Emperour shall suffer damage great."
And with these words upon his horse he faints.

CXLIX

You'd seen Rollant aswoon there in his seat,
And Oliver, who unto death doth bleed,
So much he's bled, his eyes are dim and weak;
Nor clear enough his vision, far or near,
To recognise whatever man he sees;
His companion, when each the other meets,
Above the helm jewelled with gold he beats,
Slicing it down from there to the nose-piece,
But not his head; he's touched not brow nor cheek.
At such a blow Rollant regards him keen,
And asks of him, in gentle tones and sweet:
"To do this thing, my comrade, did you mean?
This is Rollanz, who ever held you dear;
And no mistrust was ever us between."
Says Oliver: "Now can I hear you speak;
I see you not: may the Lord God you keep!
I struck you now: and for your pardon plead."
Answers Rollanz: "I am not hurt, indeed;
I pardon you, before God's Throne and here."
Upon these words, each to the other leans;
And in such love you had their parting seen.

CL

Oliver feels death's anguish on him now;
And in his head his two eyes swimming round;
Nothing he sees; he hears not any sound;
Dismounting then, he kneels upon the ground,
Proclaims his sins both firmly and aloud,
Clasps his two hands, heavenwards holds them out,
Prays God himself in Paradise to allow;
Blessings on Charles, and on Douce France he vows,
And his comrade, Rollanz, to whom he's bound.
Then his heart fails; his helmet nods and bows;
Upon the earth he lays his whole length out:
And he is dead, may stay no more, that count.
Rollanz the brave mourns him with grief profound;
Nowhere on earth so sad a man you'd found.

CLI

So Rollant's friend is dead; whom when he sees
Face to the ground, and biting it with's teeth,
Begins to mourn in language very sweet:
"Unlucky, friend, your courage was indeed!
Together we have spent such days and years;
No harmful thing twixt thee and me has been.
Now thou art dead, and all my life a grief."
And with these words again he swoons, that chief,
Upon his horse, which he calls Veillantif;
Stirrups of gold support him underneath;
He cannot fall, whichever way he lean.

CLII

Soon as Rollant his senses won and knew,
Recovering and turning from that swoon.
Bitter great loss appeared there in his view:
Dead are the Franks; he'd all of them to lose,
Save the Archbishop, and save Gualter del Hum;
He is come down out of the mountains, who
Gainst Spanish men made there a great ado;
Dead are his men, for those the pagans slew;
Will he or nill, along the vales he flew,
And called Rollant, to bring him succour soon:
"Ah! Gentle count, brave soldier, where are you?
For by thy side no fear I ever knew.
Gualter it is, who conquered Maëlgut,
And nephew was to hoary old Droün;
My vassalage thou ever thoughtest good.
Broken my spear, and split my shield in two;
Gone is the mail that on my hauberk grew;
This body of mine eight lances have gone through;
I'm dying. Yet full price for life I took."
Rollant has heard these words and understood,
Has spurred his horse, and on towards him drew.

CLIII

Grief gives Rollanz intolerance and pride;
Through the great press he goes again to strike;
To slay a score of Spaniards he contrives,
Gualter has six, the Archbishop other five.
The pagans say: "Men, these, of felon kind!
Lordings, take care they go not hence alive!
Felon he's named that does not break their line,
Recreant, who lets them any safety find!"
And so once more begin the hue and cry,
From every part they come to break the line.

CLIV

Count Rollant is a noble and brave soldier,
Gualter del Hum's a right good chevalier,
That Archbishop hath shewn good prowess there;
None of them falls behind the other pair;
Through the great press, pagans they strike again.
Come on afoot a thousand Sarrazens,
And on horseback some forty thousand men.
But well I know, to approach they never dare;
Lances and spears they poise to hurl at them,
Arrows, barbs, darts and javelins in the air.
With the first flight they've slain our Gualtïer;
Turpin of Reims has all his shield broken,
And cracked his helm; he's wounded in the head,
From his hauberk the woven mail they tear,
In his body four spear-wounds doth he bear;
Beneath him too his charger's fallen dead.
Great grief it was, when that Archbishop fell.

CLV

Turpin of Reims hath felt himself undone,
Since that four spears have through his body come;
Nimble and bold upon his feet he jumps;
Looks for Rollant, and then towards him runs,
Saying this word: "I am not overcome.

While life remains, no good vassal gives up."
He's drawn Almace, whose steel was brown and rough,
Through the great press a thousand blows he's struck:
As Charlès said, quarter he gave to none;
He found him there, four hundred else among,
Wounded the most, speared through the middle some,
Also there were from whom the heads he'd cut:
So tells the tale, he that was there says thus,
The brave Saint Giles, whom God made marvellous,
Who charters wrote for th' Minster at Loüm;
Nothing he's heard that does not know this much.

CLVI

The count Rollanz has nobly fought and well,
But he is hot, and all his body sweats;
Great pain he has, and trouble in his head,
His temples burst when he the horn sounded;
But he would know if Charles will come to them,
Takes the olifant, and feebly sounds again.
That Emperour stood still and listened then:
"My lords," said he, "Right evilly we fare!
This day Rollanz, my nephew shall be dead:
I hear his horn, with scarcely any breath.
Nimbly canter, whoever would be there!
Your trumpets sound, as many as ye bear!"
Sixty thousand so loud together blare,
The mountains ring, the valleys answer them.
The pagans hear, they think it not a jest;
Says each to each: "Carlum doth us beset."

CLVII

The pagans say: "That Emperour's at hand,
We hear their sound, the trumpets of the Franks;
If Charlès come, great loss we then shall stand,
And wars renewed, unless we slay Rollant;
All Spain we'll lose, our own clear father-land."
Four hundred men of them in helmets stand;
The best of them that might be in their ranks

Make on Rollanz a grim and fierce attack;
Gainst these the count had well enough in hand.

CLVIII

The count Rollanz, when their approach he sees
Is grown so bold and manifest and fierce
So long as he's alive he will not yield.
He sits his horse, which men call Veillantif,
Pricking him well with golden spurs beneath,
Through the great press he goes, their line to meet,
And by his side is the Archbishop Turpin.
"Now, friend, begone!" say pagans, each to each;
"These Frankish men, their horns we plainly hear;
Charle is at hand, that King in Majesty."

CLIX

The count Rollanz has never loved cowards,
Nor arrogant, nor men of evil heart,
Nor chevalier that was not good vassal.
That Archbishop, Turpins, he calls apart:
"Sir, you're afoot, and I my charger have;
For love of you, here will I take my stand,
Together we'll endure things good and bad;
I'll leave you not, for no incarnate man:
We'll give again these pagans their attack;
The better blows are those from Durendal."
Says the Archbishop: "Shame on him that holds back!
Charle is at hand, full vengeance he'll exact."

CLX

The pagans say: "Unlucky were we born!
An evil day for us did this day dawn!
For we have lost our peers and all our lords.
Charles his great host once more upon us draws,
Of Frankish men we plainly hear the horns,
"Monjoie" they cry, and great is their uproar.
The count Rollant is of such pride and force
He'll never yield to man of woman born;

Let's aim at him, then leave him on the spot!"
And aim they did: with arrows long and short,
Lances and spears and feathered javelots;
Count Rollant's shield they've broken through and bored,
The woven mail have from his hauberk torn,
But not himself, they've never touched his corse;
Veillantif is in thirty places gored,
Beneath the count he's fallen dead, that horse.
Pagans are fled, and leave him on the spot;
The count Rollant stands on his feet once more.

CLXI

Pagans are fled, enangered and enraged,
Home into Spain with speed they make their way;
The count Rollanz, he has not given chase,
For Veillantif, his charger, they have slain;
Will he or nill, on foot he must remain.
To the Archbishop, Turpins, he goes with aid;
He's from his head the golden helm unlaced,
Taken from him his white hauberk away,
And cut the gown in strips, was round his waist;
On his great wounds the pieces of it placed,
Then to his heart has caught him and embraced;
On the green grass he has him softly laid,
Most sweetly then to him has Rollant prayed:
"Ah! Gentle sir, give me your leave, I say;
Our companions, whom we so dear appraised,
Are now all dead; we cannot let them stay;
I will go seek and bring them to this place,
Arrange them here in ranks, before your face."
Said the Archbishop: "Go, and return again.
This field is yours and mine now; God be praised!"

CLXII

So Rollanz turns; through the field, all alone,
Searching the vales and mountains, he is gone;
He finds Gerin, Gerers his companion,
Also he finds Berenger and Otton,

There too he finds Anséis and Sanson,
And finds Gerard the old, of Rossillon;
By one and one he's taken those barons,
To the Archbishop with each of them he comes,
Before his knees arranges every one.
That Archbishop, he cannot help but sob,
He lifts his hand, gives benediction;
After he's said: "Unlucky, Lords, your lot!
But all your souls He'll lay, our Glorious God,
In Paradise, His holy flowers upon!
For my own death such anguish now I've got;
I shall not see him, our rich Emperor."

CLXIII

So Rollant turns, goes through the field in quest;
His companion Olivier finds at length;
He has embraced him close against his breast,
To the Archbishop returns as he can best;
Upon a shield he's laid him, by the rest;
And the Archbishop has them absolved and blest:
Whereon his grief and pity grow afresh.
Then says Rollanz: "Fair comrade Olivier,
You were the son of the good count Reinier,
Who held the march by th' Vale of Runier;
To shatter spears, through buckled shields to bear,
And from hauberks the mail to break and tear,
Proof men to lead, and prudent counsel share,
Gluttons in field to frighten and conquer,
No land has known a better chevalier."

CLXIV

The count Rollanz, when dead he saw his peers,
And Oliver, he held so very dear,
Grew tender, and began to shed a tear;
Out of his face the colour disappeared;
No longer could he stand, for so much grief,
Will he or nill, he swooned upon the field.
Said the Archbishop: "Unlucky lord, indeed!"

CLXV

When the Archbishop beheld him swoon, Rollant,
Never before such bitter grief he'd had;
Stretching his hand, he took that olifant.
Through Rencesvals a little river ran;
He would go there, fetch water for Rollant.
Went step by step, to stumble soon began,
So feeble he is, no further fare he can,
For too much blood he's lost, and no strength has;
Ere he has crossed an acre of the land,
His heart grows faint, he falls down forwards and
Death comes to him with very cruel pangs.

CLXVI

The count Rollanz wakes from his swoon once more,
Climbs to his feet; his pains are very sore;
Looks down the vale, looks to the hills above;
On the green grass, beyond his companions,
He sees him lie, that noble old baron;
'Tis the Archbishop, whom in His name wrought God;
There he proclaims his sins, and looks above;
Joins his two hands, to Heaven holds them forth,
And Paradise prays God to him to accord.
Dead is Turpin, the warrior of Charlon.
In battles great and very rare sermons
Against pagans ever a champion.
God grant him now His Benediction!

CLXVII

The count Rollant sees the Archbishop lie dead,
Sees the bowels out of his body shed,
And sees the brains that surge from his forehead;
Between his two arm-pits, upon his breast,
Crossways he folds those hands so white and fair.
Then mourns aloud, as was the custom there:
"Thee, gentle sir, chevalier nobly bred,
To th' Glorious Celestial I commend;

Ne'er shall man be, that will Him serve so well;
Since the Apostles was never such prophet,
To hold the laws and draw the hearts of men.
Now may your soul no pain nor sorrow ken,
Finding the gates of Paradise open!"

CLXVIII

Then Rollanz feels that death to him draws near,
For all his brain is issued from his ears;
He prays to God that He will call the peers,
Bids Gabriel, the angel, t' himself appear.
Takes the olifant, that no reproach shall hear,
And Durendal in the other hand he wields;
Further than might a cross-bow's arrow speed
Goes towards Spain into a fallow-field;
Climbs on a cliff; where, under two fair trees,
Four terraces, of marble wrought, he sees.
There he falls down, and lies upon the green;
He swoons again, for death is very near.

CLXIX

High are the peaks, the trees are very high.
Four terraces of polished marble shine;
On the green grass count Rollant swoons thereby.
A Sarrazin him all the time espies,
Who feigning death among the others hides;
Blood hath his face and all his body dyed;
He gets afoot, running towards him hies;
Fair was he, strong and of a courage high;
A mortal hate he's kindled in his pride.
He's seized Rollant, and the arms, were at his side,
"Charlè's nephew," he's said, "here conquered lies.
To Araby I'll bear this sword as prize."
As he drew it, something the count descried.

CLXX

So Rollant felt his sword was taken forth,
Opened his eyes, and this word to him spoke:

"Thou'rt never one of ours, full well I know."
Took the olifant, that he would not let go,
Struck him on th' helm, that jewelled was with gold,
And broke its steel, his skull and all his bones,
Out of his head both the two eyes he drove;
Dead at his feet he has the pagan thrown:
After he's said: "Culvert, thou wert too bold,
Or right or wrong, of my sword seizing hold!
They'll dub thee fool, to whom the tale is told.
But my great one, my olifant I broke;
Fallen from it the crystal and the gold."

CLXXI

Then Rollanz feels that he has lost his sight,
Climbs to his feet, uses what strength he might;
In all his face the colour is grown white.
In front of him a great brown boulder lies;
Whereon ten blows with grief and rage he strikes;
The steel cries out, but does not break outright;
And the count says: "Saint Mary, be my guide!
Good Durendal, unlucky is your plight!
I've need of you no more; spent is my pride!
We in the field have won so many fights,
Combating through so many regions wide
That Charlès holds, whose beard is hoary white!
Be you not his that turns from any in flight!
A good vassal has held you this long time;
Never shall France the Free behold his like."

CLXXII

Rollant hath struck the sardonyx terrace;
The steel cries out, but broken is no ways.
So when he sees he never can it break,
Within himself begins he to complain:
"Ah! Durendal, white art thou, clear of stain!
Beneath the sun reflecting back his rays!
In Moriane was Charlès, in the vale,
When from heaven God by His angel bade

Him give thee to a count and capitain;
Girt thee on me that noble King and great.
I won for him with thee Anjou, Bretaigne,
And won for him with thee Peitou, the Maine,
And Normandy the free for him I gained,
Also with thee Provence and Equitaigne,
And Lumbardie and all the whole Romaigne,
I won Baivere, all Flanders in the plain,
Also Burguigne and all the whole Puillane,
Costentinnople, that homage to him pays;
In Saisonie all is as he ordains;
With thee I won him Scotland, Ireland, Wales,
England also, where he his chamber makes;
Won I with thee so many countries strange
That Charlès holds, whose beard is white with age!
For this sword's sake sorrow upon me weighs,
Rather I'ld die, than it mid pagans stay.
Lord God Father, never let France be shamed!"

CLXXIII

Rollant his stroke on a dark stone repeats,
And more of it breaks off than I can speak.
The sword cries out, yet breaks not in the least,
Back from the blow into the air it leaps.
Destroy it can he not; which when he sees,
Within himself he makes a plaint most sweet:
"Ah! Durendal, most holy, fair indeed!
Relics enough thy golden hilt conceals:
Saint Peter's Tooth, the Blood of Saint Basile,
Some of the Hairs of my Lord, Saint Denise,
Some of the Robe, was worn by Saint Mary.
It is not right that pagans should thee seize,
For Christian men thy use shall ever be.
Nor any man's that worketh cowardice!
Many broad lands with thee have I retrieved
Which Charles holds, who hath the great white beard;
Wherefore that King so proud and rich is he."

CLXXIV

But Rollant felt that death had made a way
Down from his head till on his heart it lay;
Beneath a pine running in haste he came,
On the green grass he lay there on his face;
His olifant and sword beneath him placed,
Turning his head towards the pagan race,
Now this he did, in truth, that Charles might say
(As he desired) and all the Franks his race;—
'Ah, gentle count; conquering he was slain!'—
He owned his faults often and every way,
And for his sins his glove to God upraised.

CLXXV

But Rollant feels he's no more time to seek;
Looking to Spain, he lies on a sheer peak,
And with one hand upon his breast he beats:
"*Mea Culpa!* God, by Thy Virtues clean
Me from my sins, the mortal and the mean,
Which from the hour that I was born have been
Until this day, when life is ended here!"
Holds out his glove towards God, as he speaks;
Angels descend from heaven on that scene.

CLXXVI

The count Rollanz, beneath a pine he sits;
Turning his eyes towards Spain, he begins
Remembering so many divers things:
So many lands where he went conquering,
And France the Douce, the heroes of his kin,
And Charlemagne, his lord who nourished him.
Nor can he help but weep and sigh at this.
But his own self, he's not forgotten him,
He owns his faults, and God's forgiveness bids:
"Very Father, in Whom no falsehood is,
Saint Lazaron from death Thou didst remit,
And Daniel save from the lions' pit;
My soul in me preserve from all perils

And from the sins I did in life commit!"
His right-hand glove, to God he offers it;
Saint Gabriel from 's hand hath taken it.
Over his arm his head bows down and slips,
He joins his hands: and so is life finish'd.
God sent him down His angel cherubin,
And Saint Michael, we worship in peril;
And by their side Saint Gabriel alit;
So the count's soul they bare to Paradis.

Chrétien de Troyes

3

Lancelot

The trumpets that sounded in *The Song of Roland* summoned men to battle for God and feudal lord. In the centuries following Roland's exploits at Roncesvalles, medieval society became increasingly sophisticated and self-conscious. Men were concerned not only about their prowess on the field of battle but about proper deportment in court and castle. Reflecting and inspiring this changed attitude, poetry and fiction became preoccupied with social conduct. In addition to valor in knightly combats, the heroes of narratives were required to exhibit courtly behavior, refined manners, and deference to upper-class women. The result was a code of conduct which made love an ennobling ideal—a conception that has been one of the distinguishing marks of European culture. According to some scholars, the influence of this code on society was so extensive as to make the changes wrought by the Renaissance seem a mere ripple by comparison.

Romances, as the medieval world knew them, were narratives, usually in verse, of knightly adventures and supernatural occurrences in long-ago times and faraway places. Chrétien de Troyes, of whose life we know nothing save that he resided at the court of Champagne in France in the latter part of the twelfth century, was the first to put the legends of King Arthur and the knights of the Round Table into the framework of a romance. The following selection is a prose translation of Chrétien's romance, *Lancelot*. It illustrates the code of courtly love in the hero's complete submission to his lady's whims, in his devotion alike to religion and to love, and in the tension that arose from his pledging his honor to the service of both his lady and his feudal lord. The full title of this romance, *Lancelot*, or *The Knight of the Cart*, is a hint to the reader that

From the book *Arthurian Romances* by Chrétien de Troyes. Translated by W. W. Comfort. Everyman's Library Edition. [New York, 1955.] Reprinted by permission of E. P. Dutton & Co., Inc. and J. M. Dent & Sons Ltd. [Pp. 270–75, 308–10, 326–33, 358–59.]

the mysterious knight of the first section, who incurs the shame of riding in a peasant cart, is really Lancelot, worthiest of Arthur's knights and for a long time enamored of the Queen.

Since my lady of Champagne wishes me to undertake to write a romance, I shall very gladly do so, being so devoted to her service as to do anything in the world for her, without any intention of flattery. But if one were to introduce any flattery upon such an occasion, he might say, and I would subscribe to it, that this lady surpasses all others who are alive, just as the south wind which blows in May or April is more lovely than any other wind. But upon my word, I am not one to wish to flatter my lady. I will simply say: "The Countess is worth as many queens as a gem is worth of pearls and sards." Nay I shall make no comparison, and yet it is true in spite of me; I will say, however, that her command has more to do with this work than any thought or pains that I may expend upon it. . . .

Upon a certain Ascension Day King Arthur had come from Caerleon, and had held a very magnificent court at Camelot as was fitting on such a day. After the feast the King did not quit his noble companions, of whom there were many in the hall. The Queen was present, too, and with her many a courteous lady able to converse in French. And Kay, who had furnished the meal, was eating with the others who had served the food. While Kay was sitting there at meat, behold there came to court a knight, well equipped and fully armed, and thus the knight appeared before the King as he sat among his lords. He gave him no greeting, but spoke out thus: "King Arthur, I hold in captivity knights, ladies, and damsels who belong to thy dominion and household; but it is not because of any intention to restore them to thee that I make reference to them here; rather do I wish to proclaim and serve thee notice that thou hast not the strength or the resources to enable thee to secure them again. And be assured that thou shalt die before thou canst ever succour them."

The King replies that he must needs endure what he has not the power to change; nevertheless, he is filled with grief. Then the knight makes as if to go away, and turns about, without tarrying longer before the King; but after reaching the door of the hall, he does not go down the stairs, but stops and speaks from there these words: "King, if in thy court there is a single knight in whom thou hast such confidence that thou wouldst dare to entrust to him the Queen that he might escort her after me out into the woods whither I am going, I will promise to await him there, and will surrender to thee all the prisoners whom I hold in exile in my country if he is able to defend the Queen and if he succeeds in bringing her back again." Many who were in the palace heard this challenge, and the whole court was in an uproar.

Kay, too, heard the news as he sat at meat with those who served. Leaving the table, he came straight to the King, and as if greatly enraged, he began to say: "O King, I have served thee long, faithfully, and loyally; now I take my leave, and shall go away, having no desire to serve thee more." The King was grieved at what he heard, and as soon as he could, he thus replied to him: "Is this serious, or a joke?" And Kay replied: "O King, fair sire, I have no desire to jest, and I take my leave quite seriously. No other reward or wages do I wish in return for the service I have given you. My mind is quite made up to go away immediately." "Is it in anger or in spite that you wish to go?" the King inquired; "seneschal, remain at court, as you have done hitherto, and be assured that I have nothing in the world which I would not give you at once in return for your consent to stay." "Sire," says Kay, "no need of that. I would not accept for each day's pay a measure of fine pure gold."

Thereupon, the King in great dismay went off to seek the Queen. "My lady," he says, "you do not know the demand that the seneschal makes of me. He asks me for leave to go away, and says he will no longer stay at court; the reason of this I do not know. But he will do at your request what he will not do for me. Go to him now, my lady dear. Since he will not consent to stay for my sake, pray him to remain on your account, and if need be, fall at his feet, for I should never again be happy if I should lose his company." The King sends the Queen to the seneschal, and she goes to him. Finding him with the rest, she went up to him, and said: "Kay, you may be very sure that I am greatly troubled by the news I have heard of you. I am grieved to say that I have been told it is your intention to leave the King. How does this come about? What motive have you in your mind? I cannot think that you are so sensible or courteous as usual. I want to ask you to

remain: stay with us here, and grant my prayer." "Lady," he says,
"I give you thanks; nevertheless, I shall not remain." The Queen
again makes her request, and is joined by all the other knights.
And Kay informs her that he is growing tired of a service which
is unprofitable. Then the Queen prostrates herself at full length
before his feet. Kay beseeches her to rise, but she says that she will
never do so until he grants her request. Then Kay promises her
to remain, provided the King and she will grant in advance a
favour he is about to ask. "Kay," she says, "both I and he will
grant it, whatever it may be. Come now, and we shall tell him that
upon this condition you will remain." So Kay goes away with the
Queen to the King's presence. The Queen says: "I have had hard
work to detain Kay; but I have brought him here to you with the
understanding that you will do what he is going to ask." The King
sighed with satisfaction, and said that he would perform whatever
request he might make.

"Sire," says Kay, "hear now what I desire, and what is the gift
you have promised me. I esteem myself very fortunate to gain such
a boon with your consent. Sire, you have pledged your word that
you would entrust to me my lady here, and that we should go
after the knight who awaits us in the forest." Though the King is
grieved, he trusts him with the charge, for he never went back upon
his word. But it made him so ill-humoured and displeased that it
plainly showed in his countenance. The Queen, for her part, was
sorry too, and all those of the household say that Kay had made
a proud, outrageous, and mad request. Then the King took the
Queen by the hand, and said: "My lady, you must accompany Kay
without making objection." And Kay said: "Hand her over to me
now, and have no fear, for I shall bring her back perfectly happy
and safe." The King gives her into his charge, and he takes her off.
After them all the rest go out, and there is not one who is not sad.
You must know that the seneschal was fully armed, and his horse
was led into the middle of the courtyard, together with a palfrey,
as is fitting, for the Queen. The Queen walked up to the palfrey,
which was neither restive nor hard-mouthed. Grieving and sad,
with a sigh the Queen mounts, saying to herself in a low voice, so
that no one could hear: "Alas, alas, if you only knew it, I am sure
you would never allow me without interference to be led away a
step." She thought she had spoken in a very low tone; but Count
Guinable heard her, who was standing by when she mounted.

When they started away, as great a lament was made by all the men and women present as if she already lay dead upon a bier. They do not believe that she will ever in her life come back. The seneschal in his impudence takes her where that other knight is awaiting her. But no one was so much concerned as to undertake to follow him; until at last my lord Gawain thus addressed the King his uncle: "Sire," he says, "you have done a very foolish thing, which causes me great surprise; but if you will take my advice, while they are still near by, I and you will ride after them, and all those who wish to accompany us. For my part, I cannot restrain myself from going in pursuit of them at once. It would not be proper for us not to go after them, at least far enough to learn what is to become of the Queen, and how Kay is going to comport himself." "Ah, fair nephew," the King replied, "you have spoken courteously. And since you have undertaken the affair, order our horses to be led out bridled and saddled that there may be no delay in setting out."

The horses are at once brought out, all ready and with the saddles on. First the King mounts, then my lord Gawain, and all the others rapidly. Each one, wishing to be of the party, follows his own will and starts away. Some were armed, but there were not a few without their arms. My lord Gawain was armed, and he bade two squires lead by the bridle two extra steeds. And as they thus approached the forest, they saw Kay's horse running out; and they recognised him, and saw that both reins of the bridle were broken. The horse was running wild, the stirrup-straps all stained with blood, and the saddle-bow was broken and damaged. Every one was chagrined at this, and they nudged each other and shook their heads. My lord Gawain was riding far in advance of the rest of the party, and it was not long before he saw coming slowly a knight on a horse that was sore, painfully tired, and covered with sweat. The knight first saluted my lord Gawain, and his greeting my lord Gawain returned. Then the knight, recognising my lord Gawain, stopped and thus spoke to him: "You see, sir, my horse is in a sweat and in such case as to be no longer serviceable. I suppose that those two horses belong to you; now, with the understanding that I shall return the service and the favour, I beg you to let me have one or the other of them, either as a loan or outright as a gift." And he answers him: "Choose whichever you prefer." Then he who was in dire distress did not try to select the better or the fairer or the larger of the horses, but leaped quickly upon the one which was nearer to him, and rode him off. Then the one he had just left fell dead, for he had ridden him hard that day, so that he was used up and overworked.

The knight without delay goes pricking through the forest, and my lord Gawain follows in pursuit of him with all speed, until he reaches the bottom of a hill. And when he had gone some distance, he found the horse dead which he had given to the knight, and noticed that the ground had been trampled by horses, and that broken shields and lances lay strewn about, so that it seemed that there had been a great combat between several knights, and he was very sorry and grieved not to have been there. However, he did not stay there long, but rapidly passed on until he saw again by chance the knight all alone on foot, completely armed, with helmet laced, shield hanging from his neck, and with his sword girt on. He had overtaken a cart. In those days such a cart served the same purpose as does a pillory now; and in each good town where there are more than three thousand such carts nowadays, in those times there was only one, and this, like our pillories, had to do service for all those who commit murder or treason, and those who are guilty of any delinquency, and for thieves who have stolen others' property or have forcibly seized it on the roads. Whoever was convicted of any crime was placed upon a cart and dragged through all the streets, and he lost henceforth all his legal rights, and was never afterward heard, honoured, or welcomed in any court. The carts were so dreadful in those days that the saying was then first used: "When thou dost see and meet a cart, cross thyself and call upon God, that no evil may befall thee."

The knight on foot, and without a lance, walked behind the cart, and saw a dwarf sitting on the shafts, who held, as a driver does, a long goad in his hand. Then he cries out: "Dwarf, for God's sake, tell me now if thou hast seen my lady, the Queen, pass by here." The miserable, low-born dwarf would not give him any news of her, but replied: "If thou wilt get up into the cart I am driving thou shalt hear to-morrow what has happened to the Queen." Then he kept on his way without giving further heed. The knight hesitated only for a couple of steps before getting in. Yet, it was unlucky for him that he shrank from the disgrace, and did not jump in at once; for he will later rue his delay. But common sense, which is inconsistent with love's dictates, bids him refrain from getting in, warning him and counselling him to do and undertake nothing for which he may reap shame and disgrace. Reason, which dares thus speak to him, reaches only his lips, but not his heart; but love is enclosed within his heart, bidding him and urging him to mount at once upon the cart. So he jumps in, since love will have it so, feeling no concern about the shame, since he is prompted by love's commands. And my lord Gawain presses on in haste after the cart, and when he finds the knight sitting in it, his surprise is great. "Tell me," he shouted to the dwarf, "if thou knowest anything of the Queen." And he replied: "If thou art so much thy own enemy as is this knight who is sitting here, get in with him, if it be thy pleasure, and I will drive thee along with him." When my lord Gawain heard that, he considered it great foolishness, and said that he would not get in, for it would be dishonourable to exchange a horse for a cart: "Go on, and wherever thy journey lies, I will follow after thee."

[Jeered at because of his shameful ride in the peasant cart, Lancelot nevertheless perseveres in his quest. He learns that the Queen and Sir Kay are held captive in the mysterious Land of Gorre, where many of Arthur's subjects are imprisoned. After many combats, adventures, and temptations, he wins his way to the perilous entrance to Gorre. Ed.]

At the end of this very difficult bridge they dismount from their steeds and gaze at the wicked-looking stream, which is as swift and raging, as black and turgid, as fierce and terrible as if it were the devil's stream; and it is so dangerous and bottomless that anything falling into it would be as completely lost as if it fell into the salt sea. And the bridge, which spans it, is different from any other bridge; for there never was such a one as this. If any one asks of me the truth, there never was such a bad bridge, nor one whose flooring was so bad. The bridge across the cold stream consisted of a polished, gleaming sword; but the sword was stout and stiff, and was as long as two lances. At each end there was a tree-trunk in which the sword was firmly fixed. No one need fear to fall because of its breaking or bending, for its excellence was such that it could support a great weight. But the two knights who were with the third were much discouraged; for they surmised that two lions or two leopards would be found tied to a great rock at the other end of the bridge. The water and the bridge and the lions combine so to terrify them that they both tremble with fear, and say: "Fair sire, consider well what confronts you; for it is necessary and need-ful to do so. This bridge is badly made and built, and the con-struction of it is bad. If you do not change your mind in time, it will be too late to repent. You must consider which of several alternatives you will choose. Suppose that you once get across (but that cannot possibly come to pass, any more than one could hold in the winds and forbid them to blow, or keep the birds from sing-ing, or re-enter one's mother's womb and be born again—all of which is as impossible as to empty the sea of its water); but even supposing that you got across, can you think and suppose that those two fierce lions that are chained on the other side will not kill you, and suck the blood from your veins, and eat your flesh and then gnaw your bones? For my part, I am bold enough, when I even dare to look and gaze at them. If you do not take care, they will certainly devour you. Your body will soon be torn and rent apart, for they will show you no mercy. So take pity on us now, and stay here in our company! It would be wrong for you to expose yourself intentionally to such mortal peril." And he, laughing, replies to them: "Gentlemen, receive my thanks and gratitude for the concern you feel for me: it comes from your love and kind hearts. I know full well that you would not like to see any mishap come to me; but I have faith and confidence in God, that He will protect me to the end. I fear the bridge and stream no more than I fear this dry land; so I intend to prepare and make the danger-ous attempt to cross. I would rather die than turn back now."

The others have nothing more to say; but each weeps with pity and heaves a sigh. Meanwhile he prepares, as best he may, to cross the stream, and he does a very marvellous thing in removing the armour from his feet and hands. He will be in a sorry state when he reaches the other side. He is going to support himself with his bare hands and feet upon the sword, which was sharper than a scythe, for he had not kept on his feet either sole or upper or hose. But he felt no fear of wounds upon his hands or feet; he preferred to maim himself rather than to fall from the bridge and be plunged in the water from which he could never escape. In accordance with this determination, he passes over with great pain and agony, being wounded in the hands, knees, and feet. But even this suffering is sweet to him: for Love, who conducts and leads him on, assuages and relieves the pain. Creeping on his hands, feet, and knees, he proceeds until he reaches the other side. Then he recalls and recollects the two lions which he thought he had seen from the other side; but, on looking about, he does not see so much as a lizard or anything else to do him harm. He raises his hand before his face and looks at his ring, and by this test he proves that neither of the lions is there which he thought he had seen, and that he had been enchanted and deceived; for there was not a living creature there. When those who had remained behind upon the bank saw that he had safely crossed, their joy was natural; but they do not know of his injuries. He, however, considers himself fortunate not to have suffered anything worse. The blood from his wounds drips on his shirt on all sides. Then he sees before him a tower, which was so strong that never had he seen such a strong one before: indeed, it could not have been a better tower.

At the window there sat King Bademagu, who was very scrupulous and precise about matters of honour and what was right, and who was careful to observe and practise loyalty above all else; and beside him stood his son, who always did precisely the opposite so far as possible, for he found his pleasure in disloyalty, and never wearied of villainy, treason, and felony. From their point of vantage they had seen the knight cross the bridge with trouble and pain. Meleagant's colour changed with the rage and displeasure he felt; for he knows now that he will be challenged for the Queen; but his character was such that he feared no man, however strong or formidable. If he were not base and disloyal, there could no better knight be found; but he had a heart of wood, without gentleness and pity. What enraged his son and roused his ire, made the king happy and glad. The king knew of a truth that he who had crossed the bridge was much better than any one else. For no one would dare to pass over it in whom there dwelt any of that evil nature which brings more shame upon those who possess it than prowess brings of honour to the virtuous. For prowess cannot accomplish so much as wickedness and sloth can do: it is true beyond a doubt that it is possible to do more evil than good.

[Lancelot, almost beaten by Meleagant, the evil son of the King of Gorre, is so inspired by the sight of Guinevere that he triumphs and gains the promise of the Queen's release. Through a misunderstanding, Guinevere believes that Lancelot has been killed and grieves to the point of death. He meanwhile believes a false report of her death and attempts to kill himself. They are each saved, however, at the very last minute by hearing that the other is alive. *Ed.*]

. . . The Queen yearns ardently for the arrival of her lover and her joy. She has no desire this time to bear him any grudge. But rumour, which never rests but runs always unceasingly, again reaches the Queen to the effect that Lancelot would have killed himself for her sake, if he had had the chance. She is happy at the thought that this is true, but she would not have had it happen so for anything, for her sorrow would have been too great. Thereupon Lancelot arrived in haste. As soon as the king sees him, he runs to kiss and embrace him. He feels as if he ought to fly, borne along by the buoyancy of his joy. But his satisfaction is cut short by those who had taken and bound his guest, and the king tells them they have come in an evil hour, for they shall all be killed and confounded. Then they made answer that they thought he would have it so. "It is I whom you have insulted in doing your pleasure. He has no reason to complain," the king replies; "you have not shamed him at all, but only me who was protecting him. However you look at it, the shame is mine. But if you escape me now, you will see no joke in this."

When Lancelot hears his wrath, he puts forth every effort to make peace and adjust matters; when his efforts have met with success, the king takes him away to see the Queen. This time the Queen did not lower her eyes to the ground, but she went to meet him cheerfully, honouring him all she could, and making him sit down by her side. Then they talked together at length of all that was upon their hearts, and love furnished them with so much to say that topics did not lack. And when Lancelot sees how well he stands, and that all he says finds favour with the Queen, he says to her in confidence: "Lady, I marvel greatly why you received me with such a countenance when you saw me the day before yesterday, and why you would not speak a word to me: I almost died of the blow you gave me, and I had not the courage to dare to question you about it, as I now venture to do. I am ready now, lady, to make amends, when you have told me what has been the crime which has caused me such distress." Then the Queen replies: "What? Did you not hesitate for shame to mount the cart? You showed you were loath to get in, when you hesitated for two whole steps. That is the reason why I would neither address nor look at you." "May God save me from such a crime again," Lancelot replies, "and may God show me no mercy, if you were not quite right! For God's sake, lady, receive my amends at once, and tell me, for God's sake, if you can ever pardon me." "Friend, you are quite forgiven," the Queen replies; "I pardon you willingly." "Thank you for that, lady," he then says; "but I cannot tell you here all that I should like to say; I should like to talk with you more at leisure, if possible." Then the Queen indicates a window by her glance rather than with her finger, and says: "Come through the garden to-night and speak with me at yonder window, when every one inside has gone to sleep. You will not be able to get in: I shall be inside and you outside; to gain entrance will be impossible. I shall be able to touch you only with my lips or hand, but, if you please, I will stay there until morning for love of you. Our bodies cannot be joined, for close beside me in my room lies Kay the seneschal, who is still suffering from his wounds. And the door is not open, but is tightly closed and guarded well. When you come, take care to let no spy catch sight of you." "Lady," says he, "if I can help it, no spy shall see me who might think or speak evil of us." Then, having agreed upon this plan, they separate very joyfully.

Lancelot leaves the room in such a happy frame that all his past troubles are forgotten. But he was so impatient for the night to come that his restlessness made the day seem longer than a hundred ordinary days or than an entire year. If night had only come, he would gladly have gone to the trysting place. Dark and sombre night at last won its struggle with the day, and wrapped it up in its covering, and laid it away beneath its cloak. When he saw the light of day obscured, he pretended to be tired and worn, and said that, in view of his protracted vigils, he needed rest. You, who have ever done the same, may well understand and guess that he pretends to be tired and goes to bed in order to deceive the people of the house; but he cared nothing about his bed, nor would he have sought rest there for anything, for he could not have done so and would not have dared, and furthermore he would not have cared to possess the courage or the power to do so. Soon he softly rose, and was pleased to find that no moon or star was shining, and that in the house there was no candle, lamp, or lantern burning. Thus he went out and looked about, but there was no one on the watch for him, for all thought that he would sleep in his bed all night. Without escort or company he quickly went out into the garden, meeting no one on the way, and he was so fortunate as to find that a part of the garden-wall had recently fallen down. Through this break he passes quickly and proceeds to the window, where he stands, taking good care not to cough or sneeze, until the Queen arrives clad in a very white chemise. She wore no cloak or coat, but had thrown over her a short cape of scarlet cloth and shrew-mouse fur.

As soon as Lancelot saw the Queen leaning on the window-sill behind the great iron bars, he honoured her with a gentle salute. She promptly returned his greeting, for he was desirous of her, and she of him. Their talk and conversation are not of vulgar, tiresome affairs. They draw close to one another, until each holds the other's hand. But they are so distressed at not being able to come together more completely, that they curse the iron bars. Then Lancelot asserts that, with the Queen's consent, he will come inside to be with her, and that the bars cannot keep him out. And the Queen replies: "Do you not see how the bars are stiff to bend and hard to break? You could never so twist, pull or drag at them as to dislodge one of them." "Lady," says he, "have no fear of that. It would take more than these bars to keep me out. Nothing but your command could thwart my power to come to you. If you will but grant me your permission, the way will open before me. But if it is not your pleasure, then the way is so obstructed that I could not possibly pass through." "Certainly," she says, "I consent. My will need not stand in your way; but you must wait until I retire to my bed again, so that no harm may come to you, for it would be no joke or jest if the seneschal, who is sleeping here, should wake up on hearing you. So it is best for me to withdraw, for no good could come of it, if he should see me standing here." "Go then, lady," he replies; "but have no fear that I shall make any noise. I think I can draw out the bars so softly and with so little effort that no one shall be aroused."

Then the Queen retires, and he prepares to loosen the window. Seizing the bars, he pulls and wrenches them until he makes them bend and drags them from their places. But the iron was so sharp that the end of his little finger was cut to the nerve, and the first joint of the next finger was torn; but he who is intent upon something else paid no heed to any of his wounds or to the blood which trickled down. Though the window is not low, Lancelot gets through it quickly and easily. First he finds Kay asleep in his bed, then he comes to the bed of the Queen, whom he adores and before whom he kneels, holding her more dear than the relic of any saint. And the Queen extends her arms to him and, embracing him, presses him tightly against her bosom, drawing him into the bed beside her and showing him every possible satisfaction: her love and her heart go out to him. It is love that prompts her to treat him so; and if she feels great love for him, he feels a hundred thousand times as much for her. For there is no love at all in other hearts compared with what there is in his; in his heart love was so completely embodied that it was niggardly toward all other hearts. Now Lancelot possesses all he wants, when the Queen voluntarily seeks his company and love, and when he holds her in his arms, and she holds him in hers. Their sport is so agreeable and sweet, as they kiss and fondle each other, that in truth such a marvellous joy comes over them as was never heard or known. But their joy will not be revealed by me, for in a story it has no place. Yet, the most choice and delightful satisfaction was precisely that of which our story must not speak.

That night Lancelot's joy and pleasure were very great. But, to his sorrow, day comes when he must leave his mistress' side. It cost him such pain to leave her that he suffered a real martyr's agony. His heart now stays where the Queen remains; he has not the power to lead it away, for it finds such pleasure in the Queen that it has no desire to leave her: so his body goes, and his heart remains. But enough of his body stays behind to spot and stain the sheets with the blood which has fallen from his fingers. Full of sighs and tears, Lancelot leaves in great distress. He grieves that no time is fixed for another meeting, but it cannot be. Regretfully he leaves by the window through which he had entered so happily. He was so badly wounded in the fingers that they were in a sorry state; yet he straightened the bars and set them in their place again, so that from neither side, either before or behind, was it evident that any one had drawn out or bent any of the bars. When he leaves the room, he bows and acts precisely as if he were before a shrine; then he goes with a heavy heart, and reaches his lodgings without being recognised by any one. He throws himself naked upon his bed without awaking any one, and then for the first time he is surprised to notice the cuts in his fingers; but he is not at all concerned, for he is very sure that the wound was caused by dragging the window bars from the wall. Therefore he was not at all worried, for he would rather have had both arms dragged from his body than not enter through the window. But he would have been very angry and distressed, if he had thus injured and wounded himself under any other circumstances.

In the morning, within her curtained room, the Queen had fallen into a gentle sleep; she had not noticed that her sheets were spotted with blood, but she supposed them to be perfectly white and clean and presentable. Now Meleagant, as soon as he was dressed and ready, went to the room where the Queen lay. He finds her awake, and he sees the sheets spotted with fresh drops of blood, whereupon he nudges his companions and, suspicious of some mischief, looks at the bed of Kay the seneschal, and sees that his sheets are blood-stained too, for you must know that in the night his wounds had begun to bleed afresh. Then he said: "Lady, now I have found the evidence that I desired. It is very true that any man is a fool to try to confine a woman: he wastes his efforts and his pains. He who tries to keep her under guard loses her sooner than the man who takes no thought of her. A fine watch, indeed, has been kept by my father, who is guarding you on my behalf! He has succeeded in keeping you from me, but, in spite of him, Kay the seneschal has looked upon you last night, and has done what he pleased with you, as can readily be proved." "What is that?" she asks. "Since I must speak, I find blood on your sheets, which proves the fact. I know it and can prove it, because I find on both your sheets and his the blood which issued from his wounds: the evidence is very strong."

Then the Queen saw on both beds the bloody sheets, and marvelling, she blushed with shame and said: "So help me God, this blood which I see upon my sheets was never brought here by Kay, but my nose bled during the night, and I suppose it must be from my nose." In saying so, she thinks she tells the truth. "By my head," says Meleagant, "there is nothing in what you say. Swearing is of no avail, for you are taken in your guilt, and the truth will soon be proved." Then he said to the guards who were present: "Gentlemen, do not move, and see to it that the sheets are not taken from the bed until I return. I wish the king to do me justice, as soon as he has seen the truth." Then he searched until he found him, and falling at his feet, he said: "Sire, come to see what you have failed to guard. Come to see the Queen, and you shall see the certain marvels which I have already seen and tested. But, before you go, I beg you not to fail to be just and upright toward me. You know well to what danger I have exposed myself for the Queen; yet, you are no friend of mine and keep her from me under guard. This morning I went to see her in her bed, and I remarked that Kay lies with her every night. Sire, for God's sake, be not angry, if I am disgruntled and if I complain. For it is very humiliating for me to be hated and despised by one with whom Kay is allowed to lie." "Silence!" says the king; "I don't believe it." "Then come, my lord, and see the sheets and the state in which Kay has left them. Since you will not believe my words, and since you think I am lying, I will show you the sheets and the quilt covered with blood from Kay's wounds." "Come now," says the king; "I wish to see for myself, and my eyes will judge of the truth."

Then the king goes directly to the room, where the Queen got up at his approach. He sees that the sheets are blood-stained on her bed and on Kay's alike, and he says: "Lady, it is going badly now, if what my son has said is true." Then she replies: "So help me God, never even in a dream was uttered such a monstrous lie. I think Kay the seneschal is courteous and loyal enough not to commit such a deed, and besides, I do not expose my body in the market-place, nor offer it of my own free will. Surely, Kay is not the man to make an insulting proposal to me, and I have never desired and shall never desire to do such a thing myself." "Sire, I shall be much obliged to you," says Meleagant to his father, "if Kay shall be made to atone for this outrage, and the Queen's shame thus be exposed. It devolves upon you to see that justice is done, and this justice I now request and claim. Kay has betrayed King Arthur his lord, who had such confidence in him that he entrusted to him what he loved most in the world." "Let me answer, sire," says Kay, "and I shall exonerate myself. May God have no mercy upon my soul when I leave this world, if I ever lay with my lady! Indeed, I should rather be dead than ever do my lord such an ugly wrong, and may God never grant me better health than I have now but rather kill me on the spot, if such a thought ever entered my mind! But I know that my wounds bled profusely last night, and that is the reason why my sheets are stained with blood. That is why your son suspects me, but surely he has no right to do so."

And Meleagant answers him: "So help me God, the devils and demons have betrayed you. You grew too heated last night and, as a result of your exertions, your wounds have doubtless bled afresh. There is no use in your denying it; we can see it, and it is perfectly evident. It is right that he should atone for his crime, who is so plainly taken in his guilt. Never did a knight with so fair a name commit such iniquity as this, and yours is the shame for it." "Sire, sire," says Kay to the king, "I will defend the Queen and myself against the accusation of your son. He harasses and distresses me, though he has no ground to treat me so." "You cannot fight," the king replies; "you are too ill." "Sire, if you will allow it, I will fight with him, ill as I am, and will show him that I am not guilty of the crime which he imputes to me." But the Queen, having secretly sent word to Lancelot, tells the king that she will present a knight who will defend the seneschal, if Meleagant dares to urge this charge. Then Meleagant said at once: "There is no knight without exception, even were he a giant, whom I will not fight until one of us is defeated."

Then Lancelot came in, and with him such a rout of knights that the whole hall was filled with them. As soon as he had entered, in the hearing of all, both young and old, the Queen told what had happened, and said: "Lancelot, this insult has been done me by Meleagant. In the presence of all who hear his words he says I have lied, if you do not make him take it back. Last night, he asserted, Kay lay with me, because he found my sheets, like his, all stained with blood; and he says that he stands convicted, unless he will undertake his own defence, or unless some one else will fight the battle on his behalf." Lancelot says: "You need never use arguments with me. May it not please God that either you or he should be thus discredited! I am ready to fight and to prove to the extent of my power that he never was guilty of such a thought. I am ready to employ my strength in his behalf, and to defend him against this charge." Then Meleagant jumped up and said: "So help me God, I am pleased and well satisfied with that; no one need think that I object." And Lancelot said: "My lord king, I am well acquainted with suits and laws, with trials and verdicts: in a question of veracity an oath should be taken before the fight." Meleagant at once replies: "I agree to take an oath; so let the relics be brought at once, for I know well that I am right." And Lancelot answers him: "So help me God, no one who ever knew Kay the seneschal would doubt his word on such a point." Then they call for their horses, and ask that their arms be brought. This is promptly done, and when the valets had armed them, they were ready for the fight. Then the holy relics are brought forth: Meleagant steps forward, with Lancelot by his side, and both fall on their knees. Then Meleagant, laying his hands upon the relics, swears unreservedly: "So help me God and this holy relic, Kay the seneschal lay with the Queen in her bed last night and had his pleasure with her." "And I swear that thou liest," says Lancelot, "and furthermore I swear that he neither lay with her nor touched her. And may it please God to take vengeance upon him who has lied, and may He bring the truth to light! Moreover, I will take another oath and swear, whoever may dislike it or be displeased, that if I am permitted to vanquish Meleagant to-day, I will show him no mercy, so help me God and these relics here!" The king felt no joy when he heard this oath.

[The Queen allows the fight between Lancelot and Meleagant to be stopped before either is victor. She returns to Arthur's court, but Lancelot is treacherously imprisoned by Meleagant. He gains freedom long enough to participate, disguised, in the tournament presided over by the Queen, in which he willingly incurs shame by obeying her command to do his worst. But when she commands him to do his best, he triumphs over all contestants. Lancelot is imprisoned once more by Meleagant and, at last, escapes; then he challenges Meleagant to fight before King Arthur and the court. *Ed.*]

In the field there stood a sycamore as fair as any tree could be; it was wide-spread and covered a large area, and around it grew a fine border of thick fresh grass which was green at all seasons of the year. Under this fair and stately sycamore, which was planted back in Abel's time, there rises a clear spring of water which flows away hurriedly. The bed of the spring is beautiful and as bright as silver, and the channel through which the water flows is formed, I think, of refined and tested gold, and it stretches away across the field down into a valley between the woods. There it pleases the King to take his seat where nothing unpleasant is in sight. After the crowd has drawn back at the King's command, Lancelot rushes furiously at Meleagant as at one whom he hates cordially, but before striking him, he shouted with a loud and commanding voice: "Take your stand, I defy you! And take my word, this time you shall not be spared." Then he spurs his steed and draws back the distance of a bow-shot. Then they drive their horses toward each other at top speed, and strike each other so fiercely upon their resisting shields that they pierced and punctured them. But neither one is wounded, nor is the flesh touched in this first assault. They pass each other without delay, and come back at the top of their horses' speed to renew their blows on the strong, stout shields. Both of the knights are strong and brave, and both of the horses are stout and fast. So mighty are the blows they deal on the shields about their necks that the lances passed clean through, without breaking or splintering, until the cold steel reached their flesh. Each strikes the other with such force that both are borne to earth, and no breast-strap, girth, or stirrup could save them from falling backward over their saddle-bow, leaving the saddle without an occupant. The horses run riderless over hill and dale, but they kick and bite each other, thus showing their mortal hatred.

As for the knights who fell to earth, they leaped up as quickly as possible and drew their swords, which were engraved with chiselled lettering. Holding their shields before the face, they strive to wound each other with their swords of steel. Lancelot stands in no fear of him, for he knew half as much again about fencing as did his antagonist, having learned it in his youth. Both dealt such blows on the shield slung from their necks, and upon their helmets barred with gold, that they crushed and damaged them. But Lancelot presses him hard and gives him a mighty blow upon his right arm which, though encased in mail, was unprotected by the shield, severing it with one clean stroke. And when he felt the loss of his right arm, he said that it should be dearly sold. If it is at all possible, he will not fail to exact the price; he is in such pain and wrath and rage that he is well-nigh beside himself, and he has a poor opinion of himself, if he cannot score on his rival now. He rushes at him with the intent to seize him, but Lancelot forestalls his plan, for with his trenchant sword he deals his body such a cut as he will not recover from until April and May be passed. He smashes his nose-guard against his teeth, breaking three of them in his mouth. And Meleagant's rage is such that he cannot speak or say a word; nor does he deign to cry for mercy, for his foolish heart holds tight in such constraint that even now it deludes him still. Lancelot approaches and, unlacing his helmet, cuts off his head. Never more will this man trouble him: it is all over with him as he falls dead. Not a soul who was present there felt any pity at the sight. The King and all the others there are jubilant and express their joy. Happier than they ever were before, they relieve Lancelot of his arms, and lead him away exultingly.

4

Medieval Lyric Poetry

We have seen an example of the medieval epic in *The Song of Roland* and of the medieval romance in Chrétien de Troyes' *Lancelot*. Too often overlooked, however, is the gift of the Middle Ages for lyric verse, a talent that appears both in religious poems, such as the *Canticle of the Sun* by St. Francis of Assisi (1182–1226), and in more secular forms and subjects. In the songs of wandering scholars, or in the margins of manuscripts in monastic libraries (where a scribe might jot down some poem he had composed or remembered having heard), or in chance collections, we find some of the choicest medieval Latin lyrics. The poems "Let's away with study" and "When Diana lighteth late her crystal lamp" in the following selection are from a miscellaneous collection of songs, poems, and plays compiled in the thirteenth century at a Benedictine monastery in southern Germany. After the dissolution of the monastery, the manuscript remained undiscovered until early in the nineteenth century. These lyrics are especially attractive for their use of rhyme and accent (admirably preserved in the following translations), which sound so natural to the modern ear but were seldom used in Greek or Latin verse. They show yet another aspect of the Middle Ages in their intense awareness and enjoyment of the beauty of this world. The translator has termed "When Diana lighteth late her crystal lamp" the high point of medieval secular verse.

St. Francis of Assisi, "The Canticle of the Sun," in *The Writings of Saint Francis of Assisi,* trans. P. Robinson (Philadelphia: Dolphin, 1906).

Ms. of Benedictbeuern, in *Mediaeval Latin Lyrics,* trans. and ed. Helen Waddell (New York: Holt, 1933), 203, 205, 265, 267. Reprinted by permission of the author. Copyright 1933 by Henry Holt Company also Copyright 1947 by Helen Waddell.

ST. FRANCIS OF ASSISI: *The Canticle of the Sun*

Most high, omnipotent, good Lord
Praise, glory, and honour and benediction all, are Thine.
To Thee alone do they belong, most High,
And there is no man fit to mention Thee.

Praise be to Thee, my Lord, with all Thy creatures,
Especially to my worshipful brother sun,
The which lights up the day, and through him dost Thou bright-
ness give;
And beautiful is he and radiant with splendour great;
Of Thee, most High, signification gives.

Praised be my Lord, for sister moon and for the stars,
In heaven Thou hast formed them clear and precious and fair.

Praised be my Lord for brother wind
And for the air and clouds and fair and every kind of weather,
By the which Thou givest to Thy creatures nourishment.

Praised be my Lord for sister water,
The which is greatly helpful and humble and precious and pure.

Praised be my Lord for brother fire,
By the which Thou lightest up the dark.
And fair is he and gay and mighty and strong.

Praised be my Lord for our sister, mother earth,
The which sustains and keeps us
And brings forth diverse fruits with grass and flowers bright.

Praised be my Lord for those who for Thy love forgive
And weakness bear and tribulation.
Blessed those who shall in peace endure,
And by Thee, most High, shall they be crowned.

Praised be my Lord for our sister, the bodily death,
From the which no living man can flee.
Woe to them who die in mortal sin;
Blessed those who shall find themselves in Thy most holy will,
For the second death shall do them no ill.

Praise ye and bless ye my Lord, and give Him thanks,
And be subject unto Him with great humility.

MS. OF BENEDICTBEUERN: *Let's Away with Study*

Let's away with study,
  Folly's sweet.
Treasure all the pleasure
  Of our youth:
Time enough for age
  To think on Truth.
So short a day,
And life so quickly hasting,
And in study wasting
  Youth that would be gay!

'Tis our spring that slipping,
  Winter draweth near,
Life itself we're losing,
  And this sorry cheer
Dries the blood and chills the heart,
  Shrivels all delight.
Age and all its crowd of ills
  Terrifies our sight.
So short a day,
And life so quickly hasting,
And in study wasting
  Youth that would be gay!

Let us as the gods do,
  'Tis the wiser part:
Leisure and love's pleasure
  Seek the young in heart
Follow the old fashion,
  Down into the street!
Down among the maidens,
  And the dancing feet!
So short a day,
And life so quickly hasting,
And in study wasting
  Youth that would be gay!

There for the seeing
  Is all loveliness,

White limbs moving
　　Light in wantonness.
Gay go the dancers,
　　I stand and see,
Gaze, till their glances
　　Steal myself from me.
So short a day,
And life so quickly hasting,
And in study wasting
　　Youth that would be gay!

MS. OF BENEDICTBEUERN: *When Diana Lighteth*
Late Her Crystal Lamp

When Diana lighteth
Late her crystal lamp,
Her pale glory kindleth
From her brother's fire,
Little straying west winds
Wander over heaven,
Moonlight falleth,
And recalleth
With a sound of lute-strings shaken,
Hearts that have denied his reign
To love again.
Hesperus, the evening star,
To all things that mortal are,
Grants the dew of sleep.

Thrice happy Sleep!
The antidote to care,
Thou dost allay the storm
Of grief and sore despair;
Through the fast-closed gates
Thou stealest light;
Thy coming gracious is
As Love's delight.

Sleep through the wearied brain
Breathes a soft wind
From fields of ripening grain,

The sound
Of running water over clearest sand,
A millwheel turning, turning slowly round,
These steal the light
From eyes weary of sight.

Love's sweet exchange and barter, then the brain
Sinks to repose;
Swimming in strangeness of a new delight
The eyelids close;
Oh sweet the passing o'er from love to sleep.
But sweeter the awakening to love.

Under the kind branching trees
Where Philomel complains and sings
Most sweet to lie at ease,
Sweeter to take delight
Of beauty and the night
On the fresh springing grass,
With smell of mint and thyme,
And for Love's bed, the rose.
Sleep's dew doth ever bless,
But most distilled on lovers' weariness.

St. Thomas Aquinas

=== 5 ===

Summa Contra Gentiles

St. Thomas Aquinas (*ca.* 1225–1274) received his early education at the monastery of Monte Cassino and, over the objections of his family, entered the Dominican order at the age of eighteen. How little can be known during an individual's formative years about his potentialities is exemplified by the fact that Aquinas was known to his fellow students as the "Dumb Ox," but became a Doctor of Theology and was known as the "Angelic Doctor" of the medieval Church and universities. He not only lectured at Paris, Rome, and Bologna, but engaged in the affairs of the Church and wrote monumental treatises on theology. Preferring the life of scholarship to the dignity and power of office, Aquinas refused the archbishopric of Naples and the abbacy of Monte Cassino. Faithful to his duty to the Church no matter what the cost to himself, he died while journeying to a council where reconciliation of the Greek and Latin Churches was to have been discussed. Aquinas was canonized some half-century after his death. No theologian save Augustine has had a greater influence on the theology and philosophy of the Western world. By an encyclical of 1879, Pope Leo XIII directed members of the Catholic clergy to take the teachings of Aquinas as the basis of their own theological position.

Aquinas is the supreme figure in scholasticism, the medieval philosophical effort to harmonize faith and reason. In his *Summa Contra Gentiles* he distinguishes between truth discerned by human reason and that imparted by revelation—both of which are necessary to man. Revelation is contained in the Scriptures, but also comes through the teachings of the Church Fathers and the decisions of Church councils. Reason is not, for Aquinas, a product of the individual mind, but rather the "natural truth" (or "natural law") which reaches our understanding through philosophy. These two kinds of truth—reason and revelation—are complementary, for they both spring from the same source, that is, from God, the Prime Mover. The following selection, with its many quotations from the Scriptures and from Aristotle, illustrates the characteristic method of thought and proof in scholastic philosophy. It deals, in Aristotelian fashion, with the "final" cause and end (or purpose) of all things.

THAT THE END OF EVERYTHING IS A GOOD

If every agent acts for the sake of a good . . . it follows further that the end of every being is a good. For every being is ordered to its end through its action. It must be, then, that the action itself is the end, or that the end of the action is also the end of the agent. And this is its good.

. . .

Besides, that toward which a thing tends, while it is beyond the thing, and in which it rests, when it is possessed, is the end for the thing. Now, if anything lacks a proper perfection, it is moved toward it, in so far as lies within its capacity, but if it possesses it the thing rests in it. Therefore, the end of each thing is its perfection. Now, the perfection of anything is its good. So, each thing is ordered to a good as an end.

. . .

THAT ALL THINGS ARE ORDERED TO ONE END WHO IS GOD

It is, consequently, apparent that all things are ordered to one good, as to their ultimate end.

If, in fact, nothing tends toward a thing as an end, unless this thing is a good, it is therefore necessary that the good, as good, be the end. Therefore, that which is the highest good is, from the highest point of view, the end of all things. But there is only one highest good, and this is God. . . . So, all things are ordered to one good, as their end, and this is God.

Again, that which is supreme in any genus is the cause of all the members that belong in that genus; thus, fire, which is the hottest of corporeal things, is the cause of the heat of other things. Therefore, the highest good which is God is the cause of the goodness in all good things. So, also, is He the cause of every end that is an end, since whatever is an end is such because it is a good.

. . .

Moreover, in every ordered series of ends the ultimate end must be the end of all preceding ends. For instance, if a potion is mixed to be given a sick man, and it is given in order to purge him, and he is purged in order to make him thinner, and he is thinned down so that he may become healthy—then health must be the end of the thinning process, and of the purging, and of the other actions which precede it. But all things are found, in their various degrees of goodness, to be subordinated to one highest good which is the cause of all goodness. Consequently, since the good has the essential character of an end, all things are subordinated to God, as preceding ends under an ultimate end. Therefore, God must be the end of all things.

. . .

Besides, the ultimate end of any maker, as a maker, is himself; we use things made by us for our own sakes, and, if sometimes a man makes a thing for some other purpose, this has reference to his own good, either as useful, delectable, or as a good for its own sake. Now, God is the productive cause of all things, of some immediately, of others by means of other causes, as is shown in the foregoing. Therefore, He Himself is the end of all things.

. . .

HOW GOD IS THE END OF ALL THINGS

We must further investigate how God is the end of all. This will be made clear from the foregoing.

The ultimate end of all is such that He is, nonetheless, prior to all things in existing being. Now, there is a sort of end which, though it holds first place causally in the order of intention, is posterior in existing. This is the situation with an end which the agent sets up by his own action, as a physician sets up health in a sick man by his own action; this is, of course, the physician's end.

And then there is an end which takes precedence in existing being, just as it precedes in the causal order. For instance, we call that an end which one intends to obtain by his action or motion, as fire inclines upward by its motion, and a king intends to establish a city by fighting. Therefore, God is not the end of things in the sense of being something set up as an ideal, but as a pre-existing being Who is to be attained.

Again, God is at once the ultimate end of things and the first agent, as we have shown. But the end that is produced by the action of the agent cannot be the first agent; it is, rather, the effect of the agent. Therefore, God cannot be the end of things in this way, as something produced, but only as something pre-existing that is to be attained.

. . .

THAT ALL THINGS TEND TO BECOME LIKE GOD

Created things are made like unto God by the fact that they attain to divine goodness. If, then, all things tend toward God as an ultimate end, so that they may attain His goodness, it follows that the ultimate end of things is to become like God.

Again, the agent is said to be the end of the effect because the effect tends to become like the agent; hence, "the form of the generator is the end of the generating action." But God is the end of things in such a way that He is also their first agent. Therefore, all things tend to become like God as to their ultimate end.

Besides, it is quite evident that things "naturally desire to be," and if they can be corrupted by anything they naturally resist corrupting agents and tend toward a place where they may be preserved, as fire inclines upward and earth downward. Now, all things get their being from the fact that they are made like unto God, Who is subsisting being itself, for all things exist merely as participants in existing being. Therefore, all things desire as their ultimate end to be made like unto God.

Moreover, all created things are, in a sense, images of the first agent, that is, of God, "for the agent makes a product to his own likeness." Now, the function of a perfect image is to represent its prototype by likeness to it; this is why an image is made. Therefore, all things exist in order to attain to the divine likeness, as to their ultimate end.

Furthermore, everything tends through its motion or action toward a good, as its end, which we showed above. Now, a thing participates in the good precisely to the same extent that it becomes like the first goodness, which is God. So, all things tend through their movements and actions toward the divine likeness, as toward their ultimate end.

.   .   .

Of course, someone could say that the ultimate end of an intellectual substance consists, in fact, in understanding the best intelligible object—not that the best object of understanding for this or that particular intellectual substance is absolutely the best intelligible object, but that, the higher an intellectual substance is, the higher will its best object of understanding be. And so, perhaps the highest created intellectual substance may have what is absolutely best as its best intelligible object, and, consequently, its felicity will consist in understanding God, but the felicity of any lower intellectual substance will lie in the understanding of some lower intelligible object, which is, however, the highest thing understood by it. Particularly would it seem true of the human intellect that its function is not to understand absolutely the best intelligible object, because of its weakness; indeed, it stands in relation to the knowing of the greatest intelligible object, "as the owl's eye is to the sunlight."

But it seems obvious that the end of any intellectual substance, even the lowest, is to understand God. It has been shown above that the ultimate end of all things, to which they tend, is God. Though it is the lowest in the order of intellectual substances, the human intellect is, nevertheless, superior to all things that lack understanding. And so, since there should not be a less noble end for a more noble substance, the end for the human intellect will be God Himself. And an intelligent being attains his ultimate end by understanding Him, as was indicated. Therefore, the human intellect reaches God as its end, through an act of understanding.

Again, just as things devoid of understanding tend toward God as an end, by way of assimilation, so intellectual substances do so by way of cognition, as is evident from the foregoing. Now, although things devoid of understanding tend to the likeness of their proximate agents, their natural tendency does not, however, rest there, for this tendency has as its end assimilation to the highest good, as is apparent from what we have said, even though these things can only attain this likeness in a very imperfect way. Therefore, however small the amount of divine knowledge that the intellect may be able to grasp, that will be for the intellect, in regard to its ultimate end, much more than the perfect knowledge of lower objects of understanding.

Besides, a thing has the greatest desire for its ultimate end. Now, the human intellect has a greater desire, and love, and pleasure, in knowing divine matters than it has in the perfect knowledge of the lowest things, even though it can grasp but little concerning divine things. So, the ultimate end of man is to understand God, in some fashion.

Moreover, a thing inclines toward the divine likeness as to its own end. So, that whereby a thing chiefly becomes like God is its ultimate end. Now, an intellectual creature chiefly becomes like God by the fact that it is intellectual, for it has this sort of likeness over and above what other creatures have, and this likeness includes all others. In the genus of this sort of likeness a being becomes more like God by actually understanding than by habitually or potentially understanding, because God is always actually understanding. . . . And, in this actual understanding, it becomes most like God by understanding God Himself, for God understands all things in the act of understanding Himself. . . . Therefore, to understand God is the ultimate end of every intellectual substance.

Furthermore, that which is capable of being loved only for the sake of some other object exists for the sake of that other thing which is lovable simply on its own account. In fact, there is no point in going on without end in the working of natural appetite, since natural desire would then be futile, because it is impossible to get to the end of an endless series. Now, all practical sciences, arts, and powers are objects of love only because they are means to something else, for their purpose is not knowledge but operation. But the speculative sciences are lovable for their own sake, since their end is knowledge itself. Nor do we find any action in human affairs, except speculative thought, that is not directed to some other end. Even sports activities, which appear to be carried on without any purpose, have a proper end, namely, so that after our minds have been somewhat relaxed through them we may be then better able to do serious jobs. Otherwise, if sport were an end in itself, the proper thing to do would be to play all the time.

but that is not appropriate. So, the practical arts are ordered to the speculative ones, and likewise every human operation to intellectual speculation, as an end. Now, among all the sciences and arts which are thus subordinated, the ultimate end seems to belong to the one that is preceptive and architectonic in relation to the others. For instance, the art of navigation, to which the end, that is the use, of a ship pertains, is architectonic and preceptive in relation to the art of shipbuilding. In fact, this is the way that first philosophy is related to the other speculative sciences, for all the others depend on it, in the sense that they take their principles from it, and also the position to be assumed against those who deny the principles. And this first philosophy is wholly ordered to the knowing of God, as its ultimate end; that is why it is also called *divine science*. So, divine knowledge is the ultimate end of every act of human knowledge and every operation.

Again, in all agents and movers that are arranged in an order, the end of the first agent and mover must be the ultimate end of all. Thus, the end of the commander of an army is the end of all who serve as soldiers under him. Now, of all the parts of man, the intellect is found to be the superior mover, for the intellect moves the appetite, by presenting it with its object; then the intellectual appetite, that is the will, moves the sensory appetites, irascible and concupiscible, and that is why we do not obey concupiscence unless there be a command from the will; and finally, the sense appetite, with the advent of consent from the will, now moves the body. Therefore, the end of the intellect is the end of all human actions. "But the end and good of the intellect are the true"; consequently, the first truth is the ultimate end. So, the ultimate end of the whole man, and of all his operations and desires, is to know the first truth, which is God.

Besides, there is naturally present in all men the desire to know the causes of whatever things are observed. Hence, because of wondering about things that were seen but whose causes were hidden, men first began to think philosophically; when they found the cause, they were satisfied. But the search did not stop until it reached the first cause, for "then do we think that we know perfectly, when we know the first cause." Therefore, man naturally desires, as his ultimate end, to know the first cause. But the first cause of all things is God. Therefore, the ultimate end of man is to know God.

Moreover, for each effect that he knows, man naturally desires to know the cause. Now, the human intellect knows universal being. So he naturally desires to know its cause, which is God alone. . . . Now, a person has not attained his ultimate end until natural desire comes to rest. Therefore, for human happiness which is the ultimate end it is not enough to have merely any kind of intelligible knowledge; there must be divine knowledge, as an ultimate end, to terminate the natural desire. So, the ultimate end of man is the knowledge of God.

Furthermore, a body tending toward its proper place by natural appetite is moved more forcibly and swiftly as it approaches its end. Thus, Aristotle proves, in *On the Heavens* I, that natural motion in a straight line cannot go on to infinity, for then it would be no more moved later than earlier. So, a thing that tends more forcibly later than earlier, toward an objective, is not moved toward an indefinite objective, but tends toward some determinate thing. Now, we find this situation in the desire to know. The more a person knows, the more is he moved by the desire to know. Hence, man's natural desire tends, in the process of knowing, toward some definite end. Now, this can be none other than the most noble object of knowledge, which is God. Therefore, divine knowledge is the ultimate end of man.

Now, the ultimate end of man, and of every intellectual substance, is called felicity or happiness, because this is what every intellectual substance desires as an ultimate end, and for its own sake alone. Therefore, the ultimate happiness and felicity of every intellectual substance is to know God.

And so, it is said in Matthew (5:8): "Blessed are the clean of heart, for they shall see God"; and in John (17:3): "This is eternal life, that they may know Thee, the only true God."

With this view, the judgment of Aristotle is also in agreement, in the last Book of his *Ethics,* where he says that the ultimate felicity of man is "speculative, in accord with the contemplation of the best object of speculation."

St. Thomas Aquinas

6

Summa Theologica

St. Thomas Aquinas intended his second great work, the *Summa Theologica,* to be the summation of all knowledge. The 631 questions dealt with and the 10,000 objections raised (which were controverted by the use of Aristotelian logic and quotation from authority) range from the nature and attributes of God to the relationship between Christian morality and the everyday concerns of trade and commerce. "Of Cheating, Which Is Committed in Buying and Selling" and "Of the Sin of Usury" from the *Summa Theologica* reveal not only Aquinas's method and the comprehensiveness of his philosophy, but how the Church attempted to deal with a question that was becoming difficult for the Middle Ages to cope with: How to reconcile the practices of nascent capitalism with traditional economic theory and orthodox religious beliefs.

OF CHEATING, WHICH IS COMMITTED IN BUYING AND SELLING

We must now consider those sins which relate to voluntary commutations. First, we shall consider cheating, which is committed in buying and selling: secondly, we shall consider usury, which occurs in loans.

Whether It Is Lawful to Sell a Thing for More Than Its Worth?

We proceed thus to the First Article:—

Objection 1. It would seem that it is lawful to sell a thing for more than its worth. In the commutations of human life, civil

St. Thomas Aquinas, *Summa Theologica*, trans. Fathers of the English Dominican Province (New York: Benziger, 1947), 1513–14, 1516–19, 1521–22. Reprinted by permission of the publisher.

laws determine that which is just. Now according to these laws it
is just for buyer and seller to deceive one another . . . and this
occurs by the seller selling a thing for more than its worth, and
the buyer buying a thing for less than its worth. Therefore it is
lawful to sell a thing for more than its worth.

Obj. 2. Further, that which is common to all would seem to
be natural and not sinful. Now Augustine relates that the saying
of a certain jester was accepted by all, *You wish to buy for a song
and to sell at a premium,* which agrees with the saying of Prov.
xx. 14, *It is naught, it is naught, saith every buyer: and when he
is gone away, then he will boast.* Therefore it is lawful to sell a
thing for more than its worth.

Obj. 3. Further, it does not seem unlawful if that which honesty demands be done by mutual agreement. Now, according to the
Philosopher . . . in the friendship which is based on utility, the
amount of the recompense for a favor received should depend on
the utility accruing to the receiver: and this utility sometimes is
worth more than the thing given, for instance if the receiver be in
great need of that thing, whether for the purpose of avoiding a
danger, or of deriving some particular benefit. Therefore, in contracts of buying and selling, it is lawful to give a thing in return
for more than its worth.

On the contrary, It is written (Matth. vii. 12): *All things . . .
whatsoever you would that men should do to you, do you also to
them.* But no man wishes to buy a thing for more than its worth.
Therefore no man should sell a thing to another man for more
than its worth.

I answer that, It is altogether sinful to have recourse to deceit
in order to sell a thing for more than its just price, because this is
to deceive one's neighbor so as to injure him. Hence Tully says
. . . *Contracts should be entirely free from double-dealing: the
seller must not impose upon the bidder, nor the buyer upon one
that bids against him.*

But, apart from fraud, we may speak of buying and selling in
two ways. First, as considered in themselves, and from this point of
view, buying and selling seem to be established for the common
advantage of both parties, one of whom requires that which belongs to the other, and vice versa, as the Philosopher states. . . .
Now whatever is established for the common advantage, should
not be more of a burden to one party than to another, and con-

sequently all contracts between them should observe equality of thing and thing. Again, the quality of a thing that comes into human use is measured by the price given for it, for which purpose money was invented. . . . Therefore if either the price exceed the quantity of the thing's worth, or, conversely, the thing exceed the price, there is no longer the equality of justice: and consequently, to sell a thing for more than its worth, or to buy it for less than its worth, is in itself unjust and unlawful.

Secondly we may speak of buying and selling, considered as accidentally tending to the advantage of one party, and to the disadvantage of the other: for instance, when a man has great need of a certain thing, while another man will suffer if he be without it. In such a case the just price will depend not only on the thing sold, but on the loss which the sale brings on the seller. And thus it will be lawful to sell a thing for more than it is worth in itself, though the price paid be not more than it is worth to the owner. Yet if the one man derive a great advantage by becoming possessed of the other man's property, and the seller be not at a loss through being without that thing, the latter ought not to raise the price, because the advantage accruing to the buyer, is not due to the seller, but to a circumstance affecting the buyer. Now no man should sell what is not his, though he may charge for the loss he suffers.

On the other hand if a man find that he derives great advantage from something he has bought, he may, of his own accord, pay the seller something over and above: and this pertains to his honesty.

Reply Obj. 1. As stated above . . . human law is given to the people among whom there are many lacking virtue, and it is not given to the virtuous alone. Hence human law was unable to forbid all that is contrary to virtue; and it suffices for it to prohibit whatever is destructive of human intercourse, while it treats other matters as though they were lawful, not by approving of them, but by not punishing them. Accordingly, if without employing deceit the seller disposes of his goods for more than their worth, or the buyer obtain them for less than their worth, the law looks upon this as licit, and provides no punishment for so doing, unless the excess be too great, because then even human law demands restitution to be made, for instance if a man be deceived in regard to more than half the amount of the just price of a thing.

On the other hand the Divine law leaves nothing unpunished

that is contrary to virtue. Hence, according to the Divine law, it is reckoned unlawful if the equality of justice be not observed in buying and selling: and he who has received more than he ought must make compensation to him that has suffered loss, if the loss be considerable. I add this condition, because the just price of things is not fixed with mathematical precision, but depends on a kind of estimate, so that a slight addition or subtraction would not seem to destroy the equality of justice.

Reply Obj. 2. As Augustine says . . . *this jester, either by looking into himself or by his experience of others, thought that all men are inclined to wish to buy for a song and sell at a premium. But since in reality this is wicked, it is in every man's power to acquire that justice whereby he may resist and overcome this inclination.* And then he gives the example of a man who gave the just price for a book to a man who through ignorance asked a low price for it. Hence it is evident that this common desire is not from nature but from vice, wherefore it is common to many who walk along the broad road of sin.

Reply Obj. 3. In commutative justice we consider chiefly real equality. On the other hand, in friendship based on utility we consider equality of usefulness, so that the recompense should depend on the usefulness accruing, whereas in buying it should be equal to the thing bought.

•   •   •

Whether, in Trading, It Is Lawful to Sell a Thing at a Higher Price Than What Was Paid for It?

We proceed thus to the Fourth Article:—

Objection 1. It would seem that it is not lawful, in trading, to sell a thing for a higher price than we paid for it. For Chrysostom says on Matth. xxi. 12: *He that buys a thing in order that he may sell it, entire and unchanged, at a profit, is the trader who is cast out of God's temple.* Cassiodorus speaks in the same sense in his commentary on Ps. lxx. 15, *Because I have not known learning,* or *trading* according to another version: *What is trade,* says he, *but buying at a cheap price with the purpose of retailing at a higher price?* and he adds: *Such were the tradesmen whom Our Lord cast out of the temple.* Now no man is cast out of the temple except for a sin. Therefore such like trading is sinful.

Obj. 2. Further, it is contrary to justice to sell goods at a higher price than their worth, or to buy them for less than their value, as shown above. . . . Now if you sell a thing for a higher price than you paid for it, you must either have bought it for less than its value, or sell it for more than its value. Therefore this cannot be done without sin.

Obj. 3. Further, Jerome says . . . *Shun, as you would the plague, a cleric who from being poor has become wealthy, or who, from being a nobody has become a celebrity.* Now trading would not seem to be forbidden to clerics except on account of its sinfulness. Therefore it is a sin in trading, to buy at a low price and to sell at a higher price.

On the contrary, Augustine commenting on Ps. lxx. 15, *Because I have not known learning,* says: *The greedy tradesman blasphemes over his losses; he lies and perjures himself over the price of his wares. But these are vices of the man, not of the craft, which can be exercised without these vices.* Therefore trading is not in itself unlawful.

I answer that, A tradesman is one whose business consists in the exchange of things. According to the Philosopher . . . exchange of things is twofold; one, natural as it were, and necessary, whereby one commodity is exchanged for another, or money taken in exchange for a commodity, in order to satisfy the needs of life. Such like trading, properly speaking, does not belong to tradesmen, but rather to housekeepers or civil servants who have to provide the household or the state with the necessaries of life. The other kind of exchange is either that of money for money, or of any commodity for money, not on account of the necessities of life, but for profit, and this kind of exchange, properly speaking, regards tradesmen, according to the Philosopher. . . . The former kind of exchange is commendable because it supplies a natural need: but the latter is justly deserving of blame, because, considered in itself, it satisfies the greed for gain, which knows no limit and tends to infinity. Hence trading, considered in itself, has a certain debasement attaching thereto, in so far as, by its very nature, it does not imply a virtuous or necessary end. Nevertheless gain which is the end of trading, though not implying, by its nature, anything virtuous or necessary, does not, in itself, connote anything sinful or contrary to virtue: wherefore nothing prevents gain from being directed to some necessary or even virtuous end, and thus trading becomes lawful. Thus, for instance, a man may intend the moderate gain which he seeks to acquire by trading for the upkeep of his household, or for the assistance of the needy: or again, a man may take to trade for some public advantage, for instance, lest his country lack the necessaries of life, and seek gain, not as an end, but as payment for his labor.

Reply Obj. 1. The saying of Chrysostom refers to the trading which seeks gain as a last end. This is especially the case where a man sells something at a higher price without its undergoing any change. For if he sells at a higher price something that has changed for the better, he would seem to receive the reward of his labor. Nevertheless the gain itself may be lawfully intended, not as a last end, but for the sake of some other end which is necessary or virtuous, as stated above.

Reply Obj. 2. Not everyone that sells at a higher price than he bought is a tradesman, but only he who buys that he may sell at a profit. If, on the contrary, he buys not for sale but for possession, and afterwards, for some reason wishes to sell, it is not a trade transaction even if he sell at a profit. For he may lawfully do this, either because he has bettered the thing, or because the value of the thing has changed with the change of place or time, or on account of the danger he incurs in transferring the thing from one place to another, or again in having it carried by another. In this sense neither buying nor selling is unjust.

Reply Obj. 3. Clerics should abstain not only from things that are evil in themselves, but even from those that have an appearance of evil. This happens in trading, both because it is directed to worldly gain, which clerics should despise, and because trading is open to so many vices, since *a merchant is hardly free from sins of the lips* (Ecclus. xxvi. 28). There is also another reason, because trading engages the mind too much with worldly cares, and consequently withdraws it from spiritual cares; wherefore the Apostle says (2 Tim. ii. 4): *No man being a soldier to God entangleth himself with secular businesses.* Nevertheless it is lawful for clerics to engage in the first mentioned kind of exchange, which is directed to supply the necessaries of life, either by buying or by selling.

OF THE SIN OF USURY

We must now consider the sin of usury, which is committed in loans. . . .

Whether It Is a Sin to Take Usury for Money Lent?

We proceed thus to the First Article:—

Objection 1. It would seem that it is not a sin to take usury for money lent. For no man sins through following the example of Christ. But Our Lord said of Himself (Luke xix. 23): *At My coming I might have exacted it,* i.e. the money lent, *with usury.* Therefore it is not a sin to take usury for lending money.

Obj. 2. Further, according to Ps. xviii. 8, *The law of the Lord is unspotted,* because, to wit, it forbids sin. Now usury of a kind is allowed in the Divine law, according to Deut. xxiii. 19, 20. *Thou shalt not fenerate to thy brother money, nor corn, nor any other thing, but to the stranger:* nay more, it is even promised as a reward for the observance of the Law, according to Deut. xxviii. 12: *Thou shalt fenerate to many nations, and shalt not borrow of any one.* Therefore it is not a sin to take usury.

Obj. 3. Further, in human affairs justice is determined by civil laws. Now civil law allows usury to be taken. Therefore it seems to be lawful.

Obj. 4. Further, the counsels are not binding under sin. But, among other counsels we find (Luke vi. 35): *Lend, hoping for nothing thereby.* Therefore it is not a sin to take usury.

Obj. 5. Further, it does not seem to be in itself sinful to accept a price for doing what one is not bound to do. But one who has money is not bound in every case to lend it to his neighbor. Therefore it is lawful for him sometimes to accept a price for lending it.

Obj. 6. Further, silver made into coins does not differ specifically from silver made into a vessel. But it is lawful to accept a price for the loan of a silver vessel. Therefore it is also lawful to accept a price for the loan of a silver coin. Therefore usury is not in itself a sin.

Obj. 7. Further, anyone may lawfully accept a thing which its owner freely gives him. Now he who accepts the loan, freely gives the usury. Therefore he who lends may lawfully take the usury.

On the contrary, It is written (Exod. xxii. 25): *If thou lend money to any of thy people that is poor, that dwelleth with thee, thou shalt not be hard upon them as an extortioner, nor oppress them with usuries.*

I answer that, To take usury for money lent is unjust in itself, because this is to sell what does not exist, and this evidently leads to inequality which is contrary to justice.

In order to make this evident, we must observe that there are certain things the use of which consists in their consumption: thus we consume wine when we use it for drink, and we consume wheat when we use it for food. Wherefore in such like things the use of the thing must not be reckoned apart from the thing itself, and whoever is granted the use of the thing, is granted the thing itself; and for this reason, to lend things of this kind is to transfer the ownership. Accordingly if a man wanted to sell wine separately from the use of the wine, he would be selling the same thing twice, or he would be selling what does not exist, wherefore he would evidently commit a sin of injustice. In like manner he commits an injustice who lends wine or wheat, and asks for double payment, viz. one, the return of the thing in equal measure, the other, the price of the use, which is called usury.

On the other hand, there are things the use of which does not consist in their consumption: thus to use a house is to dwell in it, not to destroy it. Wherefore in such things both may be granted: for instance, one man may hand over to another the ownership of his house while reserving to himself the use of it for a time, or vice versa, he may grant the use of the house, while retaining the ownership. For this reason a man may lawfully make a charge for the use of his house, and, besides this, revendicate the house from the person to whom he has granted its use, as happens in renting and letting a house.

Now money, according to the Philosopher . . . was invented chiefly for the purpose of exchange: and consequently the proper and principal use of money is its consumption or alienation whereby it is sunk in exchange. Hence it is by its very nature unlawful to take payment for the use of money lent, which payment is known as usury: and just as a man is bound to restore other ill-gotten goods, so is he bound to restore the money which he has taken in usury.

Reply Obj. 1. In this passage usury must be taken figuratively for the increase of spiritual goods which God exacts from us, for

He wishes us ever to advance in the goods which we receive from Him: and this is for our own profit not for His.

Reply Obj. 2. The Jews were forbidden to take usury from their brethren, i.e. from other Jews. By this we are given to understand that to take usury from any man is evil simply, because we ought to treat every man as our neighbor and brother, especially in the state of the Gospel, whereto all are called. Hence it is said without any distinction in Ps. xiv. 5: *He that hath not put out his money to usury,* and (Ezech. xviii. 8): *Who hath not taken usury.* They were permitted, however, to take usury from foreigners, not as though it were lawful, but in order to avoid a greater evil, lest, to wit, through avarice to which they were prone according to Is. lvi. 11, they should take usury from the Jews who were worshippers of God.

Where we find it promised to them as a reward, *Thou shalt fenerate to many nations,* etc., fenerating is to be taken in a broad sense for lending, as in Ecclus. xxix. 10, where we read: *Many have refused to fenerate, not out of wickedness,* i.e. they would not lend. Accordingly the Jews are promised in reward an abundance of wealth, so that they would be able to lend to others.

Reply Obj. 3. Human laws leave certain things unpunished, on account of the condition of those who are imperfect, and who would be deprived of many advantages, if all sins were strictly forbidden and punishments appointed for them. Wherefore human law has permitted usury, not that it looks upon usury as harmonizing with justice, but lest the advantage of many should be hindered. Hence it is that in civil law it is stated that *those things according to natural reason and civil law which are consumed by being used, do not admit of usufruct,* and that *the senate did not (nor could it) appoint a usufruct to such things, but established a quasi-usufruct,* namely by permitting usury. Moreover the Philosopher, led by natural reason, says . . . that *to make money by usury is exceedingly unnatural.*

Reply Obj. 4. A man is not always bound to lend, and for this reason it is placed among the counsels. Yet it is a matter of precept not to seek profit by lending: although it may be called a matter of counsel in comparison with the maxims of the Pharisees, who deemed some kinds of usury to be lawful, just as love of one's enemies is a matter of counsel. Or again, He speaks here not of the hope of usurious gain, but of the hope which is put in man.

For we ought not to lend or do any good deed through hope in man, but only through hope in God.

Reply Obj. 5. He that is not bound to lend, may accept repayment for what he has done, but he must not exact more. Now he is repaid according to equality of justice if he is repaid as much as he lent. Wherefore if he exacts more for the usufruct of a thing which has no other use but the consumption of its substance, he exacts a price of something non-existent: and so his exaction is unjust.

Reply Obj. 6. The principal use of a silver vessel is not its consumption, and so one may lawfully sell its use while retaining one's ownership of it. On the other hand the principal use of silver money is sinking it in exchange, so that it is not lawful to sell its use and at the same time expect the restitution of the amount lent. It must be observed, however, that the secondary use of silver vessels may be an exchange, and such use may not be lawfully sold. In like manner there may be some secondary use of silver money; for instance, a man might lend coins for show, or to be used as security.

Reply Obj. 7. He who gives usury does not give it voluntarily simply, but under a certain necessity, in so far as he needs to borrow money which the owner is unwilling to lend without usury.

· · ·

Whether It Is Lawful to Borrow Money Under a Condition of Usury?

We proceed thus to the Fourth Article:—

Objection 1. It would seem that it is not lawful to borrow money under a condition of usury. For the Apostle says (Rom. i. 32) that they *are worthy of death . . . not only they that do* these sins, *but they also that consent to them that do them.* Now he that borrows money under a condition of usury consents in the sin of the usurer, and gives him an occasion of sin. Therefore he sins also.

Obj. 2. Further, for no temporal advantage ought one to give another an occasion of committing a sin: for this pertains to active scandal, which is always sinful, as stated above. . . . Now he that seeks to borrow from a usurer gives him an occasion of sin. Therefore he is not to be excused on account of any temporal advantage.

Obj. 3. Further, it seems no less necessary sometimes to deposit one's money with a usurer than to borrow from him. Now it seems altogether unlawful to deposit one's money with a usurer, even as it would be unlawful to deposit one's sword with a madman, a maiden with a libertine, or food with a glutton. Neither therefore is it lawful to borrow from a usurer.

On the contrary, He that suffers injury does not sin, according to the Philosopher . . . wherefore justice is not a mean between two vices, as stated in the same book. . . . Now a usurer sins by doing an injury to the person who borrows from him under a condition of usury. Therefore he that accepts a loan under a condition of usury does not sin.

I answer that, It is by no means lawful to induce a man to sin, yet it is lawful to make use of another's sin for a good end, since even God uses all sin for some good, since He draws some good from every evil. . . . Hence when Publicola asked whether it were lawful to make use of an oath taken by a man swearing by false gods (which is a manifest sin, for he gives Divine honor to them) Augustine . . . answered that he who uses, not for a bad but for a good purpose, the oath of a man that swears by false gods, is a party, not to his sin of swearing by demons, but to his good compact whereby he kept his word. If however he were to induce him to swear by false gods, he would sin.

Accordingly we must also answer to the question in point that it is by no means lawful to induce a man to lend under a condition of usury: yet it is lawful to borrow for usury from a man who is ready to do so and is a usurer by profession; provided the borrower have a good end in view, such as the relief of his own or another's need. Thus too it is lawful for a man who has fallen among thieves to point out his property to them (which they sin in taking) in order to save his life, after the example of the ten men who said to Ishmael (Jerem. xli. 8): *Kill us not: for we have stores in the field.*

Reply Obj. 1. He who borrows for usury does not consent to the usurer's sin but makes use of it. Nor is it the usurer's acceptance of usury that pleases him, but his lending, which is good.

Reply Obj. 2. He who borrows for usury gives the usurer an occasion, not for taking usury, but for lending; it is the usurer who finds an occasion of sin in the malice of his heart. Hence there is passive scandal on his part, while there is no active scandal on the part of the person who seeks to borrow. Nor is this passive scandal a reason why the other person should desist from borrowing if he is in need, since this passive scandal arises not from weakness or ignorance but from malice.

Reply Obj. 3. If one were to entrust one's money to a usurer lacking other means of practising usury; or with the intention of making a greater profit from his money by reason of the usury, one would be giving a sinner matter for sin, so that one would be a participator in his guilt. If, on the other hand, the usurer to whom one entrusts one's money has other means of practising usury, there is no sin in entrusting it to him that it may be in safer keeping, since this is to use a sinner for a good purpose.

Dante Alighieri

—— 7 ——

The Divine Comedy: The Inferno

Dante Alighieri (1265–1321), greatest of the Italian poets, was born in
Florence of a family that had originally been of the feudal class, but for
several generations before Dante's birth had belonged to the urban com-
mercial class. As a youth he was caught up in intellectual interests and,
under the influence of the scholar Brunetto Latini, mastered the literature and philosophy of the ancient world. A friend of the poets and
artists of his time, Dante knew the famous painter Giotto well and was
a member of the culturally aggressive society of Florence.

His life was repeatedly (and usually adversely) affected by the civil turmoil of his native city, which reflected the larger struggle between the
papacy and the Holy Roman Empire. Holding public office for a while,
Dante became involved in this civic strife and later was banished on pain
of being burned alive if he returned to Florence. Dante wandered thereafter from city to city, taking service with successive patrons until he
retired to Ravenna, where he died.

Dante's greatest work, *The Divine Comedy*, begun about 1300, has tra-
ditionally entitled him to rank among the greatest poets of all time.
Dante called his poem the *Commedia;* the epithet "Divina" was added
some two centuries later. A comedy only in the medieval sense of having
a fortunate ending, the poem describes the experiences of the human soul
after death; Dante recounts his own pilgrimage—under the tutelage of
the Roman poet Vergil—through Hell and up the mount of Purgatory,
until at last he arrives in Paradise, where he is welcomed by the soul
of his idealized Beatrice.

Thoroughly learned in the medieval scholasticism of St. Thomas

From *The Inferno* by Dante, translated by John Ciardi, copyright 1954 by
John Ciardi, published by arrangement with The New American Library of
World Literature, Inc., New York. [Pp. 28–32, 34–39, 42–46, 49–54, 283–87.] This
is part of the Mentor Classics Edition of *The Divine Comedy* in Mr. Ciardi's
translation. *The Inferno* and *The Purgatorio* have already been published, and
The Paradiso is scheduled to appear Fall, 1964.

Aquinas, skilled in Latin poetry (although he wrote his *Comedy* in Italian), and familiar with the symbolism of medieval art and legend (the leopard, lion, and wolf of the first canto, for instance, probably represent lust, violence, and fraud), Dante combines these elements of his knowledge in the poem. The following selection is taken from *The Inferno,* the first part of the *Comedy,* as translated by John Ciardi, one of America's most distinguished contemporary poets. In it Dante narrates his encounters with the great men of the classic past who, according to medieval belief, could not receive salvation because they had lived before Christ's redemption of mankind. They are not punished but remain in "limbo." The cantos omitted from the selection tell of Dante's witnessing the punishments visited upon sinners in the lower circles of Hell. In the final canto of *The Inferno,* Dante emerges at last from the pit of Hell on Easter morn and sees again the stars of Heaven. Freed from despair, he goes on toward the ascent to Paradise, which he narrates in *The Purgatorio* and *The Paradiso*.

CANTO I

Midway in our life's journey, I went astray
    from the straight road and woke to find myself
    alone in a dark wood. How shall I say

what wood that was! I never saw so drear,
    so rank, so arduous a wilderness!
    Its very memory gives a shape to fear.

Death could scarce be more bitter than that place!
    But since it came to good, I will recount
    all that I found revealed there by God's grace.

How I came to it I cannot rightly say,
    so drugged and loose with sleep had I become
    when I first wandered there from the True Way.

But at the far end of that valley of evil
    whose maze had sapped my very heart with fear!
    I found myself before a little hill

and lifted up my eyes. Its shoulders glowed
   already with the sweet rays of that planet
   whose virtue leads men straight on every road,

and the shining strengthened me against the fright
   whose agony had wracked the lake of my heart
   through all the terrors of that piteous night.

Just as a swimmer, who with his last breath
   flounders ashore from perilous seas, might turn
   to memorize the wide water of his death—

so did I turn, my soul still fugitive
   from death's surviving image, to stare down
   that pass that none had ever left alive.

And there I lay to rest from my heart's race
   till calm and breath returned to me. Then rose
   and pushed up that dead slope at such a pace

each footfall rose above the last. And lo!
   almost at the beginning of the rise
   I faced a spotted Leopard, all tremor and flow

and gaudy pelt. And it would not pass, but stood
   so blocking my every turn that time and again
   I was on the verge of turning back to the wood.

This fell at the first widening of the dawn
   as the sun was climbing Aries with those stars
   that rode with him to light the new creation.

Thus the holy hour and the sweet season
   of commemoration did much to arm my fear
   of that bright murderous beast with their good omen.

Yet not so much but what I shook with dread
   at sight of a great Lion that broke upon me
   raging with hunger, its enormous head

held high as if to strike a mortal terror
   into the very air. And down his track,
   a She-Wolf drove upon me, a starved horror

ravening and wasted beyond all belief.
  She seemed a rack for avarice, gaunt and craving.
  Oh many the souls she has brought to endless grief!

She brought such heaviness upon my spirit
  at sight of her savagery and desperation,
  I died from every hope of that high summit.

And like a miser—eager in acquisition
  but desperate in self-reproach when Fortune's wheel
  turns to the hour of his loss—all tears and attrition

I wavered back; and still the beast pursued,
  forcing herself against me bit by bit
  till I slid back into the sunless wood.

And as I fell to my soul's ruin, a presence
  gathered before me on the discolored air,
  the figure of one who seemed hoarse from long silence.

At sight of him in that friendless waste I cried:
  "Have pity on me, whatever thing you are,
  whether shade or living man." And it replied:

"Not man, though man I once was, and my blood
  was Lombard, both my parents Mantuan.
  I was born, though late, *sub Julio,* and bred

in Rome under Augustus in the noon
  of the false and lying gods. I was a poet
  and sang of old Anchises' noble son

who came to Rome after the burning of Troy.
  But you—why do *you* return to these distresses
  instead of climbing that shining Mount of Joy

which is the seat and first cause of man's bliss?"
  "And are you then that Virgil and that fountain
  of purest speech?" My voice grew tremulous:

"Glory and light of poets! now may that zeal
  and love's apprenticeship that I poured out
  on your heroic verses serve me well!

For you are my true master and first author,
  the sole maker from whom I drew the breath
  of that sweet style whose measures have brought me
    honor.

See there, immortal sage, the beast I flee.
  For my soul's salvation, I beg you, guard me from her,
  for she has struck a mortal tremor through me."

And he replied, seeing my soul in tears:
  "He must go by another way who would escape
  this wilderness, for that mad beast that fleers

before you there, suffers no man to pass.
  She tracks down all, kills all, and knows no glut,
  but, feeding, she grows hungrier than she was.

She mates with any beast, and will mate with more
  before the Greyhound comes to hunt her down.
  He will not feed on lands nor loot, but honor

and love and wisdom will make straight his way.
  He will rise between Feltro and Feltro, and in him
  shall be the resurrection and new day

of that sad Italy for which Nisus died,
  and Turnus, and Euryalus, and the maid Camilla.
  He shall hunt her through every nation of sick pride

till she is driven back forever to Hell
  whence Envy first released her on the world.
  Therefore, for your own good, I think it well

you follow me and I will be your guide
  and lead you forth through an eternal place.
  There you shall see the ancient spirits tried

in endless pain, and hear their lamentation
  as each bemoans the second death of souls.
  Next you shall see upon a burning mountain

souls in fire and yet content in fire,
  knowing that whensoever it may be
  they yet will mount into the blessed choir.

To which, if it is still your wish to climb,
    a worthier spirit shall be sent to guide you.
    With her shall I leave you, for the King of Time,

who reigns on high, forbids me to come there
    since, living, I rebelled against his law.
    He rules the waters and the land and air

and there holds court, his city and his throne.
    Oh blessed are they he chooses!" And I to him:
    "Poet, by that God to you unknown,

lead me this way. Beyond this present ill
    and worse to dread, lead me to Peter's gate
    and be my guide through the sad halls of Hell."

And he then: "Follow." And he moved ahead
in silence, and I followed where he led.

CANTO II

The light was departing. The brown air drew down
    all the earth's creatures, calling them to rest
    from their day-roving, as I, one man alone,

prepared myself to face the double war
    of the journey and the pity, which memory
    shall here set down, nor hesitate, nor err.

O Muses! O High Genius! Be my aid!
    O Memory, recorder of the vision,
    here shall your true nobility be displayed!

Thus I began: "Poet, you who must guide me,
    before you trust me to that arduous passage,
    look to me and look through me—can I be worthy?

You sang how the father of Sylvius, while still
    in corruptible flesh won to that other world,
    crossing with mortal sense the immortal sill.

But if the Adversary of all Evil
    weighing his consequence and who and what
    should issue from him, treated him so well—

that cannot seem unfitting to thinking men,
since he was chosen father of Mother Rome
and of her Empire by God's will and token.

Both, to speak strictly, were founded and foreknown
as the established Seat of Holiness
for the successors of Great Peter's throne.

In that quest, which your verses celebrate,
he learned those mysteries from which arose
his victory and Rome's apostolate.

There later came the chosen vessel, Paul,
bearing the confirmation of that Faith
which is the one true door to life eternal.

But I—how should I dare? By whose permission?
I am not Aeneas. *I* am not Paul.
Who could believe me worthy of the vision?

How, then, may I presume to this high quest
and not fear my own brashness? You are wise
and will grasp what my poor words can but suggest."

As one who unwills what he wills, will stay
strong purposes with feeble second thoughts
until he spells all his first zeal away—

so I hung back and balked on that dim coast
till thinking had worn out my enterprise,
so stout at starting and so early lost.

"I understand from your words and the look in your eyes,"
that shadow of magnificence answered me,
"your soul is sunken in that cowardice

that bears down many men, turning their course
and resolution by imagined perils,
as his own shadow turns the frightened horse.

To free you of this dread I will tell you all
of why I came to you and what I heard
when first I pitied you. I was a soul

among the souls of Limbo, when a Lady
   so blessed and so beautiful, I prayed her
   to order and command my will, called to me.

Her eyes were kindled from the lamps of Heaven.
   Her voice reached through me, tender, sweet, and low.
   An angel's voice, a music of its own:

'O gracious Mantuan whose melodies
   live in earth's memory and shall live on
   till the last motion ceases in the skies,

my dearest friend, and fortune's foe, has strayed
   onto a friendless shore and stands beset
   by such distresses that he turns afraid

from the True Way, and news of him in Heaven
   rumors my dread he is already lost.
   I come, afraid that I am too-late risen.

Fly to him and with your high counsel, pity,
   and with whatever need be for his good
   and soul's salvation, help him, and solace me.

It is I, Beatrice, who send you to him.
   I come from the blessed height for which I yearn.
   Love called me here. When amid Seraphim

I stand again before my Lord, your praises
   shall sound in Heaven.' She paused, and I began:
   'O Lady of that only grace that raises

feeble mankind within its mortal cycle
   above all other works God's will has placed
   within the heaven of the smallest circle;

so welcome is your command that to my sense,
   were it already fulfilled, it would yet seem tardy.
   I understand, and am all obedience.

But tell me how you dare to venture thus
   so far from the wide heaven of your joy
   to which your thoughts yearn back from this abyss.'

'Since what you ask,' she answered me, 'probes near
  the root of all, I will say briefly only
  how I have come through Hell's pit without fear.

Know then, O waiting and compassionate soul,
  that is to fear which has the power to harm,
  and nothing else is fearful even in Hell.

I am so made by God's all-seeing mercy
  your anguish does not touch me, and the flame
  of this great burning has no power upon me.

There is a Lady in Heaven so concerned
  for him I send you to, that for her sake
  the strict decree is broken. She has turned

and called Lucia to her wish and mercy
  saying: 'Thy faithful one is sorely pressed;
  in his distresses I commend him to thee.'

Lucia, that soul of light and foe of all
  cruelty, rose and came to me at once
  where I was sitting with the ancient Rachel,

saying to me: 'Beatrice, true praise of God,
  why dost thou not help him who loved thee so
  that for thy sake he left the vulgar crowd?

Dost thou not hear his cries? Canst thou not see
  the death he wrestles with beside that river
  no ocean can surpass for rage and fury?

No soul of earth was ever as rapt to seek
  its good or flee its injury as I was—
  when I had heard my sweet Lucia speak—

to descend from Heaven and my blessed seat
  to you, laying my trust in that high speech
  that honors you and all who honor it.'

She spoke and turned away to hide a tear
  that, shining, urged me faster. So I came
  and freed you from the beast that drove you there,

blocking the near way to the Heavenly Height.
And now what ails you? Why do you lag? Why
this heartsick hesitation and pale fright

when three such blessed Ladies lean from Heaven
in their concern for you and my own pledge
of the great good that waits you has been given?"

As flowerlets drooped and puckered in the night
turn up to the returning sun and spread
their petals wide on his new warmth and light—

just so my wilted spirits rose again
and such a heat of zeal surged through my veins
that I was born anew. Thus I began:

"Blesséd be that Lady of infinite pity,
and blesséd be thy taxed and courteous spirit
that came so promptly on the word she gave thee.

Thy words have moved my heart to its first purpose.
My Guide! My Lord! My Master! Now lead on:
one will shall serve the two of us in this."

He turned when I had spoken, and at his back
I entered on that hard and perilous track.

CANTO III

I AM THE WAY INTO THE CITY OF WOE.
I AM THE WAY TO A FORSAKEN PEOPLE.
I AM THE WAY INTO ETERNAL SORROW.

SACRED JUSTICE MOVED MY ARCHITECT.
I WAS RAISED HERE BY DIVINE OMNIPOTENCE,
PRIMORDIAL LOVE AND ULTIMATE INTELLECT.

ONLY THOSE ELEMENTS TIME CANNOT WEAR
WERE MADE BEFORE ME, AND BEYOND TIME I STAND.
ABANDON ALL HOPE YE WHO ENTER HERE.

These mysteries I read cut into stone
above a gate. And turning I said: "Master,
what is the meaning of this harsh inscription?"

And he then as initiate to novice:
"Here must you put by all division of spirit
and gather your soul against all cowardice.

This is the place I told you to expect.
Here you shall pass among the fallen people,
souls who have lost the good of intellect."

So saying, he put forth his hand to me,
and with a gentle and encouraging smile
he led me through the gate of mystery.

Here sighs and cries and wails coiled and recoiled
on the starless air, spilling my soul to tears.
A confusion of tongues and monstrous accents toiled

in pain and anger. Voices hoarse and shrill
and sounds of blows, all intermingled, raised
tumult and pandemonium that still

whirls on the air forever dirty with it
as if a whirlwind sucked at sand. And I,
holding my head in horror, cried: "Sweet Spirit,

what souls are these who run through this black haze?"
And he to me: "These are the nearly soulless
whose lives concluded neither blame nor praise.

They are mixed here with that despicable corps
of angels who were neither for God nor Satan,
but only for themselves. The High Creator

scourged them from Heaven for its perfect beauty,
and Hell will not receive them since the wicked
might feel some glory over them." And I:

"Master, what gnaws at them so hideously
their lamentation stuns the very air?"
"They have no hope of death," he answered me,

"and in their blind and unattaining state
their miserable lives have sunk so low
that they must envy every other fate.

No word of them survives their living season.
  Mercy and Justice deny them even a name.
  Let us not speak of them: look, and pass on."

I saw a banner there upon the mist.
  Circling and circling, it seemed to scorn all pause.
  So it ran on, and still behind it pressed

a never-ending rout of souls in pain.
  I had not thought death had undone so many
  as passed before me in that mournful train.

And some I knew among them; last of all
  I recognized the shadow of that soul
  who, in his cowardice, made the Great Denial.

At once I understood for certain: these
  were of that retrograde and faithless crew
  hateful to God and to His enemies.

These wretches never born and never dead
  ran naked in a swarm of wasps and hornets
  that goaded them the more the more they fled,

and made their faces stream with bloody gouts
  of pus and tears that dribbled to their feet
  to be swallowed there by loathsome worms and maggots.

Then looking onward I made out a throng
  assembled on the beach of a wide river,
  whereupon I turned to him: "Master, I long

to know what souls these are, and what strange usage
  makes them as eager to cross as they seem to be
  in this infected light." At which the Sage:

"All this shall be made known to you when we stand
  on the joyless beach of Acheron." And I
  cast down my eyes, sensing a reprimand

in what he said, and so walked at his side
  in silence and ashamed until we came
  through the dead cavern to that sunless tide.

There, steering toward us in an ancient ferry
    came an old man with a white bush of hair,
    bellowing: "Woe to you depraved souls! Bury

here and forever all hope of Paradise:
    I come to lead you to the other shore,
    into eternal dark, into fire and ice.

And you who are living yet, I say begone
    from these who are dead." But when he saw me stand
    against his violence he began again:

"By other windings and by other steerage
    shall you cross to that other shore. Not here! Not here!
    A lighter craft than mine must give you passage."

And my Guide to him: "Charon, bite back your spleen:
    this has been willed where what is willed must be,
    and is not yours to ask what it may mean."

The steersman of that marsh of ruined souls,
    who wore a wheel of flame around each eye,
    stifled the rage that shook his woolly jowls.

But those unmanned and naked spirits there
    turned pale with fear and their teeth began to chatter
    at sound of his crude bellow. In despair

they blasphemed God, their parents, their time on earth,
    the race of Adam, and the day and the hour
    and the place and the seed and the womb that gave them
        birth.

But all together they drew to that grim shore
    where all must come who lose the fear of God.
    Weeping and cursing they come for evermore,

and demon Charon with eyes like burning coals
    herds them in, and with a whistling oar
    flails on the stragglers to his wake of souls.

As leaves in autumn loosen and stream down
    until the branch stands bare above its tatters
    spread on the rustling ground, so one by one

the evil seed of Adam in its Fall
    cast themselves, at his signal, from the shore
    and streamed away like birds who hear their call.

So they are gone over that shadowy water,
    and always before they reach the other shore
    a new noise stirs on this, and new throngs gather.

"My son," the courteous Master said to me,
    "all who die in the shadow of God's wrath
    converge to this from every clime and country.

And all pass over eagerly, for here
    Divine Justice transforms and spurs them so
    their dread turns wish: they yearn for what they fear.

No soul in Grace comes ever to this crossing;
    therefore if Charon rages at your presence
    you will understand the reason for his cursing."

When he had spoken, all the twilight country
    shook so violently, the terror of it
    bathes me with sweat even in memory:

the tear-soaked ground gave out a sigh of wind
    that spewed itself in flame on a red sky,
    and all my shattered senses left me. Blind,

like one whom sleep comes over in a swoon,
I stumbled into darkness and went down.

CANTO IV

A monstrous clap of thunder broke apart
    the swoon that stuffed my head; like one awakened
    by violent hands, I leaped up with a start.

And having risen; rested and renewed,
    I studied out the landmarks of the gloom
    to find my bearings there as best I could.

And I found I stood on the very brink of the valley
    called the Dolorous Abyss, the desolate chasm
    where rolls the thunder of Hell's eternal cry,

so depthless-deep and nebulous and dim
　　that stare as I might into its frightful pit
　　it gave me back no feature and no bottom.

Death-pale, the Poet spoke: "Now let us go
　　into the blind world waiting here below us.
　　I will lead the way and you shall follow."

And I, sick with alarm at his new pallor,
　　cried out, "How can I go this way when you
　　who are my strength in doubt turn pale with terror?"

And he: "The pain of these below us here,
　　drains the color from my face for pity,
　　and leaves this pallor you mistake for fear.

Now let us go, for a long road awaits us."
　　So he entered and so he led me in
　　to the first circle and ledge of the abyss.

No tortured wailing rose to greet us here
　　but sounds of sighing rose from every side,
　　sending a tremor through the timeless air,

a grief breathed out of untormented sadness,
　　the passive state of those who dwelled apart,
　　men, women, children—a dim and endless congress.

And the Master said to me: "You do not question
　　what souls these are that suffer here before you?
　　I wish you to know before you travel on

that these were sinless. And still their merits fail,
　　for they lacked Baptism's grace, which is the door
　　of the true faith *you* were born to. Their birth fell

before the age of the Christian mysteries,
　　and so they did not worship God's Trinity
　　in fullest duty. I am one of these.

For such defects are we lost, though spared the fire
　　and suffering Hell in one affliction only:
　　that without hope we live on in desire."

I thought how many worthy souls there were
  suspended in that Limbo, and a weight
  closed on my heart for what the noblest suffer.

"Instruct me, Master and most noble Sir,"
  I prayed him then, "better to understand
  the perfect creed that conquers every error:

has any, by his own or another's merit,
  gone ever from this place to blessedness?"
  He sensed my inner question and answered it:

"I was still new to this estate of tears
  when a Mighty One descended here among us,
  crowned with the sign of His victorious years.

He took from us the shade of our first parent,
  of Abel, his pure son, of ancient Noah,
  of Moses, the bringer of law, the obedient.

Father Abraham, David the King,
  Israel with his father and his children,
  Rachel, the holy vessel of His blessing,

and many more He chose for elevation
  among the elect. And before these, you must know,
  no human soul had ever won salvation."

We had not paused as he spoke, but held our road
  and passed meanwhile beyond a press of souls
  crowded about like trees in a thick wood.

And we had not traveled far from where I woke
  when I made out a radiance before us
  that struck away a hemisphere of dark.

We were still some distance back in the long night,
  yet near enough that I half-saw, half-sensed,
  what quality of souls lived in that light.

"O ornament of wisdom and of art,
  what souls are these whose merit lights their way
  even in Hell. What joy sets them apart?"

And he to me: "The signature of honor
　　they left on earth is recognized in Heaven
　　and wins them ease in Hell out of God's favor."

And as he spoke a voice rang on the air:
　　"Honor the Prince of Poets; the soul and glory
　　that went from us returns. He is here! He is here!"

The cry ceased and the echo passed from hearing;
　　I saw four mighty presences come toward us
　　with neither joy nor sorrow in their bearing.

"Note well," my Master said as they came on,
　　"that soul that leads the rest with sword in hand
　　as if he were their captain and champion.

It is Homer, singing master of the earth.
　　Next after him is Horace, the satirist,
　　Ovid is third, and Lucan is the fourth.

Since all of these have part in the high name
　　the voice proclaimed, calling me Prince of Poets,
　　the honor that they do me honors them."

So I saw gathered at the edge of light
　　the masters of that highest school whose song
　　outsoars all others like an eagle's flight.

And after they had talked together a while,
　　they turned and welcomed me most graciously,
　　at which I saw my approving Master smile.

And they honored me far beyond courtesy,
　　for they included me in their own number,
　　making me sixth in that high company.

So we moved toward the light, and as we passed
　　we spoke of things as well omitted here
　　as it was sweet to touch on there. At last

we reached the base of a great Citadel
　　circled by seven towering battlements
　　and by a sweet brook flowing round them all.

This we passed over as if it were firm ground.
    Through seven gates I entered with those sages
    and came to a green meadow blooming round.

There with a solemn and majestic poise
    stood many people gathered in the light,
    speaking infrequently and with muted voice.

Past that enameled green we six withdrew
    into a luminous and open height
    from which each soul among them stood in view.

And there directly before me on the green
    the master souls of time were shown to me.
    I glory in the glory I have seen!

Electra stood in a great company
    among whom I saw Hector and Aeneas
    and Caesar in armor with his falcon's eye.

I saw Camilla, and the Queen Amazon
    across the field. I saw the Latian King
    seated there with his daughter by his throne.

And the good Brutus who overthrew the Tarquin:
    Lucrezia, Julia, Marcia, and Cornelia;
    and, by himself apart, the Saladin.

And raising my eyes a little I saw on high
    Aristotle, the master of those who know,
    ringed by the great souls of philosophy.

All wait upon him for their honor and his.
    I saw Socrates and Plato at his side
    before all others there. Democritus

who ascribes the world to chance, Diogenes,
    and with him there Thales, Anaxagoras,
    Zeno, Heraclitus, Empedocles.

And I saw the wise collector and analyst—
    Dioscorides I mean. I saw Orpheus there,
    Tully, Linus, Seneca the moralist,

Euclid the geometer, and Ptolemy,
　Hippocrates, Galen, Avicenna,
　and Averrhoës of the Great Commentary.

I cannot count so much nobility;
　my longer theme pursues me so that often
　the word falls short of the reality.

The company of six is reduced by four.
　My Master leads me by another road
　out of that serenity to the roar

and trembling air of Hell. I pass from light
into the kingdom of eternal night.

CANTO XXXIV

"On march the banners of the King of Hell,"
　my Master said. "Toward us. Look straight ahead:
　can you make him out at the core of the frozen shell?"

Like a whirling windmill seen afar at twilight,
　or when a mist has risen from the ground—
　just such an engine rose upon my sight

stirring up such a wild and bitter wind
　I cowered for shelter at my Master's back,
　there being no other windbreak I could find.

I stood now where the souls of the last class
　(with fear my verses tell it) were covered wholly;
　they shone below the ice like straws in glass.

Some lie stretched out; others are fixed in place
　upright, some on their heads, some on their soles;
　another, like a bow, bends foot to face.

When we had gone so far across the ice
　that it pleased my Guide to show me the foul creature
　which once had worn the grace of Paradise,

he made me stop, and, stepping aside, he said:
　"Now see the face of Dis! This is the place
　where you must arm your soul against all dread."

Do not ask, Reader, how my blood ran cold
    and my voice choked up with fear. I cannot write it:
    this is a terror that cannot be told.

I did not die, and yet I lost life's breath:
    imagine for yourself what I became,
    deprived at once of both my life and death.

The Emperor of the Universe of Pain
    jutted his upper chest above the ice;
    and I am closer in size to the great mountain

the Titans make around the central pit,
    than they to his arms. Now, starting from this part,
    imagine the whole that corresponds to it!

If he was once as beautiful as now
    he is hideous, and still turned on his Maker,
    well may he be the source of every woe!

With what a sense of awe I saw his head
    towering above me! for it had three faces:
    one was in front, and it was fiery red;

the other two, as weirdly wonderful,
    merged with it from the middle of each shoulder
    to the point where all converged at the top of the skull;

the right was something between white and bile;
    the left was about the color that one finds
    on those who live along the banks of the Nile.

Under each head two wings rose terribly,
    their span proportioned to so gross a bird:
    I never saw such sails upon the sea.

They were not feathers—their texture and their form
    were like a bat's wings—and he beat them so
    that three winds blew from him in one great storm:

it is these winds that freeze all Cocytus.
    He wept from his six eyes, and down three chins
    the tears ran mixed with bloody froth and pus.

In every mouth he worked a broken sinner
    between his rake-like teeth. Thus he kept three
    in eternal pain at his eternal dinner.

For the one in front the biting seemed to play
    no part at all compared to the ripping: at times
    the whole skin of his back was flayed away.

"That soul that suffers most," explained my Guide,
    "is Judas Iscariot, he who kicks his legs
    on the fiery chin and has his head inside.

Of the other two, who have their heads thrust forward,
    the one who dangles down from the black face
    is Brutus: note how he writhes without a word.

And there, with the huge and sinewy arms, is the soul
    of Cassius.—But the night is coming on
    and we must go, for we have seen the whole."

Then, as he bade, I clasped his neck, and he,
    watching for a moment when the wings
    were opened wide, reached over dexterously

and seized the shaggy coat of the king demon;
    then grappling matted hair and frozen crusts
    from one tuft to another, clambered down.

When we had reached the joint where the great thigh
    merges into the swelling of the haunch,
    my Guide and Master, straining terribly,

turned his head to where his feet had been
    and began to grip the hair as if he were climbing;
    so that I thought we moved toward Hell again.

"Hold fast!" my Guide said, and his breath came shrill
    with labor and exhaustion. "There is no way
    but by such stairs to rise above such evil."

At last he climbed out through an opening
    in the central rock, and he seated me on the rim;
    then joined me with a nimble backward spring.

I looked up, thinking to see Lucifer
as I had left him, and I saw instead
his legs projecting high into the air.

Now let all those whose dull minds are still vexed
by failure to understand what point it was
I had passed through, judge if I was perplexed.

"Get up. Up on your feet," my Master said.
"The sun already mounts to middle tierce,
and a long road and hard climbing lie ahead."

It was no hall of state we had found there,
but a natural animal pit hollowed from rock
with a broken floor and a close and sunless air.

"Before I tear myself from the Abyss,"
I said when I had risen, "O my Master,
explain to me my error in all this:

where is the ice? and Lucifer—how has he
been turned from top to bottom: and how can the sun
have gone from night to day so suddenly?"

And he to me: "You imagine you are still
on the other side of the center where I grasped
the shaggy flank of the Great Worm of Evil

which bores through the world—you *were* while I climbed
          down,
but when I turned myself about, you passed
the point to which all gravities are drawn.

You are under the other hemisphere where you stand;
the sky above us is the half opposed
to that which canopies the great dry land.

Under the mid-point of that other sky
the Man who was born sinless and who lived
beyond all blemish, came to suffer and die.

You have your feet upon a little sphere
  which forms the other face of the Judecca.
  There it is evening when it is morning here.

And this gross Fiend and Image of all Evil
  who made a stairway for us with his hide
  is pinched and prisoned in the ice-pack still.

On this side he plunged down from heaven's height,
  and the land that spread here once hid in the sea
  and fled North to our hemisphere for fright;

and it may be that moved by that same fear,
  the one peak that still rises on this side
  fled upward leaving this great cavern here."

Down there, beginning at the further bound
  of Beelzebub's dim tomb, there is a space
  not known by sight, but only by the sound

of a little stream descending through the hollow
  it has eroded from the massive stone
  in its endlessly entwining lazy flow.

My Guide and I crossed over and began
  to mount that little known and lightless road
  to ascend into the shining world again.

He first, I second, without thought of rest
  we climbed the dark until we reached the point
  where a round opening brought in sight the blest

and beauteous shining of the Heavenly cars.
And we walked out once more beneath the Stars.

Dante Alighieri

8

De Monarchia

The Latin treatise *De Monarchia*, written between 1310 and 1316, contains Dante's mature political ideas and summarizes the arguments for one side of the chief political controversy of the Middle Ages: Was the pope or the emperor the supreme temporal ruler? Put another way, the question was whether the state was to be independent or under the control of the Church. The popes had claimed authority over secular rulers by virtue of their appointment by God as His vicars on earth. The popes also claimed that, since they were responsible for the fate of men's souls in the hereafter, they ought to have control over what men do in this world to enhance their chances of salvation. Dante, employing the method of scholasticism, which deduces specific points from generally accepted principles, rejects these arguments. In the following selection he argues for the necessity of a temporal monarchy and attempts to prove logically that the emperor receives his power direct from God. His argument that the Roman people rightfully exercised their dominion is omitted, however, as being of less importance to his thesis.

First, we must ascertain what temporal Monarchy is in its idea, as I may say, and in its purpose. Temporal Monarchy, called also the Empire, we define as a single Principality extending over all peoples in time, or in those things and over those things which are measured by time. Concerning it three main questions arise. First, we may ask and seek to prove whether it is necessary for the well-

The De Monarchia of Dante Alighieri, trans. Aurelia Henry (Boston: Houghton Mifflin, 1904), 5–6, 18–21, 24–26, 137, 164, 166–68, 170–74, 196–206.

being of the world; secondly, whether the Roman people rightfully appropriated the office of Monarchy; and thirdly, whether the authority of Monarchy derives from God directly, or from another, a minister or vicar of God.

. . .

Resuming what was said in the beginning, I repeat, there are three main questions asked and debated in regard to temporal Monarchy, which is more commonly termed the Empire, and it is my purpose to make inquiry concerning these in the order cited, according to the principle now enunciated. And so let the first question be whether temporal Monarchy is necessary for the well-being of the world. The necessity of temporal Monarchy can be gainsaid with no force of reason or authority, and can be proved by the most powerful and patent arguments, of which the first is taken on the testimony of the Philosopher in the *Politics*. There this venerable authority asserts that when several things are ordained for one end, one of them must regulate or rule, and the others submit to regulation or rule. This, indeed, not only because of the author's glorious name, but because of inductive reasoning, demands credence.

If we consider the individual man, we shall see that this applies to him, for, when all his faculties are ordered for his happiness, the intellectual faculty itself is regulator and ruler of all others; in no way else can man attain to happiness. If we consider the household, whose end is to teach its members to live rightly, there is need for one called the *pater-familias*, or for some one holding his place, to direct and govern, according to the Philosopher when he says, "Every household is ruled by its eldest." It is for him, as Homer says, to guide and make laws for those dwelling with him. From this arises the proverbial curse, "May you have an equal in your house." If we consider the village, whose aim is adequate protection of persons and property, there is again needed for governing the rest either one chosen for them by another, or one risen to preëminence from among themselves by their consent; otherwise, they not only obtain no mutual support, but sometimes the whole community is destroyed by many striving for first place. Again, if we consider the city, whose end is to insure comfort and sufficiency in life, there is need for undivided rule in rightly directed governments, and in those wrongly directed as well; else the end of civil life is missed, and the city ceases to be what it was. Finally, if we consider the individual kingdom, whose end is that of the city with greater promise of tranquillity, there must be one king to direct and govern. If not, not only the inhabitants of the kingdom fail of their end, but the kingdom lapses into ruin, in agreement with that word of infallible truth, "Every kingdom divided against itself is brought to desolation." If, then, this is true of these instances, and of all things ordained for a single end, it is true of the statement assumed above.

We are now agreed that the whole human race is ordered for one end, as already shown. It is meet, therefore, that the leader and lord be one, and that he be called Monarch, or Emperor. Thus it becomes obvious that for the well-being of the world there is needed a Monarchy, or Empire.

.   .   .

Further, mankind is a whole with relation to certain parts, and is a part with relation to a certain whole. It is a whole, of course, with relation to particular kingdoms and nations, as was shown above, and it is a part with relation to the whole universe, as is self-evident. Therefore, in the manner in which the constituent parts of collective humanity correspond to humanity as a whole, so, we say, collective humanity corresponds as a part to its larger whole. That the constituent parts of collective humanity correspond to humanity as a whole through the one only principle of submission to a single Prince, can be easily gathered from what has gone before. And therefore humanity corresponds to the universe itself, or to its Prince, who is God and Monarch, simply through one only principle, namely, the submission to a single Prince. We conclude from this that Monarchy is necessary to the world for its well-being.

And everything is well, nay, best disposed which acts in accordance with the intention of the first agent, who is God. This is self-evident, save to such as deny that divine goodness attains the summit of perfection. It is of the intention of God that all things should represent the divine likeness in so far as their peculiar nature is able to receive it. For this reason it was said, "Let us make man in our image, after our likeness." Although "in our image" cannot be said of things inferior to man, nevertheless, "after our likeness" can be said of all things, for the entire universe is nought else than a footprint of divine goodness. The human race, therefore, is ordered well, nay, is ordered for the best, when according to the utmost of its power it becomes like unto God. But the human race is most like unto God when it is most one, for the principle of unity dwells in Him alone. Wherefore it is written, "Hear, O Israel, the Lord our God is one Lord."

But the human race is most one when all are united together, a state which is manifestly impossible unless humanity as a whole becomes subject to one Prince, and consequently comes most into accordance with that divine intention which we showed at the beginning of this chapter is the good, nay, is the best disposition of mankind.

． ． ．

The question pending investigation, then, concerns two great luminaries, the Roman Pontiff and the Roman Prince: and the point at issue is whether the authority of the Roman Monarch, who, as proved in the second book, is rightful Monarch of the world, derives from God directly, or from some vicar or minister of God, by whom I mean the successor of Peter, veritable keeper of the keys of the kingdom of heaven.

． ． ．

Those men to whom the entire subsequent discussion is directed assert that the authority of the Empire depends on the authority of the Church, just as the inferior artisan depends on the architect. They are drawn to this by divers opposing arguments, some of which they take from Holy Scripture, and some from certain acts performed by the Chief Pontiff, and by the Emperor himself; and they endeavor to make their conviction reasonable.

． ． ．

From the same gospel they quote the saying of Christ to Peter, "Whatsoever thou shalt loose on earth shall be loosed in heaven," and understand this saying to refer alike to all the Apostles, according to the text of Matthew and John. They reason from this that the successor of Peter has been granted of God power to bind and loose all things, and then infer that he has power to loose the laws and decrees of the Empire, and to bind the laws and decrees of the temporal kingdom. Were this true, their inference would be correct.

But we must reply to it by making a distinction against the major premise of the syllogism which they employ. Their syllogism is this: Peter had power to bind and loose all things; the successor of Peter has like power with him; therefore the successor of Peter has power to loose and bind all things. From this they infer that he has power to loose and bind the laws and decrees of the Empire.

I concede the minor premise, but the major only with distinction. Wherefore I say that "all," the symbol of the universal, which is implied in "whatsoever," is never distributed beyond the scope of the distributed term. When I say, "All animals run," the distribution of "all" comprehends whatever comes under the genus "animal." But when I say, "All men run," the symbol of the universal only refers to whatever comes under the term "man." And when I say, "All grammarians run," the distribution is narrowed still further.

Therefore we must always determine what it is over which the symbol of the universal is distributed; then, from the recognized nature and scope of the distributed term, will be easily apparent the extent of the distribution. Now, were "whatsoever" to be understood absolutely when it is said, "Whatsoever thou shalt bind," he would certainly have the power they claim; nay, he would have even greater power, he would be able to loose a wife from her husband, and, while the man still lived, bind her to another—a thing he can in no wise do. He would be able to absolve me, while impenitent—a thing which God himself cannot do.

So it is evident that the distribution of the term under discussion is to be taken, not absolutely, but relatively to something else. A consideration of the concession to which the distribution is subjoined will make manifest this related something. Christ said to Peter, "I will give unto thee the keys of the kingdom of heaven"; that is, I will make thee doorkeeper of the kingdom of heaven. Then he adds, "and whatsoever," that is, "everything which," and He means thereby, "Everything which pertains to that office thou shalt have power to bind and loose." And thus the symbol of the universal which is implied in "whatsoever" is limited in its distribution to the prerogative of the keys of the kingdom of heaven. Understood thus, the proposition is true, but understood absolutely, it is obviously not. Therefore I conclude that although the successor of Peter has authority to bind and loose in accordance with the requirements of the prerogative granted to Peter, it does not follow, as they claim, that he has authority to bind and loose the decrees or statutes of Empire, unless they prove that this also belongs to the office of the keys. But we shall demonstrate farther on that the contrary is true.

They quote also the words in Luke which Peter addressed to Christ, saying, "Behold, here are two swords," and they assert that the two ruling powers were predicted by those two swords, and because Peter declared they were "where he was," that is, "with him," they conclude that according to authority these two ruling powers abide with Peter's successor.

To refute this we must show the falsity of the interpretation on which the argument is based. Their assertion that the two swords which Peter designated signify the two ruling powers before spoken of, we deny outright, because such an answer would have been at variance with Christ's meaning, and because Peter replied in haste, as usual, with regard to the mere external significance of things.

A consideration of the words preceding it and of the cause of the words will show that such an answer would have been inconsistent with Christ's meaning. Let it be called to mind that this response was made on the day of the feast, which Luke mentions earlier, saying, "Then came the day of unleavened bread, when the passover must be killed." At this feast Christ had already foretold His impending passion, in which He must be parted from His disciples. Let it be remembered also that when these words were uttered, all the twelve disciples were together; wherefore a little after the words just quoted Luke says, "And when the hour was come, He sat down, and the twelve Apostles with him." Continuing the discourse from this place he reaches the words, "When I sent you without purse, and scrip, and shoes, lacked ye anything?" And they answered, "Nothing." Then said He unto them, "But now, he that hath a purse, let him take it, and likewise his scrip: and he that hath no sword, let him sell his garment, and buy one." The meaning of Christ is clear enough here. He did not say, "Buy or procure two swords," but "twelve"; for it was in order that each of the twelve disciples might have one that He said to them, "He that hath no sword, let him buy one." And He spake thus to forewarn them of the persecution and contempt the future should bring, as though he would say, "While I was with you ye were welcomed, now shall ye be turned away. It behooves you, therefore, to prepare for yourselves those things which before I denied to you, but for which there is present need." If Peter's reply to these words had carried the meaning ascribed to it, the meaning would have been at variance with that of Christ, and Christ would have censured Him, as he did oftentimes, for his witless answers. However, He did not do so, but assented, saying to him, "It is enough," meaning, "I speak because of necessity; but if each cannot have a sword, two will suffice."

And that Peter usually spoke of the external significance of things is shown in his quick and unthinking presumption, impelled, I believe, not only by the sincerity of his faith, but by the purity and simplicity of his nature. To this characteristic presumption all those who write of Christ bear witness.

First, Matthew records that when Jesus had inquired of the disciples: "Whom say ye that I am?" before all the others Peter replied, "Thou art Christ, the Son of the living God." He also records that when Christ was telling His disciples how He must go to Jerusalem and suffer many things, Peter took Him and began to rebuke Him, saying, "Be it far from thee, Lord: this shall not be unto thee." Then Christ, turning to him, said in reproof, "Get thee behind me, Satan." Matthew also writes that on the Mount of Transfiguration, in the presence of Christ, Moses, and Elias, and the two sons of Zebedee, Peter said, "Lord, it is good for us to be here. If thou wilt, let us make here three tabernacles, one for thee, one for Moses, and one for Elias." Matthew further writes that when the disciples were on the ship in the night, and Christ walked on the water, Peter said, "Lord, if it be thou, bid me come unto thee on the water." And that when Christ predicted how all His disciples should be offended because of Him, Peter answered, "Though all men shall be offended because of thee, yet will I never be offended." And afterwards, "Though I should die with thee, yet will I not deny thee." And this statement Mark confirms, while Luke writes that, just before the words we have quoted concerning the swords, Peter had said to Christ, "Lord, I am ready to go with thee, both into prison and to death."

John tells of him, that when Christ desired to wash his feet, Peter asked, "Lord, dost thou wash my feet?" and then said, "Thou shalt never wash my feet." He further relates how Peter smote with his sword the servant of the High Priest, an account in which the four Evangelists agree. And John tells how when Peter came to the sepulchre and saw the other disciples lingering at the door, he entered in straightway; and again when after the resurrection Jesus stood on the shore and Peter "heard that it was the Lord, he girt his fisher's coat unto him (for he was naked), and did cast himself into the sea." Lastly, he recounts that when Peter saw John, he said to Jesus, "Lord, and what shall this man do?"

It is a source of joy to have summed up this evidence of our Head Shepherd, in praise of his singleness of purpose. From all this it is obvious that when he spoke of the two swords, his answer to Christ was unambiguous in meaning.

Even if the words of Christ and Peter are to be accepted typically, they cannot be interpreted in the sense these men claim, but rather as referring to the sword concerning which Matthew writes: "Think not that I am come to send peace on earth: I came not to send peace, but a sword. For I am come to set a man at variance against his father," and what follows. This He accomplished in word and deed, wherefore Luke tells Theophilus of all "that Jesus began to do and teach." Such was the sword Christ enjoined them to buy, and Peter made answer that already they had two with them. As we have shown, they were ready for words and for works to bring to pass those things which Christ proclaimed He had come to do by the sword.

. . .

Although by the method of reduction to absurdity it has been shown . . . that the authority of Empire has not its source in the Chief Pontiff, yet it has not been fully proved, save by an inference, that its immediate source is God, seeing that if the authority does not depend on the Vicar of God, we conclude that it depends on God Himself. For a perfect demonstration of the proposition we must prove directly that the Emperor, or Monarch, of the world has immediate relationship to the Prince of the universe, who is God.

In order to realize this, it must be understood that man alone of all beings holds the middle place between corruptibility and incorruptibility, and is therefore rightly compared by philosophers to the horizon which lies between the two hemispheres. Man may be considered with regard to either of his essential parts, body or soul. If considered in regard to the body alone, he is perishable; if in regard to the soul alone, he is imperishable. So the Philosopher spoke well of its incorruptibility when he said in the second book *on the Soul,* "And this only can be separated as a thing eternal from that which perishes."

If man holds a middle place between the perishable and imperishable, then, inasmuch as every mean shares the nature of the extremes, man must share both natures. And inasmuch as every nature is ordained for a certain ultimate end, it follows that there exists for man a twofold end, in order that as he alone of all beings partakes of the perishable and the imperishable, so he alone of all beings should be ordained for two ultimate ends. One end is for that in him which is perishable, the other for that which is imperishable.

Ineffable Providence has thus designed two ends to be contemplated of man: first, the happiness of this life, which consists in the activity of his natural powers, and is prefigured by the terrestrial Paradise; and then the blessedness of life everlasting, which consists in the enjoyment of the countenance of God, to which man's natural powers may not attain unless aided by divine light, and which may be symbolized by the celestial Paradise.

To these states of blessedness, just as to diverse conclusions, man must come by diverse means. To the former we come by the teachings of philosophy, obeying them by acting in conformity with the moral and intellectual virtues; to the latter through spiritual teachings which transcend human reason, and which we obey by acting in conformity with the theological virtues, Faith, Hope, and Charity. Now the former end and means are made known to us by human reason, which the philosophers have wholly explained to us; and the latter by the Holy Spirit, which has revealed to us supernatural but essential truth through the Prophets and Sacred Writers, through Jesus Christ, the coeternal Son of God, and through His disciples. Nevertheless, human passion would cast all these behind, were not men, like horses astray in their brutishness, held to the road by bit and rein.

Wherefore a twofold directive agent was necessary to man, in accordance with the twofold end; the Supreme Pontiff to lead the human race to life eternal by means of revelation, and the Emperor to guide it to temporal felicity by means of philosophic instruction. And since none or few—and these with exceeding difficulty—could attain this port, were not the waves of seductive desire calmed, and mankind made free to rest in the tranquillity of peace, therefore this is the goal which he whom we call the guardian of the earth and Roman Prince should most urgently seek; then would it be possible for life on this mortal threshing-floor to pass in freedom and peace. The order of the world follows the order inherent in the revolution of the heavens. To attain this order it is necessary that instruction productive of liberality and peace should be applied by the guardian of the realm, in due place and time, as dispensed by Him who is the ever present Watcher of the whole order of the heavens. And He alone foreordained this order, that by it in His providence He might link together all things, each in its own place.

If this is so, and there is none higher than He, only God elects and only God confirms. Whence we may further conclude that neither those who are now, nor those who in any way whatsoever have been, called Electors have the right to be so called; rather should they be entitled heralds of divine providence. Whence it is that those in whom is vested the dignity of proclamation suffer dissension among themselves at times, when, all or part of them being shadowed by the clouds of passion, they discern not the face of God's dispensation.

It is established, then, that the authority of temporal Monarchy descends without mediation from the fountain of universal authority. And this fountain, one in its purity of source, flows into multifarious channels out of the abundance of its excellence.

Methinks I have now approached close enough to the goal I had set myself, for I have taken the kernels of truth from the husks of falsehood, in that question which asked whether the office of Monarchy was essential to the welfare of the world, and in the next which made inquiry whether the Roman people rightfully appropriated the Empire, and in the last which sought whether the authority of the Monarch derived from God immediately, or from some other. But the truth of this final question must not be restricted to mean that the Roman Prince shall not be subject in some degree to the Roman Pontiff, for felicity that is mortal is ordered in a measure after felicity that is immortal. Wherefore let Caesar honor Peter as a first-born son should honor his father, so that, refulgent with the light of paternal grace, he may illumine with greater radiance the earthly sphere over which he has been set by Him who alone is Ruler of all things spiritual and temporal.

Geoffrey Chaucer

9

Canterbury Tales: The Prologue

Geoffrey Chaucer (*ca.* 1340–1400), the first of the great English poets, affords an example of the cosmopolitan, sophisticated quality of medieval literature at its best. At ease in the literary conventions of French, Italian, and Latin poetry, Chaucer was also successful in the world of practical affairs. In his youth he had seen military service in France and had been a member of diplomatic missions to France and Italy. Although Chaucer's many government posts and sinecures may not have been bestowed on him for his literary achievements, there can be no doubt that, during his lifetime, he enjoyed wide acclaim as a writer.

Chaucer's masterpiece, *Canterbury Tales,* was composed during the latter years of the fourteenth century. It is, on the one hand, a glorification of the medieval ideal society composed of clergy, nobility, and commoners; on the other hand, it is a shrewd depiction of individual follies and vices, which suggest a decline in medieval society and its institutions.

The setting of the *Tales* is a pilgrimage of some thirty persons, drawn from the various ranks of society, to visit the shrine of St. Thomas à Becket, a twelfth-century martyr and defender of the Church. Each pilgrim is to tell two stories on the road to Canterbury and two on the return journey. Chaucer identifies the pilgrims in medieval fashion, noting their dress and emblems of rank. Thus, his characters represent a cross section of the society of the time. Furthermore, his skill in characterization creates a gallery of distinct, vivid individuals. These sketches comprise *The Prologue,* most of which is given in the following selection.

The stories usually suit the character of the narrator and range from the elegant stylizations of courtly romance in *The Knight's Tale* to the crude anecdotes of the miller and the reeve. Although Chaucer never completed his collection of stories (only twenty-three pilgrims get their

From Geoffrey Chaucer's *Canterbury Tales,* rendered into modern English by J. U. Nicolson. Copyright 1934 by Covici, Friede, Inc. Reprinted by permission of Crown Publishers, Inc. [Pp. 1–22.]

turn), he succeeds in presenting a picture of medieval society and, in a broader sense, the whole range of human behavior.

When April with his showers sweet with fruit
The drought of March has pierced unto the root
And bathed each vein with liquor that has power
To generate therein and sire the flower;
When Zephyr also has, with his sweet breath,
Quickened again, in every holt and heath,
The tender shoots and buds, and the young sun
Into the Ram one half his course has run,
And many little birds make melody
That sleep through all the night with open eye
(So Nature pricks them on to ramp and rage)—
Then do folk long to go on pilgrimage,
And palmers to go seeking out strange strands,
To distant shrines well known in sundry lands.
And specially from every shire's end
Of England they to Canterbury wend,
The holy blessed martyr there to seek
Who helped them when they lay so ill and weak.
   Befell that, in that season, on a day
In Southwark, at the Tabard, as I lay
Ready to start upon my pilgrimage
To Canterbury, full of devout homage,
There came at nightfall to that hostelry
Some nine and twenty in a company
Of sundry persons who had chanced to fall
In fellowship, and pilgrims were they all
That toward Canterbury town would ride.
The rooms and stables spacious were and wide,
And well we there were eased, and of the best.
And briefly, when the sun had gone to rest,
So had I spoken with them, every one,
That I was of their fellowship anon,
And made agreement that we'd early rise
To take the road, as you I will apprise.

But none the less, whilst I have time and space,
Before yet farther in this tale I pace,
It seems to me accordant with reason
To inform you of the state of every one
Of all of these, as it appeared to me,
And who they were, and what was their degree,
And even how arrayed there at the inn;
And with a knight thus will I first begin.

THE KNIGHT

A knight there was, and he a worthy man,
Who, from the moment that he first began
To ride about the world, loved chivalry,
Truth, honour, freedom and all courtesy.
Full worthy was he in his liege-lord's war,
And therein had he ridden (none more far)
As well in Christendom as heathenesse,
And honoured everywhere for worthiness.
At Alexandria, he, when it was won;
Full oft the table's roster he'd begun
Above all nations' knights in Prussia.
In Latvia raided he, and Russia,
No christened man so oft of his degree.
In far Granada at the siege was he
Of Algeciras, and in Belmarie.
At Ayas was he and at Satalye
When they were won; and on the Middle Sea
At many a noble meeting chanced to be.
Of mortal battles he had fought fifteen,
And he'd fought for our faith at Tramissene
Three times in lists, and each time slain his foe.
This self-same worthy knight had been also
At one time with the lord of Palatye
Against another heathen in Turkey:
And always won he sovereign fame for prize.
Though so illustrious, he was very wise
And bore himself as meekly as a maid.
He never yet had any vileness said,

In all his life, to whatsoever wight.
He was a truly perfect, gentle knight.
But now, to tell you all of his array,
His steeds were good, but yet he was not gay.
Of simple fustian wore he a jupon.
Sadly discoloured by his habergeon;
For he had lately come from his voyage
And now was going on this pilgrimage.

THE SQUIRE

With him there was his son, a youthful squire,
A lover and a lusty bachelor,
With locks well curled, as if they'd laid in press.
Some twenty years of age he was, I guess.
In stature he was of an average length,
Wondrously active, aye, and great of strength.
He'd ridden sometime with the cavalry
In Flanders, in Artois, and Picardy,
And borne him well within that little space
In hope to win thereby his lady's grace.
Prinked out he was, as if he were a mead,
All full of fresh-cut flowers white and red.
Singing he was, or fluting, all the day;
He was as fresh as is the month of May.
Short was his gown, with sleeves both long and wide.
Well could he sit on horse, and fairly ride.
He could make songs and words thereto indite,
Joust, and dance too, as well as sketch and write.
So hot he loved that, while night told her tale,
He slept no more than does a nightingale.
Courteous he, and humble, willing and able,
And carved before his father at the table.

THE YEOMAN

A yeoman had he, nor more servants, no,
At that time, for he chose to travel so;

And he was clad in coat and hood of green.
A sheaf of peacock arrows bright and keen
Under his belt he bore right carefully
(Well could he keep his tackle yeomanly:
His arrows had no draggled feathers low),
And in his hand he bore a mighty bow.
A cropped head had he and a sun-browned face.
Of woodcraft knew he all the useful ways.
Upon his arm he bore a bracer gay,
And at one side a sword and buckler, yea,
And at the other side a dagger bright,
Well sheathed and sharp as spear point in the light;
On breast a Christopher of silver sheen.
He bore a horn in baldric all of green;
A forester he truly was, I guess.

THE PRIORESS

There was also a nun, a prioress,
Who, in her smiling, modest was and coy;
Her greatest oath was but "By Saint Eloy!"
And she was known as Madam Eglantine.
Full well she sang the services divine,
Intoning through her nose, becomingly;
And fair she spoke her French, and fluently,
After the school of Stratford-at-the-Bow,
For French of Paris was not hers to know.
At table she had been well taught withal,
And never from her lips let morsels fall,
Nor dipped her fingers deep in sauce, but ate
With so much care the food upon her plate
That never driblet fell upon her breast.
In courtesy she had delight and zest.
Her upper lip was always wiped so clean
That in her cup was no iota seen
Of grease, when she had drunk her draught of wine.
Becomingly she reached for meat to dine.
And certainly delighting in good sport,
She was right pleasant, amiable—in short.

She was at pains to counterfeit the look
Of courtliness, and stately manners took.
And would be held worthy of reverence.
 But, to say something of her moral sense,
She was so charitable and piteous
That she would weep if she but saw a mouse
Caught in a trap, though it were dead or bled.
She had some little dogs, too, that she fed
On roasted flesh, or milk and fine white bread.
But sore she'd weep if one of them were dead,
Or if men smote it with a rod to smart:
For pity ruled her, and her tender heart.
Right decorous her pleated wimple was;
Her nose was fine; her eyes were blue as glass;
Her mouth was small and therewith soft and red;
But certainly she had a fair forehead;
It was almost a full span broad, I own,
For, truth to tell, she was not undergrown.
Neat was her cloak, as I was well aware.
Of coral small about her arm she'd bear
A string of beads and gauded all with green;
And therefrom hung a brooch of golden sheen
Whereon there was first written a crowned "A,"
And under, *Amor vincit omnia.*
Another little NUN with her had she,
Who was her chaplain; and of PRIESTS she'd three.

THE MONK

A monk there was, one made for mastery,
An outrider, who loved his venery;
A manly man, to be an abbot able.
Full many a blooded horse had he in stable:
And when he rode men might his bridle hear
A-jingling in the whistling wind as clear,
Aye, and as loud as does the chapel bell
Where this brave monk was master of the cell.
The rule of Maurus or Saint Benedict,
By reason it was old and somewhat strict,

This said monk let such old things slowly pace
And followed new-world manners in their place.
He cared not for that text a clean-plucked hen
Which holds that hunters are not holy men;
Nor that a monk, when he is cloisterless,
Is like unto a fish that's waterless;
That is to say, a monk out of his cloister.
But this same text he held not worth an oyster;
And I said his opinion was right good.
What? Should he study as a madman would
Upon a book in cloister cell? Or yet
Go labour with his hands and swink and sweat,
As Austin bids? How shall the world be served?
Let Austin have his toil to him reserved.
Therefore he was a rider day and night;
Greyhounds he had, as swift as bird in flight.
Since riding and the hunting of the hare
Were all his love, for no cost would he spare.
I saw his sleeves were purfled at the hand
With fur of grey, the finest in the land;
Also, to fasten hood beneath his chin,
He had of good wrought gold a curious pin:
A love-knot in the larger end there was.
His head was bald and shone like any glass,
And smooth as one anointed was his face.
Fat was this lord, he stood in goodly case.
His bulging eyes he rolled about, and hot
They gleamed and red, like fire beneath a pot;
His boots were soft; his horse of great estate.
Now certainly he was a fine prelate:
He was not pale as some poor wasted ghost.
A fat swan loved he best of any roast.
His palfrey was as brown as is a berry.

THE FRIAR

A friar there was, a wanton and a merry,
A limiter, a very festive man.
In all the Orders Four is none that can

Equal his gossip and his fair language.
He had arranged full many a marriage
Of women young, and this at his own cost.
Unto his order he was a noble post.
Well liked by all and intimate was he
With franklins everywhere in his country,
And with the worthy women of the town:
For at confessing he'd more power in gown
(As he himself said) than a good curate,
For of his order he was licentiate.
He heard confession gently, it was said,
Gently absolved too, leaving naught of dread.
He was an easy man to give penance
When knowing he should gain a good pittance;
For to a begging friar, money given
Is sign that any man has been well shriven.
For if one gave (he dared to boast of this),
He took the man's repentance not amiss.
For many a man there is so hard of heart
He cannot weep however pains may smart.
Therefore, instead of weeping and of prayer,
Men should give silver to poor friars all bare.
His tippet was stuck always full of knives
And pins, to give to young and pleasing wives.
And certainly he kept a merry note:
Well could he sing and play upon the rote.
At balladry he bore the prize away.
His throat was white as lily of the May;
Yet strong he was as ever champion.
In towns he knew the taverns, every one,
And every good host and each barmaid too—
Better than begging lepers, these he knew.
For unto no such solid man as he
Accorded it, as far as he could see,
To have sick lepers for acquaintances.
There is no honest advantageousness
In dealing with such poverty-stricken curs;
It's with the rich and with big victuallers.
And so, wherever profit might arise,
Courteous he was and humble in men's eyes.

There was no other man so virtuous.
He was the finest beggar of his house;
A certain district being farmed to him,
None of his brethren dared approach its rim;
For though a widow had no shoes to show,
So pleasant was his *In principio*,
He always got a farthing ere he went.
He lived by pickings, it is evident.
And he could romp as well as any whelp.
On love days could he be of mickle help.
For there he was not like a cloisterer,
With threadbare cope as is the poor scholar,
But he was like a lord or like a pope.
Of double worsted was his semi-cope,
That rounded like a bell, as you may guess.
He lisped a little, out of wantonness,
To make his English soft upon his tongue;
And in his harping, after he had sung,
His two eyes twinkled in his head as bright
As do the stars within the frosty night.
This worthy limiter was named Hubert.

THE MERCHANT

There was a merchant with forked beard, and girt
In motley gown, and high on horse he sat,
Upon his head a Flemish beaver hat;
His boots were fastened rather elegantly.
His spoke his notions out right pompously,
Stressing the times when he had won, not lost.
He would the sea were held at any cost
Across from Middleburgh to Orwell town.
At money-changing he could make a crown.
This worthy man kept all his wits well set;
There was no one could say he was in debt,
So well he governed all his trade affairs
With bargains and with borrowings and with shares.
Indeed, he was a worthy man withal,
But, sooth to say, his name I can't recall.

THE CLERK

A clerk from Oxford was with us also,
Who'd turned to getting knowledge, long ago.
As meagre was his horse as is a rake,
Nor he himself too fat, I'll undertake,
But he looked hollow and went soberly.
Right threadbare was his overcoat; for he
Had got him yet no churchly benefice,
Nor was so worldly as to gain office.
For he would rather have at his bed's head
Some twenty books, all bound in black and red,
Of Aristotle and his philosophy
Than rich robes, fiddle, or gay psaltery.
Yet, and for all he was philosopher,
He had but little gold within his coffer;
But all that he might borrow from a friend
On books and learning he would swiftly spend,
And then he'd pray right busily for the souls
Of those who gave him wherewithal for schools.
Of study took he utmost care and heed.
Not one word spoke he more than was his need;
And that was said in fullest reverence
And short and quick and full of high good sense.
Pregnant of moral virtue was his speech;
And gladly would he learn and gladly teach.

THE LAWYER

A sergeant of the law, wary and wise,
Who'd often gone to Paul's walk to advise,
There was also, compact of excellence.
Discreet he was, and of great reverence;
At least he seemed so, his words were so wise.
Often he sat as justice in assize,
By patent or commission from the crown;
Because of learning and his high renown,
He took large fees and many robes could own.
So great a purchaser was never known.

All was fee simple to him, in effect,
Wherefore his claims could never be suspect.
Nowhere a man so busy of his class,
And yet he seemed much busier than he was.
All cases and all judgments could he cite
That from King William's time were apposite.
And he could draw a contract so explicit
Not any man could fault therefrom elicit;
And every statute he'd verbatim quote.
He rode but badly in a medley coat,
Belted in a silken sash, with little bars,
But of his dress no more particulars.

THE FRANKLIN

There was a franklin in his company;
White was his beard as is the white daisy.
Of sanguine temperament by every sign,
He loved right well his morning sop in wine.
Delightful living was the goal he'd won,
For he was Epicurus' very son,
That held opinion that a full delight
Was true felicity, perfect and right.
A householder, and that a great, was he;
Saint Julian he was in his own country.
His bread and ale were always right well done;
A man with better cellars there was none.
Baked meat was never wanting in his house,
Of fish and flesh, and that so plenteous
It seemed to snow therein both food and drink
Of every dainty that a man could think.
According to the season of the year
He changed his diet and his means of cheer.
Full many a fattened partridge did he mew,
And many a bream and pike in fish-pond too.
Woe to his cook, except the sauces were
Poignant and sharp, and ready all his gear.
His table, waiting in his hall alway,
Stood ready covered through the livelong day.

At county sessions was he lord and sire,
And often acted as a knight of shire.
A dagger and a trinket-bag of silk
Hung from his girdle, white as morning milk.
He had been sheriff and been auditor;
And nowhere was a worthier vavasor.

THE HABERDASHER, THE CARPENTER, THE WEAVER, THE DYER, AND THE ARRAS-MAKER

A haberdasher and a carpenter,
An arras-maker, dyer, and weaver
Were with us, clothed in similar livery,
All of one sober, great fraternity.
Their gear was new and well adorned it was;
Their weapons were not cheaply trimmed with brass,
But all with silver; chastely made and well
Their girdles and their pouches too, I tell.
Each man of them appeared a proper burgess
To sit in guildhall on a high dais.
And each of them, for wisdom he could span,
Was fitted to have been an alderman;
For chattels they'd enough, and, too, of rent;
To which their goodwives gave a free assent,
Or else for certain they had been to blame.
It's good to hear "Madam" before one's name,
And go to church when all the world may see,
Having one's mantle borne right royally.

THE COOK

A cook they had with them, just for the nonce,
To boil the chickens with the marrow-bones,
And flavour tartly and with galingale.
Well could he tell a draught of London ale.
And he could roast and seethe and broil and fry,
And make a good thick soup, and bake a pie.

But very ill it was, it seemed to me,
That on his shin a deadly sore had he;
For sweet blanc-mange, he made it with the best.

THE SAILOR

There was a sailor, living far out west;
For aught I know, he was of Dartmouth town.
He sadly rode a hackney, in a gown,
Of thick rough cloth falling to the knee.
A dagger hanging on a cord had he
About his neck, and under arm, and down.
The summer's heat had burned his visage brown;
And certainly he was a good fellow.
Full many a draught of wine he'd drawn, I trow,
Of Bordeaux vintage, while the trader slept.
Nice conscience was a thing he never kept.
If that he fought and got the upper hand,
By water he sent them home to every land.
But as for craft, to reckon well his tides,
His currents and the dangerous watersides,
His harbours, and his moon, his pilotage,
There was none such from Hull to far Carthage.
Hardy, and wise in all things undertaken,
By many a tempest had his beard been shaken.
He knew well all the havens, as they were,
From Gottland to the Cape of Finisterre,
And every creek in Brittany and Spain;
His vessel had been christened *Madeleine*.

THE PHYSICIAN

With us there was a doctor of physic;
In all this world was none like him to pick
For talk of medicine and surgery;
For he was grounded in astronomy.
He often kept a patient from the pall
By horoscopes and magic natural.
Well could he tell the fortune ascendent
Within the houses for his sick patient.

He knew the cause of every malady,
Were it of hot or cold, of moist or dry,
And where engendered, and of what humour;
He was a very good practitioner.
The cause being known, down to the deepest root,
Anon he gave to the sick man his boot.
Ready he was, with his apothecaries,
To send him drugs and all electuaries;
By mutual aid much gold they'd always won—
Their friendship was a thing not new begun.
Well read was he in Esculapius,
And Deiscorides, and in Rufus,
Hippocrates, and Hali, and Galen,
Serapion, Rhazes, and Avicen,
Averrhoës, Gilbert, and Constantine,
Bernard, and Gatisden, and John Damascene.
In diet he was measured as could be,
Including naught of superfluity,
But nourishing and easy. It's no libel
To say he read but little in the Bible.
In blue and scarlet he went clad, withal,
Lined with a taffeta and with sendal;
And yet he was right chary of expense;
He kept the gold he gained from pestilence.
For gold in physic is a fine cordial,
And therefore loved he gold exceeding all.

THE WIFE OF BATH

There was a housewife come from Bath, or near,
Who—sad to say—was deaf in either ear.
At making cloth she had so great a bent
She bettered those of Ypres and even of Ghent.
In all the parish there was no goodwife
Should offering make before her, on my life;
And if one did, indeed, so wroth was she
It put her out of all her charity.
Her kerchiefs were of finest weave and ground;
I dare swear that they weighed a full ten pound

Which, of a Sunday, she wore on her head.
Her hose were of the choicest scarlet red,
Close gartered, and her shoes were soft and new.
Bold was her face, and fair, and red of hue.
She'd been respectable throughout her life,
With five churched husbands bringing joy and strife,
Not counting other company in youth;
But thereof there's no need to speak, in truth.
Three times she'd journeyed to Jerusalem;
And many a foreign stream she'd had to stem;
At Rome she'd been, and she'd been in Boulogne,
In Spain at Santiago, and at Cologne.
She could tell much of wandering by the way:
Gap-toothed was she, it is no lie to say.
Upon an ambler easily she sat,
Well wimpled, aye, and over all a hat
As broad as is a buckler or a targe;
A rug was tucked around her buttocks large,
And on her feet a pair of sharpened spurs.
In company well could she laugh her slurs.
The remedies of love she knew, perchance,
For of that art she'd learned the old, old dance.

THE PARSON

There was a good man of religion, too,
A country parson, poor, I warrant you;
But rich he was in holy thought and work.
He was a learned man also, a clerk,
Who Christ's own gospel truly sought to preach;
Devoutly his parishioners would he teach.
Benign he was and wondrous diligent,
Patient in adverse times and well content,
As he was ofttimes proven; always blithe,
He was right loath to curse to get a tithe,
But rather would he give, in case of doubt,
Unto those poor parishioners about,
Part of his income, even of his goods.
Enough with little, coloured all his moods.

Wide was his parish, houses far asunder,
But never did he fail, for rain or thunder,
In sickness, or in sin, or any state,
To visit to the farthest, small and great,
Going afoot, and in his hand a stave.
This fine example to his flock he gave,
That first he wrought and afterwards he taught;
Out of the gospel then that text he caught,
And this figure he added thereunto—
That, if gold rust, what shall poor iron do?
For if the priest be foul, in whom we trust,
What wonder if a layman yield to lust?
And shame it is, if priest take thought for keep,
A shitty shepherd, shepherding clean sheep.
Well ought a priest example good to give,
By his own cleanness, how his flock should live.
He never let his benefice for hire,
Leaving his flock to flounder in the mire,
And ran to London, up to old Saint Paul's
To get himself a chantry there for souls,
Nor in some brotherhood did he withhold;
But dwelt at home and kept so well the fold
That never wolf could make his plans miscarry;
He was a shepherd and not mercenary.
And holy though he was, and virtuous,
To sinners he was not impiteous,
Nor haughty in his speech, nor too divine,
But in all teaching prudent and benign.
To lead folk into Heaven but by stress
Of good example was his busyness.
But if some sinful one proved obstinate,
Be who it might, of high or low estate,
Him he reproved, and sharply, as I know.
There is nowhere a better priest, I trow.
He had no thirst for pomp or reverence,
Nor made himself a special, spiced conscience,
But Christ's own lore, and His apostles' twelve
He taught, but first he followed it himselve.

THE PLOWMAN

With him there was a plowman, was his brother,
That many a load of dung, and many another
Had scattered, for a good true toiler, he,
Living in peace and perfect charity.
He loved God most, and that with his whole heart
At all times, though he played or plied his art,
And next, his neighbour, even as himself.
He'd thresh and dig, with never thought of pelf,
For Christ's own sake, for every poor wight,
All without pay, if it lay in his might.
He paid his taxes, fully, fairly, well,
Both by his own toil and by stuff he'd sell.
In a tabard he rode upon a mare.

There were also a reeve and miller there;
A summoner, manciple and pardoner,
And these, beside myself, made all there were.

THE MILLER

The miller was a stout churl, be it known,
Hardy and big of brawn and big of bone;
Which was well proved, for when he went on lam
At wrestling, never failed he of the ram.
He was a chunky fellow, broad of build;
He'd heave a door from hinges if he willed,
Or break it through, by running, with his head.
His beard, as any sow or fox, was red,
And broad it was as if it were a spade.
Upon the coping of his nose he had
A wart, and thereon stood a tuft of hairs,
Red as the bristles in an old sow's ears;
His nostrils they were black and very wide.
A sword and buckler bore he by his side.
His mouth was like a furnace door for size.
He was a jester and could poetize,
But mostly all of sin and ribaldries.
He could steal corn and full thrice charge his fees;

And yet he had a thumb of gold, begad.
A white coat and blue hood he wore, this lad.
A bagpipe he could blow well, be it known,
And with that same he brought us out of town.

THE MANCIPLE

There was a manciple from an inn of court,
To whom all buyers might quite well resort
To learn the art of buying food and drink;
For whether he paid cash or not, I think
That he so knew the markets, when to buy,
He never found himself left high and dry.
Now is it not of God a full fair grace
That such a vulgar man has wit to pace
The wisdom of a crowd of learned men?
Of masters had he more than three times ten,
Who were in law expert and curious;
Whereof there were a dozen in that house
Fit to be stewards of both rent and land
Of any lord in England who would stand
Upon his own and live in manner good,
In honour, debtless (save his head were wood),
Or live as frugally as he might desire;
These men were able to have helped a shire
In any case that ever might befall;
And yet this manciple outguessed them all.

THE REEVE

The reeve he was a slender, choleric man,
Who shaved his beard as close as razor can.
His hair was cut round even with his ears;
His top was tonsured like a pulpiteer's.
Long were his legs, and they were very lean,
And like a staff, with no calf to be seen.
Well could he manage granary and bin;
No auditor could ever on him win.
He could foretell, by drought and by the rain,
The yielding of his seed and of his grain.

His lord's sheep and his oxen and his dairy,
His swine and horses, all his stores, his poultry,
Were wholly in this steward's managing;
And, by agreement, he'd made reckoning
Since his young lord of age was twenty years;
Yet no man ever found him in arrears.
There was no agent, hind, or herd who'd cheat
But he knew well his cunning and deceit;
They were afraid of him as of the death.
His cottage was a good one, on a heath;
By green trees shaded with this dwelling-place.
Much better than his lord could he purchase.
Right rich he was in his own private right,
Seeing he'd pleased his lord, by day or night,
By giving him, or lending, of his goods,
And so got thanked—but yet got coats and hoods.
In youth he'd learned a good trade, and had been
A carpenter, as fine as could be seen.
This steward sat a horse that well could trot,
And was all dapple-grey, and was named Scot.
A long surcoat of blue did he parade,
And at his side he bore a rusty blade.
Of Norfolk was this reeve of whom I tell,
From near a town that men call Badeswell.
Bundled he was like friar from chin to croup,
And ever he rode hindmost of our troop.

THE SUMMONER

A summoner was with us in that place,
Who had a fiery-red, cherubic face,
For eczema he had; his eyes were narrow
As hot he was, and lecherous, as a sparrow;
With black and scabby brows and scanty beard;
He had a face that little children feared.
There was no mercury, sulphur, or litharge,
No borax, ceruse, tartar, could discharge,
Nor ointment that could cleanse enough, or bite,
To free him of his boils and pimples white,

Nor of the bosses resting on his cheeks.
Well loved he garlic, onions, aye and leeks,
And drinking of strong wine as red as blood.
Then would he talk and shout as madman would.
And when a deal of wine he'd poured within,
Then would he utter no word save Latin.
Some phrases had he learned, say two or three,
Which he had garnered out of some decree;
No wonder, for he'd heard it all the day;
And all you know right well that even a jay
Can call out "Wat" as well as can the pope.
But when, for aught else, into him you'd grope,
'Twas found he'd spent his whole philosophy;
Just *"Questio quid juris"* would he cry.
He was a noble rascal, and a kind;
A better comrade 'twould be hard to find.
Why, he would suffer, for a quart of wine,
Some good fellow to have his concubine
A twelve-month, and excuse him to the full
(Between ourselves, though, he could pluck a gull).
And if he chanced upon a good fellow,
He would instruct him never to have awe,
In such a case, of the archdeacon's curse,
Except a man's soul lie within his purse;
For in his purse the man should punished be.
"The purse is the archdeacon's Hell," said he.
But well I know he lied in what he said,
A curse ought every guilty man to dread
(For curse can kill, as absolution save),
And 'ware *significavit* to the grave.
In his own power had he, and at ease,
The boys and girls of all the diocese,
And knew their secrets, and by counsel led.
A garland had he set upon his head,
Large as a tavern's wine-bush on a stake;
A buckler had he made of bread they bake.

THE PARDONER

With him there rode a gentle pardoner
Of Rouncival, his friend and his compeer;
Straight from the court of Rome had journeyed he.
Loudly he sang "Come hither, love, to me,"
The summoner joining with a burden round;
Was never horn of half so great a sound.
This pardoner had hair as yellow as wax,
But lank it hung as does a strike of flax;
In wisps hung down such locks as he'd on head,
And with them he his shoulders overspread;
But thin they dropped, and stringy, one by one.
But as to hood, for sport of it, he'd none,
Though it was packed in wallet all the while.
It seemed to him he went in latest style,
Dishevelled, save for cap, his head all bare.
As shiny eyes he had as has a hare.
He had a fine veronica sewed to cap.
His wallet lay before him in his lap,
Stuffed full of pardons brought from Rome all hot.
A voice he had that bleated like a goat.
No beard had he, nor ever should he have,
For smooth his face as he'd just had a shave;
I think he was a gelding or a mare.
But in his craft, from Berwick unto Ware,
Was no such pardoner in any place.
For in his bag he had a pillowcase
The which, he said, was Our True Lady's veil:
He said he had a piece of the very sail
That good Saint Peter had, what time he went
Upon the sea, till Jesus changed his bent.
He had a latten cross set full of stones,
And in a bottle had he some pig's bones.
But with these relics, when he came upon
Some simple parson, then this paragon
In that one day more money stood to gain
Than the poor dupe in two months could attain.

And thus, with flattery and suchlike japes,
He made the parson and the rest his apes.
But yet, to tell the whole truth at the last,
He was, in church, a fine ecclesiast.
Well could he read a lesson or a story,
But best of all he sang an offertory;
For well he knew that when that song was sung,
Then might he preach, and all with polished tongue,
To win some silver, as he right well could;
Therefore he sang so merrily and so loud.

Now have I told you briefly, in a clause,
The state, the array, the number, and the cause
Of the assembling of this company
In Southwark, at this noble hostelry
Known as the Tabard Inn, hard by the Bell.

Thomas à Kempis

=================== *10* ===================

The Imitation of Christ

Thomas à Kempis (1380–1471) was born in the town of Kempen in western Germany. Early in his schooling he showed a special inclination toward mysticism, and throughout his life he preferred solitude or, as he put it, "books and quiet corners." Joining the Augustinian order of monks, Thomas became a priest and subprior and remained in the monastery of Mount St. Agnes (at Zwolle) until his death at the age of ninety-one.

During this lifetime in the monastery, Thomas must have spent most of his time in the library and scriptorium, copying manuscripts and composing devotional works, the most important of which is *The Imitation of Christ* (1441). The storms of theological controversy, the troubles of the Great Schism, and the wars of France, England, and the Holy Roman Empire left no mark upon his work. Thomas was, according to his brother monks, "simple in worldly affairs"; in fact, he failed at his job as prior of the monastery and had to be demoted to subprior. This gentle unworldliness was a part of his mysticism. Thomas's sense of nearness to God afforded him assurance in the troublesome controversies of his time. The simple piety of his book has made it so popular that, beginning with an English version that appeared during his lifetime, it has been translated into more languages than any other book save the Bible, and it is widely admired by both Catholics and Protestants. The selection that follows is of particular interest, for it is from an American edition of a translation made by John Wesley, founder of modern Methodism. Wesley said that the *Imitation* was one of his chief guides and inspirations.

───────────────   ───────────────

Thomas à Kempis, *The Imitation of Christ*, in *An Extract of the Christian's Pattern; or, a Treatise on the Imitation of Christ*, trans. John Wesley (Baltimore: Lewis, 1840), 7–13, 24–31, 51–53, 63–65.

OF THE IMITATION OF CHRIST,
AND CONTEMPT OF ALL THE VANITIES OF THE WORLD

He that followeth me, walketh not in darkness, saith the Lord. These are the words of Christ, by which we are admonished, that we ought to imitate his life and manners, if we would be truly enlightened and delivered from all blindness of heart.

Let therefore our chief endeavor be to meditate upon the life of Jesus Christ.

What will it avail thee to dispute sublimely of the Trinity, if thou be void of humility, and art thereby displeasing to the Trinity?

Truly, sublime words do not make a man holy and just; but a virtuous life maketh him dear to God.

I had rather feel compunction, than know the definition thereof.

If thou didst know the whole Bible, and the sayings of all the philosophers by heart, what would all that profit thee without the love of God?

Vanity of vanities! all is vanity, but to love God and serve him only.

It is therefore vanity to seek after perishing riches.

It is also vanity to seek honors.

It is vanity to follow the desires of the flesh, and to labor for that for which thou must afterwards suffer grievous punishment.

It is vanity to wish to live long, and to be careless to live well.

It is vanity to mind this present life, and not those things which are to come.

It is vanity to set thy love on that which speedily passeth away, and not to hasten thither where everlasting joys remain.

OF THINKING HUMBLY OF OURSELVES

All men naturally desire to know; but what availeth knowledge without the fear of God?

Surely, an humble husbandman that serveth God, is better than a proud philosopher, that, neglecting himself, studies the course of the heavens.

He that knoweth himself, is vile in his own eyes, and is not pleased with the praises of men.

If I understood all things in the world, and had not charity, what would that help me in the sight of God, who will judge me according to my deeds.

Cease from an inordinate desire of knowing, for therein is much distraction and deceit.

There are many things, to know which doth little profit the soul.

And he is very unwise, that minds any other things than those that tend to the welfare of his soul.

Many words do not satisfy the soul: but a pure conscience giveth confidence towards God.

The more thou knowest, and the better thou understandest, the more grievously shalt thou be judged, unless thy life be the more holy.

Be not therefore lifted up; but rather let the knowledge given thee make thee afraid.

If thou thinkest that thou knowest much, yet there are many more things which thou knowest not.

Be not over wise, but rather acknowledge thine own ignorance.

If thou wilt know any thing profitably, love to be unknown, and of no account.

* * *

It is great wisdom to esteem ourselves nothing, and to think always well and highly of others.

* * *

OF THE DOCTRINE OF TRUTH

Happy is he whom truth itself teacheth, not by figures, and words that pass away; but by an immediate communication of itself.

Our own opinion and our own sense often deceive us, and discern little.

What availeth it to dispute about hidden things, for being ignorant of which we shall not be reproved at the day of judgment?

It is great folly to neglect things profitable and to think of curious or hurtful things.

* * *

He to whom the Eternal Word speaketh, is delivered from a world of vain notions.

From the One Word are all things, and all speak that one, and this is he, who also speaketh unto us.

No man understandeth or judgeth rightly without him.

He to whom all things are one, who reduceth all things to one, and seeth all things in one may be stable in heart, and remain peaceable in God.

O God, the Truth, make me one with thee in everlasting love.

. . .

I am weary of reading and hearing many things; in thee is all that I desire.

Let all creatures be silent in thy sight; speak thou alone unto me.

The more simple any one is, the more doth he understand without labor; because he receiveth the light of knowledge from above.

A pure, simple, and stable spirit is not dissipated, though it be employed in many works; because it does all to the glory of God, and seeks not itself in any thing it doth.

What hinders and troubles thee but the unmortified affections of thine own heart?

Who hath a sharper combat than he who laboreth to overcome himself?

This ought to be our business, to conquer ourselves, and daily to advance in holiness.

All perfection in this life hath some imperfection mixed with it: and no knowledge of ours is without some darkness.

An humble knowledge of thyself, is a surer way to God than a deep search after science.

Yet knowledge is not to be blamed, it being good in itself, and ordained by God; but a good conscience and a virtuous life is always to be preferred before it.

O if men bestowed as much labor in the rooting out of vices, as they do in the moving of questions, there would not be so great wickedness, nor so much hurt done in the world.

Surely at the day of judgment we shall not be examined what we have read, but what we have done; not how well we have spoken, but how religiously we have lived.

Tell me where are now all those doctors and masters with whom thou wast well acquainted, whilst they lived and flourished in learning?

Now others possess their preferments, and perhaps do scarce

ever think of them. In their life time they seemed something, but now they are not spoken of.

O how quickly doth the glory of the world pass away! O that their life had been answerable to their learning! Then had their study been to good purpose.

How many perish in this world, because they rather choose to be great than humble? Therefore they become vain in their imaginations.

He is truly great, that is great in love.

He is truly great, that is little in his own eyes, and that maketh no account of any height of honor.

He is truly wise, that accounteth all earthly things as dung, that he may win Christ.

And he is truly learned that doth the will of God, and forsaketh his own will.

* * *

OF WORKS DONE OUT OF CHARITY

The outward work without charity profiteth nothing; but whatsoever is done out of charity, be it ever so little and contemptible in the sight of the world, is wholly fruitful.

For God weigheth more with how much love one worketh than how much he doeth.

He doeth much that loveth much.

He doeth much that doeth a thing well.

He doeth well that serveth his neighbor and not his own will.

Often it seemeth to be charity, and it is rather carnality; because natural inclination, self-will, hope of reward, and desire of our own interest, are motives that men are rarely free from.

He that hath true and perfect charity seeketh himself in nothing; but only desireth in all things that God should be exalted.

He envieth none, because he seeketh not his own satisfaction: neither rejoiceth in himself, but chooses God only for his portion.

He attributes nothing that is good to any man, but wholly referreth it unto God, from whom, as from the fountain, all things proceed: in whom finally all the saints rest.

O that he had but one spark of true charity he would certainly discern that all earthly things are full of vanity.

OF BEARING WITH THE DEFECTS OF OTHERS

Those things that a man cannot amend in himself, or in others, he ought to suffer patiently until God orders things otherwise.

Think that perhaps it is better so for thy trial and patience.

If one that is once or twice warned will not give over, contend not with him; but commit all to God, that his will may be done, and his name honored in all his servants, who well knoweth how to turn evil into good.

Study to be patient in bearing with the defects and infirmities of others, of what sort soever they be; for that thou thyself also hast many, which must be suffered by others.

If thou canst not make thyself such a one as thou wouldst, how canst thou expect to have another in all things to thy liking?

We would willingly have others perfect, and yet we amend not our own faults.

We would have others exactly corrected, and will not be corrected ourselves.

The liberty of others displeaseth us, and yet we will not have our desires denied.

Thus it appears how seldom we weigh our neighbors in the same balance with ourselves.

If all men were perfect, what should we have to suffer of our neighbor for God.

But now God hath thus ordained it, that we may learn to bear one another's burdens; for no man is without fault; no man but hath his burden; no man is self-sufficient; no man has wisdom enough for himself; but we ought to bear with one another, comfort, help, instruct and admonish one another.

Occasions of adversity best discover how great virtue each one hath.

For occasions make not a man frail, but show what he is.

OF THE EXAMPLES OF THE HOLY FATHERS

Consider the lively examples of the holy fathers, in whom true religion shone, and thou shalt see how little it is, and almost nothing, which we do now.

Alas! what is our life if it be compared to theirs.

These saints and friends of *Christ* served the Lord in hunger and thirst, in cold and nakedness, in labor, and weariness, in watchings and fastings, in persecutions and many reproaches.

O how many grievous tribulations suffered the apostles, martyrs, confessors, virgins, and all the rest that would follow the steps of *Christ*.

They hated their lives in this world, that they might possess their souls in everlasting life.

O how strict and self-renouncing a life led those holy fathers in the wilderness! How long and grievous temptations suffered they! How often were they assaulted by the enemy! What frequent and fervent prayers offered they to God! How rigorous an abstinence did they daily use! How great zeal and care had they of their spiritual proficiency! How strong a combat had they for the overcoming of their lusts! How pure and upright an intention did they preserve unto God!

All the day they labored and spent part of the night in prayer; although even while they labored they did not cease from mental prayer.

They spent all their time usefully; all their hours of devotion seemed short, and by reason of the great sweetness they felt in contemplation they forgot the necessity of corporeal refreshments.

They renounced all riches, dignities, honors, friends and kinsfolk; they desired to have nothing of the world; they took no care of any thing more than was necessary for the sustenance of life.

They were poor in earthly things, but rich in grace.

Outwardly they wanted, but inwardly were refreshed with divine consolation.

They were strangers to the world; but friends to God.

They seemed to themselves as nothing, and were despised by the world; but they were precious in the eyes of God.

They were grounded in humility, walked in love and patience, and therefore profited daily in spirit.

Help me, O Lord, in thy holy service, and grant that I may now this day begin perfectly; for that which I have done hitherto is nothing.

Much diligence is necessary to him that will profit much.

If he that firmly purposeth often faileth; what shall he do that seldom or feebly purposeth anything?

It may fall out sundry ways that we break our resolution, and a little omission of spiritual exercises seldom passes without some loss.

The purpose of just men depends not so much upon their own wisdom as upon the grace of God, on whom they always rely in whatsoever they take in hand.

For man doth propose, but God doth dispose; neither is the way of man in himself.

If any accustomed exercise be sometimes omitted, either for some act of piety, or profit to thy brother, it may easily afterward be recovered again.

But to omit it out of sloth, or carelessness, is very blameable, and will be found pernicious.

We must diligently search into and regulate both the outward and inward man; because both contribute to our advancement.

Gird thy loins like a man against the assaults of the devil; bridle thy appetite, and thou wilt the more easily bridle all the motions of the flesh.

Be thou at no time idle altogether; but either reading, or writing, or praying, or meditating, or endeavoring something for the public good.

Blessed is that servant, whom, when his Lord cometh, he shall find watching; verily I say unto you, he shall make him ruler over all his goods.

OF THE LOVE OF SOLITUDE AND SILENCE

Seek a convenient time to retire into thyself.

Meddle not with curiosities.

Read such things as may rather yield compunction of heart than busy thy head.

If thou wilt withdraw thyself from superfluous talk and useless visits, as also from hearkening after news and rumors, thou shalt find sufficient leisure to meditate on good things.

One said, "As often as I have been among men, I returned like a man"; and this we often find true, when we have been long in company.

It is easier not to speak at all than not to speak more than we should.

It is easier to keep at home than to be sufficiently upon our guard when we are abroad.

He, therefore, that intends to attain to inward and spiritual things, must, with Jesus, retire from the multitude.

No man safely goes abroad, but he who is willing to stay at home.

No man ruleth safely, but he that is willing to be ruled.

No man safely commands, but he that hath learned readily to obey.

No man safely rejoiceth, unless he hath within him the testimony of a good conscience.

And yet the security of the saints was always full of the fear of God.

Neither were they less careful and humble in themselves, because they shone outwardly with grace and great virtues.

These have often, through confidence in themselves, fallen into the greatest dangers who have been in the greatest esteem among men.

Wherefore it is most profitable to many not to be altogether free from temptations, lest they should be too secure, lest they should be puffed up with pride, or too freely inclined to worldly comforts.

O how good a conscience would he keep, that would never seek after transitory joy, nor entangle himself with the things of this world.

·   ·   ·

OF A PURE MIND AND SIMPLE INTENTION

Simplicity and purity are the two wings by which a man is lifted up above all earthly things.

Simplicity is in the intention; purity in the affection: simplicity tends to God; purity apprehends and tastes him.

No good acton will hinder thee, if thou be inwardly free from inordinate affection.

If thou intend and seek nothing but the will of God, and the good of thy neighbor, thou shalt enjoy eternal liberty.

If thy heart was right, then every creature would be a looking-glass of life and a book of holy doctrine.

There is no creature so little and abject that represents not the goodness of God.

If thou wert inwardly pure, thou wouldst see and understand all things without any impediment.

A pure heart penetrateth heaven and hell.

Such as every one is inwardly, so he judgeth outwardly.

If there be joy in the world, surely a man of pure heart possesseth it. And if there be anywhere tribulation and affliction, an evil conscience feels it.

As iron put into the fire loseth its rust and becometh all bright like fire, so he that wholly turneth himself unto God is purified from all slothfulness and is changed into the likeness of God.

When a man beginneth to grow lukewarm, then he is afraid of a little labor.

But when a man beginneth to overcome himself, then he esteemeth those things light which before seemed grievous unto him.

OF THE CONSIDERATION OF ONE'S SELF

We should not trust too much to ourselves because we have often neither grace nor understanding.

There is but little light in us, and that we quickly lose by negligence. We reprehend small things in others, and pass over greater in ourselves.

We quickly feel and weigh what we suffer from others, but we mind not what others suffer from us.

He that doth well and rightly considers his own work will find little cause to judge hardly of another.

The inward Christian preferreth the care of himself before all other cares.

He that diligently attendeth unto himself easily holds his peace concerning others.

Thou willst never be inwardly religious unless thou pass over other men's matters and look especially to thyself.

If thou attend wholly unto God and thyself, thou wilt be little moved with whatsoever thou seest abroad.

Where art thou when thou art not with thyself? And when thou hast run over all, what hast thou profited if thou hast neglected thyself?

If thou desirest peace of mind, thou must reject all other cares, and look only to thyself.

Thou shalt profit much, if thou keep thyself free from all temporal cares.

Thou shalt greatly fail, if thou esteem any thing of this world.

Let nothing be great, nothing high, nothing pleasing to thee, but only God himself, or that which is of God.

Esteem all comfort vain which proceedeth from any creature.

A soul that loveth God despiseth all things but God.

· · ·

OF THANKFULNESS FOR THE GRACE OF GOD

Why seekest thou rest since thou art born to labor?

Dispose thyself to patience rather than to comfort; and to the bearing of the cross rather than to joy.

What worldly man would not willingly receive spiritual joy and comfort if he could always have it?

For spiritual comfort exceeds all the delight of the world and pleasures of the flesh.

False freedom of mind and trust in ourselves are very contrary to heavenly visitations.

God doth well in giving the grace of consolation; but man doth evil in not returning all again unto God with thanksgiving.

And therefore the gifts of grace cannot flow in us, because we are not thankful to the giver and return them not wholly to the fountain.

For grace ever attends him that is thankful; and from the proud shall be taken that which is given to the humble.

All that is high is not holy; nor all that is sweet good; nor every desire pure; nor every thing that is dear unto us grateful to God.

I willingly accept that grace, whereby I may ever become more humble and careful, and more ready to renounce myself.

He that is taught by the gift of grace, and instructed by the withdrawing thereof, will not dare to attribute any good to himself but will acknowledge himself poor and naked.

Give unto God that which is God's, and ascribe unto thyself that which is thine own; that is, give thanks to God for his grace, and acknowledge that nothing is thine, but only sin and the punishment due thereto.

Set thyself always in the lowest place, and the highest shall be given thee; for thou canst not be in the highest till thou hast been in the lowest.

The chief saints before God are the least in their own eyes; and how much the more glorious so much the more humble.

Those that are firmly settled and grounded in God can [in] no way be proud.

Be, therefore, thankful for the least gift, so shalt thou receive greater.

Let the least appear unto thee very great and the most contemned as an especial gift.

If thou considerest the worth of the giver, no gift will seem little or of too mean esteem. For that is not little which is given by the most high God.

Yes, if he should give punishment and stripes, it ought to be grateful; for he doth it always for our welfare, whatsoever he permitteth to befall us.

He that desireth to keep the grace of God, let him be thankful for the grace given, and patient for the taking away thereof. Let him pray that it may return. Let him be wary and humble lest he lose it.

11

Everyman

Medieval drama was originally an addition to the Church's liturgy for some special day's observance, such as the Easter service when the clergy might reenact the scene at the tomb; gradually, however, it became an independent form. Although separate from the rituals of the Church, drama continued throughout the Middle Ages to be exclusively religious. In many towns, especially in England, plays were entrusted to the care of guilds. Presented on wagon stages rolled from place to place in the streets during the celebrations of the great Church festivals, the plays often took the form of a sequence of scenes illustrating Bible narratives: the Creation, the Flood (given, naturally, by the carpenters' guild; after all, who would be better skilled at building the ark?), the Nativity, and so on. They came to include some secular matter, as, for instance, the comic interludes of the *Shepherds' Play*, in which the rustic clowning of the shepherds and a thieving cottager accompany the story of the Nativity.

The fifteenth century witnessed the full flowering of medieval drama. Audiences in streets and innyards could enjoy not only dramatizations of Bible stories, but plays telling of miraculous incidents in the lives of the saints. Strolling companies of professionals also put on "morality plays," in which personified abstractions like Faith, Hope, and Charity contested with World, Flesh, and Devil for the soul of man. This view of the world as a testing place, where man learns through suffering how to set his feet upon the path of salvation, was congenial to the medieval mind. In the play *Everyman*, originally Dutch but translated and produced in several English versions before the close of the fifteenth century, we find in simple but moving terms the universal experience of mankind encountering death and divine judgment. The following translation preserves, for the most part, the word order and erratic rhyme pattern of the original. The spelling, however, has been modernized.

Everyman, in *Dodsley's Old Plays*, ed. W. C. Hazlitt (London: Reeves & Turner, 1874), I, 100–42. (This is an adaptation.)

144

DRAMATIS PERSONAE

GOD	GOODS	STRENGTH
DEATH	GOOD DEEDS	DISCRETION
EVERY-MAN	KNOWLEDGE	FIVE WITS
FELLOWSHIP	CONFESSION	ANGEL
KINDRED	BEAUTY	DOCTOR

GOD speaks

GOD   I perceive here in my majesty,
How that all creatures be to me unkind,
Living without dread in worldly prosperity:
Of spiritual sight the people be so blind,
Drowned in sin, they know me not for their God;
In worldly riches is all their mind,
They fear not my righteousness, the sharp rod;
My love that I showed when I for them died
They forget clean, and shedding of my blood red;
I hanged between two it cannot be denied;
To give them life I suffered to be dead;
I healed their feet, with thorns hurt was my head;
I could do no more than I did truly,
And now I see the people do clean forsake me:
They use the seven deadly sins damnable,
As pride, covetousness, wrath and lechery,
Now in the world be made commendable:
And thus they leave of angels the heavenly company,
Every man liveth so after his own pleasure,
And yet of their life they be nothing sure:
I see the more that I them forbear
The worse they be from year to year;
All that liveth decayeth fast,
Therefore I will in all the haste
Have a reckoning of every man's person;
For, if I leave the people thus alone
In their life and wicked tempests,
Verily they will become much worse than beasts:

For now one would by envy another up eat;
Charity they do all clean forget:
I hoped well that every man
In my glory should make his mansion,
And thereto I had them all elect;
But now I see, like traitors deject,
They thank me not for the pleasure that I to them meant,
Nor yet for their being that I them have lent:
I proffered the people great multitude of mercy,
And few there be that asketh it heartily;
They be so encumbered with worldly riches,
That needs on them I must do justice,
On every man living without fear.—
Where art thou, Death, thou mighty messenger?

    DEATH Almighty God, I am here at your will,
Your commandment to fulfill.

    GOD Go thou to Every-man,
And show him in my name,
A pilgrimage he must on him take,
Which he in nowise may escape;
And that he bring with him a sure reckoning,
Without delay or any tarrying.

    DEA. Lord, I will in the world go run over all,
And cruelly out search both great and small;
Every man will I beset that liveth beastly,
Out of God's laws, and dreadeth not folly:
He that loveth riches I will strike with my dart
His sight to blind, and from heaven to depart,
Except that alms be his good friend,
In hell for to dwell world without end.
Lo, yonder I see Every-man walking:
Full little he thinketh on my coming;
His mind is on fleshly lusts, and his treasure;
And great pain it shall cause him to endure
Before the Lord heaven king.—
Every-man, stand still: whither art thou going
Thus gayly? hast thou thy maker forgot?

    EVERY-MAN Why asketh thou?
Wouldst thou know?

    DEA. Yes, sir, I will show you;

In great haste I am sent to thee
From God out of his majesty.

EVER. What, sent to me!

DEA. Yes, certainly:
Though thou have forgot him here,
He thinketh on thee in the heavenly sphere;
As, ere we depart, thou shalt know.

EVER. What desireth God of me?

DEA. That shall I show thee;
A reckoning he will needs have
Without any longer respite.

. . .

EVER. Full unready I am such reckoning to give:
I know thee not; what messenger art thou?

DEA. I am Death, that no man dreadeth;
For every man I rest, and no man spareth,
For it is God's commandment
That all to me should be obedient.

EVER. O Death, thou comest when I had thee least in
mind:
In thy power it lieth me to save;
Yet of my good will I give thee, if thou will be kind,
Yea, a thousand pounds shalt thou have.
And defer this matter till another day.

DEA. Every-man, it may not be by no way;
I set not by gold, silver nor riches,
Nor by pope, emperor, king, duke nor princes;
For, if I would receive gifts great,
All the world I might get;
But my custom is clean contrary:
I give thee no respite, come hence, and not tarry.

EVER. Alas, shall I have no longer respite?
I may say, Death giveth no warning:
To think on thee it maketh my heart sick;
For all unready is my book of reckoning:
But twelve years if I might have abiding,
My accounting book I would make so clear
That my reckoning I should not need to fear.
Wherefore, Death, I pray thee for God's mercy,
Spare me till I be provided of remedy.

DEA. Thee availeth not to cry, weep and pray:
But haste thee lightly that thou were going this journey:
And prove thy friends if thou can;
For, know thou well, the tide abideth no man,
And in the world each living creature
For Adam's sin must die of nature.

EVER. Death, if I should this pilgrimage take,
And my reckoning surely make,
Show me, for Saint Charity,
Should I not come again shortly?

DEA. No, Every-man, if thou be once there,
Thou mayst never more come here,
Trust me verily.

EVER. O gracious God, in the high seat celestial,
Have mercy on me in this most need.—
Shall I have no company from this vale terrestrial
Of mine acquaintance that way me to lead?

DEA. Yea, if any be so hardy,
That would go with thee, and bear thee company:
Hie thee that thou were gone to God's magnificence,
Thy reckoning to give before his presence.
What, thinkest thou thy life is given thee,
And thy worldly goods also?

EVER. I had thought so, verily.

DEA. Nay, nay; it was but lent thee,
For as soon as thou art gone,
Another awhile shall have it, and then go therefrom,
Even as thou hast done.
Every-man, thou art mad! Thou hast thy wits five;
And here on earth will not amend thy life;
For suddenly I do come.

EVER. O wretched caitiff, whither shall I flee,
That I might escape this endless sorrow!—
Now, gentle Death, spare me till to-morrow,
That I may amend me
With good advisement.

DEA. Nay, thereto I will not consent,
Nor no man will I respite;
But to the heart suddenly I shall smite
Without any advisement.

And now out of thy sight I will me hie;
See thou make thee ready shortly,
For thou mayst say, this is the day
That no man living may escape away.

   EVER.   Alas! I may well weep with sighs deep:
Nor have I no manner of company
To help me in my journey, and me to keep;
And also my writing is full unready.
How shall I do now for to excuse me!

. . .

To whom were I best my complaint to make?
What, if I to Fellowship thereof spake,
And showed him of this sudden chance!
For in him is all my reliance;
We have in the world so many a day
Been good friends in sport and play.
I see him yonder, certainly;
I trust that he will bear me company,
Therefore to him will I speak to ease my sorrow.
Well met, good Fellowship; and good-morrow.

FELLOWSHIP speaks

   FELLOWSHIP   Every-man, good-morrow by this day:
Sir, why lookest thou so piteously?
If anything be amiss, I pray thee, me say,
That I may help to remedy.

. . .

   EVER.   Then be you a good friend at need;
I have found you true here before.

   FEL.   And so ye shall evermore;
For, in faith, if thou go to hell,
I will not forsake thee by the way.

   EVER.   Ye speak like a good friend, I believe you well;
I shall deserve it if I may.

   FEL.   I speak of no deserving, by this day;
For he that will say and nothing do,
Is not worthy with good company to go:

Therefore show me the grief of your mind,
As to your friend most lovingly and kind.

    EVER.   I shall show you how it is
Commanded, I am to go a journey,
A long way, hard and dangerous;
And give a straight account without delay
Before the high judge Adonai:
Wherefore I pray you, bear me company,
As ye have promised, in this journey.

    FEL.   That is matter, indeed; promise is **duty,**
But if I should take such a voyage on me,
I know it well it should be to my pain:
Also it makes me afraid certain.
But let us take counsel here as well as **we can,**
For your words would fear a strong man.

    EVER.   Why, ye said—if I had need,
Ye would me never forsake quick indeed,
Though it were to hell truly.

    FEL.   So I said, certainly;
But such pleasures be set aside, the **sooth to say,**
And also if we took such a journey,
When should we come again?

    EVER.   Nay, never again till the day of **doom.**

    FEL.   In faith, then will not I come there:
Who hath you these tidings brought?

    EVER.   Indeed, Death was with me here.

    FEL.   Now, by God that all hath **bought,**
If Death were the messenger,
For no man that is living to-day
I will not go that loath journey,
Not for the father that begat me.

    EVER.   Ye promised otherwise, pardy.

    FEL.   I know well I said so truly,
And yet if thou wilt eat and drink, and make **good cheer,**
Or haunt to women the lusty company,
I would not forsake you while the day is clear,
Trust me verily.

    EVER.   Yea, thereto ye would be ready:
To go to mirth, solace and play.

Your mind will sooner apply
Than to bear me company in my long journey.
    FEL. Now, in good faith, I will not that way;
But if thou will murder, or any man kill,
In that I will help thee with a good-will.

           • • •

    EVER. Whither away, Fellowship? will you forsake me?
    FEL. Yes, by my say; to God I betake thee.
    EVER. Farewell, good Fellowship; for this my heart is
    sore:
Adieu forever, I shall see thee no more.
    FEL. In faith, Every-man, farewell now at the end;
For you I will remember that parting is mourning.
    EVER. Alack! shall we thus depart, indeed?
Aye! Lady, help, without any more comfort,
Lo, Fellowship forsaketh me in my most need:
For help in this world whither shall I resort?
Fellowship here before with me would merry make;
And now little sorrow for me doth he take.
It is said, in prosperity men friends may find,
Which in adversity be full unkind.
Now, whither for succor shall I flee,
Since that Fellowship hath forsaken me?
To my kinsmen I will truly,
Praying them to help me in my necessity;
I believe that they will do so;
For kind will creep where it may not go.
I will go say; for yonder I see them go:—
Where be ye now, my friends and kinsmen?
    KINDRED Here be we now at your commandment:
Cousin, I pray you, show us your intent
In any wise, and not spare.

           • • •

    EVER. Gramercy, my friends and kinsmen kind;
Now shall I show you the grief of my mind.
I was commanded by a messenger,
That is a high king's chief officer;
He bade me go a pilgrimage to my pain,
And, I know well, I shall never come again:

Also I must give a reckoning straight;
For I have a great enemy that hath me in wait,
Which intendeth me for to hinder.

    KIN.   What account is that which ye must render?
That would I know.

    EVER.   Of all my works I must show,
How I have lived, and my days spent;
Also of ill deeds that I have used
In my time this life was me lent,
And of all virtues that I have refused:
Therefore I pray you, go thither with me
To help to make my account, for Saint Charity.

    KIN.   What, to go thither? Is that the matter?
Nay, Every-man, I had rather fast on bread and water,
All this five year and more.

    EVER.   Alas, that ever I was born!
For now shall I never be merry,
If that you forsake me.

    KIN.   Aye, sir; what, ye be a merry man:
Take good heart to you, and make no moan.
But one thing I warn you, by Saint Ann,
As for me ye shall go alone.

    EVER.   My Kindred, will you not with me go?

    KIN.   No, by our Lady, I have the cramp in my toe:
Trust not to me; for, so God me speed,
I will deceive you in your most need.

                  . . .

    EVER.   Aye, Jesus, is all come here to?
Lo, fair words maketh fools vain;
They promise, and nothing will do certain.
My kinsmen promised me faithfully
For to abide with me steadfastly;
And now fast away do they flee:
Even so Fellowship promised me.
What friend were best me of to provide?
I lose my time here longer to abide;
Yet in my mind a thing there is,—
All my life I have loved riches;
If that my good now help me might,

He would make my heart full light:
I will speak to him in this distress.—
Where art thou, my Goods and Riches?
   GOODS Who calleth me? Every-man? what, hast thou
      haste?
I lie here in corners trussed and piled so high,
And in chests I am locked so fast,
Also sacked in bags, thou mayst see with thine eye,
I cannot stir; in packs low I lie:
What would ye have, lightly me say?
   EVER. Come hither, Good, in all the haste thou may;
For of counsel I must desire thee.
   GOODS Sir, if ye in the world have sorrow or adversity,
That can I help you to remedy shortly.
   EVER. It is another disease that grieveth me;
In this world it is not, I tell thee so,
I am sent for another way to go,
To give a straight account general
Before the highest Jupiter of all:
And all my life I have had joy and pleasure in thee,
Therefore I pray thee go with me;
For, peradventure, thou mayst before God Almighty
My reckoning help to clean and purify,
For it is said ever among
That money maketh all right that is wrong.
   GOODS Nay, Every-man, I sing another song;
I follow no man on such voyages,
For, if I went with thee,
Thou should fare much the worse for me:
For because on me thou did set thy mind,
Thy reckoning I have made blotted and blind,
That thine account thou cannot make truly;
And that hast thou for the love of me.
   EVER. That would grieve me full sore,
When I should come to that fearful answer:
Up, let us go thither together.
   GOODS Nay, not so; I am too brittle, I may not endure:
I will follow no man one foot be ye sure.
   EVER. Alas, I have thee loved, and had great pleasure
All my life days on good and treasure.

GOODS   That is to thy damnation without lessening,
For my love is contrary to the love everlasting;
But if thou had me loved moderately during,
As, to the poor give part of me,
Then shouldst thou not in this dolor be,
Nor in this great sorrow and care.

EVER.   Lo, now was I deceived ere I was aware,
And all I suppose was misspending of time.

GOODS   What, thinkest thou that I am thine?

EVER.   I had thought so.

GOODS   Nay, Every-man, I say no:
As for a while I was lent thee;
A season thou hast had me in prosperity;
My condition is man's soul to kill,
If I save one, a thousand I do spill:
Believest thou that I will follow thee?
Nay, from this world not verily.

EVER.   I had believed otherwise.

GOODS   Therefore to thy soul Good is a thief,
For when thou art dead, this is my guise,
Another to deceive in this same wise,
As I have done thee, and all to his soul's reprieve.

EVER.   O false Good, cursed thou be,
Thou traitor to God that has deceived me,
And caught me in thy snare.

GOODS   Mary, thou brought thyself in care,
Whereof I am glad,
I must needs laugh, I cannot be sad.

EVER.   Aye, Good, thou hast had long my hearty love;
I gave thee that which should be the Lord's above:
But wilt thou not go with me, indeed?
I pray thee truth to say.

GOODS   No, so God me speed;
Therefore farewell, and have good-day.

EVER.   O, to whom shall I make my moan!

.   .   .

Of whom shall I now counsel take?
I think that I shall never speed
Till that I go to my Good-deed;

But, alas! she is so weak
That she can neither go nor speak:
Yet will I venture on her now.—
My Good-deeds, where be you?

    GOOD-DEEDS Here I lie, cold in the ground;
Thy sins hath me so bound,
That I cannot stir.

    EVER. O Good-deeds, I stand in fear;
I must you pray of counsel,
For help now should come right well.

    GOOD-DEEDS Every-man, I have understanding,
That ye be summoned an account to make
Before Messias of Jerusalem king,
And you do wish that journey with you will I take.

    EVER. Therefore I come to you my moan to make:
I pray you, that ye will go with me.

    GOOD-DEEDS I would full fain, but I can not stand verily.

    EVER. Why, has there anything on you fall?

    GOOD-DEEDS Yes, sir, I may thank you of all;
If ye had perfectly cheered me,
Your book of count full ready had been.
Look, the books of your works and deeds eke;
Aye, see how they lie under the feet,
To your soul's heaviness.

    EVER. Our Lord Jesus help me,
For one letter here I cannot see.

    GOOD-DEEDS There is a blind reckoning in time of distress.

    EVER. Good-deeds, I pray you, help me in this need,
Or else I am forever damned, indeed;
Therefore help me to make reckoning
Before the Redeemer of all thing,
That king is, and was, and ever shall.

    GOOD-DEEDS Every-man, I am sorry for your fall,
And fain would I help you if I were able.

    EVER. Good-deeds, your counsel I pray you give me.

    GOOD-DEEDS That shall I do verily:
Though that on my feet I may not go,
I have a sister that shall with you also,
Called Knowledge, which shall with you abide,
To help you make that dreadful reckoning.

KNOWLEDGE   Every-man, I will go with thee, and be thy
   guide,
In thy most need to go by thy side.
   EVER.   In good condition I am now in everything,
And am whole content with this good thing,
Thanked be God my creator.
   GOOD-DEEDS   And when he hath brought you there,
Where thou shalt heal thee of thy smart,
Then go you with your reckoning and your good deeds
   together,
For to make you joyful at heart
Before the blessed Trinity.
   EVER.   My Good-deeds, gramercy;
I am well content certainly
With your words sweet.
   KNO.   Now go we together lovingly
To Confession, that cleansing river.
   EVER.   For joy I weep: I would we were there;
But, I pray you, give me perception,
Where dwelleth that holy man Confession?
   KNO.   In the house of salvation;
We shall find him in that place,
That shall us comfort by God's grace.—
Lo, this is Confession: kneel down, and ask mercy;
For he is in good conceit with God Almighty.
   EVER.   O glorious fountain that all uncleanliness doth
   clarify,
Wash from me the spots of vice unclean,
That on me no sin may be seen;
I come with Knowledge for my redemption,
Redempt with heart and full contrition,
For I am commanded a pilgrimage to take,
And great accounts before God to make.
Now I pray you, Shrift, mother of salvation,
Help my good deeds for my piteous exclamation.
   CON.   I know your sorrows well, Every-man:
Because with Knowledge ye come to me,
I will you comfort as well as I can;
And a precious jewel I will give thee,
Called penance, voider of adversity:

Therewith shall your body chastised be
With abstinence and perseverance in God's service;
Here shall you receive that scourge of me,
Which is penance strong that ye must endure,
To remember thy Saviour was scourged for thee
With sharp scourges, and suffered it patiently:
So must thou, ere thou escape that painful pilgrimage.—
Knowledge, keep him in this voyage,
And by that time Good-deeds will be with thee;
But in any wise be seeker of mercy,
For your time draweth fast; if ye will saved be,
Ask God mercy, and he will grant truly:
When with the scourge of penance man doth him bind,
The oil of forgiveness then shall he find.

    EVER. Thanked be God for his gracious work;
For now I will my penance begin:
This hath rejoiced and lighted my heart,
Though the knots be painful and hard within.

    KNO. Every-man, look your penance that ye fulfill,
What pain that ever it to you be;
And Knowledge shall give you counsel at will,
How your account ye shall make clearly.

    EVER. O eternal God, O heavenly figure,
O way of righteousness, O goodly vision,
Which descended down in a virgin pure
Because he would Every-man redeem,
Which Adam forfeited by his disobedience,
O blessed Godhead elect and high divine,
Forgive my grievous offence;
Here I cry thee mercy in this presence:
O ghostly treasure, O ransomer and redeemer
Of all the world, hope and conduiter,
Mirror of joy, foundator of mercy,
Which illumineth heaven and earth thereby,
Hear my clamorous complaint, though it late be,
Receive my prayers; unworthy in this heavy life
Though I be, a sinner most abominable,
Yet let my name be written in Moses' table.—
O Mary, pray to the maker of all things
Me for to help at my ending,

And save me from the power of my enemy;
For Death assaileth me strongly:
And, Lady, that I may by means of thy prayer
Of your son's glory be a partner,
By the means of his passion, I it crave;
I beseech you, help my soul to save.—
Knowledge, give me the scourge of penance,
My flesh therewith shall give acquaintance;
I will now begin, if God give me grace.

    KNO. Every-man, God give you time and space:
Thus I bequeath you in the hands of our Saviour;
Now may you make your reckoning sure.

    EVER. In the name of the holy Trinity,
My body sore punished shall be,
Take this body for the sin of the flesh;
Also thou delightest to go gay and fresh;
And in the way of damnation thou did me bring,
Therefore suffer now strokes of punishing:
Now of penance I will wade the water clear,
To save me from purgatory that sharp fire.

    GOOD-DEEDS I thank God, now I can walk and go,
And am delivered of my sickness and woe;
Therefore with Every-man I will go, and not spare,
His good works I will help him to declare.

    KNO. Now, Every-man, be merry and glad;
Your Good-deeds cometh now, ye may not be sad:
Now is your Good-deeds whole and sound,
Going upright upon the ground.

    EVER. My heart is light, and shall be evermore;
Now will I smite faster than I did before.

    GOOD-DEEDS Every-man, pilgrim, my special friend,
Blessed be thou without end;
For thee is prepared the eternal glory:
Ye have me made whole and sound,
Therefore I will abide by thee in every stound.

    EVER. Welcome, my Good-deeds, now I hear thy voice
I weep for very sweetness of love.

    KNO. Be no more sad, but ever rejoice,
God seeth thy living in his throne above;
Put on this garment to thy behove,

Which is wet with your tears,
Or else before God you may it miss,
When ye to your journey's end come shall.

    EVER.   Gentle Knowledge, what do ye it call?

    KNO.   It is a garment of sorrow,
From pain it will you borrow;
Contrition it is,
That getteth forgiveness,
It pleaseth God passing well.

    GOOD-DEEDS   Every-man, will you wear it for your heal?

    EVER.   Now blessed be Jesus, Mary's son;
For now have I on true contrition:
And let us go now without tarrying.—
Good-deeds, have we clear our reckoning?

    GOOD-DEEDS   Yea, indeed, I have it here.

[Everyman confesses his sins to the priest and receives extreme unction.
Accompanied by Knowledge, Discretion, Strength, Beauty, and Five-Wits,
he comes to his grave, where all save Good-Deeds bid him farewell. *Ed.*]

    EVER.   Methink, alas! that I must be gone
To make my reckoning, and my debts pay;
For, I see, my time is nigh spent away.—
Take example, all ye that this do hear or see,
How they that I love best do forsake me;
Except my Good-deeds, that abideth truly.

    GOOD-DEEDS   All earthly things is but vanity,
Beauty, Strength and Discretion do man forsake,
Foolish friends, and kinsmen, that fair spake;
All fleeth save Good-deeds, and that am I.

    EVER.   Have mercy on me, God most mighty,—
And stand by me thou mother and maid, holy Mary.

    GOOD-DEEDS   Fear not, I will speak for thee.

    EVER.   Here I cry God mercy.

    GOOD-DEEDS   Shorten our end and diminish our pain:
Let us go, and never come again.

    EVER.   Into thy hands, Lord, my soul I commend,
Receive it, Lord, that it be not lost;
As thou me boughtest, so me defend,
And save me from the fiend's boast,

That I may appear with that blessed host
That shall be saved at the day of doom.

. . .

KNO.   Now hath he suffered that we all shall endure,
The Good-deeds shall make all sure;
Now hath he made ending:
Me thinketh that I hear angels sing,
And make great joy and melody,
Where every man's soul received shall be.

THE ANGEL   Come, excellent elect spouse to Jesus,
Here above thou shalt go,
Because of thy singular virtue:
Now the soul is taken the body from,
Thy reckoning is crystal clear;
Now shalt thou into the heavenly sphere,
Unto which all ye shall come
That liveth well before the day of doom.

DOCTOR   This moral men may have in mind;
Ye hearers, take it of worth, old and young,
And forsake pride, for he deceiveth you in the end,
And remember Beauty, Five-wits, Strength and Discretion,
They all at the last do Every-man forsake,
Save his Good-deeds, there doth he take:
But beware, and if they be small,
Before God he hath no help at all;
None excuse may be there for Every-man:
Alas! how shall he do then,
For after death amends may no man make;
For then mercy and pity doth him forsake;
If his reckoning be not clean when he doth come,
God will say—*Ite, maledicti, in ignem aeternum:*
And he that hath his account whole and sound,
High in heaven he shall be crowned;
Unto which place God bring us all thither,
That we may live body and soul together;
Thereto help the Trinity:
Amen, say ye, for Saint Charity.

Petrarch

12

Letter to Posterity

Petrarch (1304–1374) or, to use the Italian form of his name, Francesco Petrarca, is often termed the founder of humanism. By his inexhaustible industry in scholarship he brought the mind of western Europe into sympathetic contact with classical antiquity. He was also the first to collect a private library of any size and to advocate the preservation of Greek and Latin manuscripts. In his life and work humanism is well illustrated. The orator, the poet, and the scholar (Petrarch was skilled in all these roles) of that time were, in effect, obliged to pursue and disseminate learning, secure individual integrity, and harmonize classical genius with divine revelation. Classical learning, requiring the study and preparation of accurate texts of the works of Greek and Roman writers, was a necessary means to perfect man's intellect and civilize his habits. Although Petrarch himself failed to master Greek, the following generation of scholars made knowledge of Greek a necessary attainment for the learned man. In the ensuing centuries humanism came to mean the cultivation of the human personality so that the individual, with liberated intelligence and talent, could lead a life of dignity, self-reliance, and creativeness.

Of Florentine parentage, Petrarch lived by choice at Avignon, the seat of the papacy during the greater part of the fourteenth century, and was often a guest in the palaces of despots and princes in Italy. For the most part, however, he followed a life of solitary study. Petrarch is best known today for his Italian sonnets to Laura, utilizing the conventional chivalrous love poetry of southern France, to which he added concepts of Platonic idealism. His contemporaries knew him more for his Latin epic, *Africa,* modeled on Vergil's *Aeneid,* and for his patriotic odes honoring Italy. In a spectacular ceremony in Rome in 1341, he was crowned with a laurel wreath as the foremost poet and scholar of his time.

"Francesco Petrarca to Posterity," in *Petrarch, the First Modern Scholar and Man of Letters,* by James Harvey Robinson (New York: Putnam, 1898), 59–76.

The selection that follows is an autobiographical fragment, written about 1351, revealing the pride and self-consciousness as well as the devotion to scholarship and intellectual integrity of the man who, more than any other, merits the title of inaugurator of the Renaissance.

Greeting.—It is possible that some word of me may have come to you, though even this is doubtful, since an insignificant and obscure name will scarcely penetrate far in either time or space. If, however, you should have heard of me, you may desire to know what manner of man I was, or what was the outcome of my labours, especially those of which some description or, at any rate, the bare titles may have reached you.

To begin with myself, then, the utterances of men concerning me will differ widely, since in passing judgment almost every one is influenced not so much by truth as by preference, and good and evil report alike know no bounds. I was, in truth, a poor mortal like yourself, neither very exalted in my origin, nor, on the other hand, of the most humble birth, but belonging, as Augustus Caesar says of himself, to an ancient family. As to my disposition, I was not naturally perverse or wanting in modesty, however the contagion of evil associations may have corrupted me. My youth was gone before I realised it; I was carried away by the strength of manhood; but a riper age brought me to my senses and taught me by experience the truth I had long before read in books, that youth and pleasure are vanity—nay, that the Author of all ages and times permits us miserable mortals, puffed up with emptiness, thus to wander about, until finally, coming to a tardy consciousness of our sins, we shall learn to know ourselves. In my prime I was blessed with a quick and active body, although not exceptionally strong; and while I do not lay claim to remarkable personal beauty, I was comely enough in my best days. I was possessed of a clear complexion, between light and dark, lively eyes, and for long years a keen vision, which however deserted me, contrary to my hopes, after I reached my sixtieth birthday, and forced me, to my great annoyance, to resort to glasses. Although I had previously enjoyed perfect health, old age brought with it the usual array of discomforts.

My parents were honourable folk, Florentine in their origin, of medium fortune, or, I may as well admit it, in a condition verging upon poverty. They had been expelled from their native city, and consequently I was born in exile, at Arezzo, in the year 1304 of this latter age which begins with Christ's birth, July the twentieth, on a Monday, at dawn. I have always possessed an extreme contempt for wealth; not that riches are not desirable in themselves, but because I hate the anxiety and care which are invariably associated with them. I certainly do not long to be able to give gorgeous banquets. I have, on the contrary, led a happier existence with plain living and ordinary fare than all the followers of Apicius, with their elaborate dainties. So-called *convivia,* which are but vulgar bouts, sinning against sobriety and good manners, have always been repugnant to me. I have ever felt that it was irksome and profitless to invite others to such affairs, and not less so to be bidden to them myself. On the other hand, the pleasure of dining with one's friends is so great that nothing has ever given me more delight than their unexpected arrival, nor have I ever willingly sat down to table without a companion. Nothing displeases me more than display, for not only is it bad in itself, and opposed to humility, but it is troublesome and distracting.

I struggled in my younger days with a keen but constant and pure attachment, and would have struggled with it longer had not the sinking flame been extinguished by death—premature and bitter, but salutary. I should be glad to be able to say that I had always been entirely free from irregular desires, but I should lie if I did so. I can, however, conscientiously claim that, although I may have been carried away by the fire of youth or by my ardent temperament, I have always abhorred such sins from the depths of my soul. As I approached the age of forty, while my powers were unimpaired and my passions were still strong, I not only abruptly threw off my bad habits, but even the very recollection of them, as if I had never looked upon a woman. This I mention as among the greatest of my blessings, and I render thanks to God, who freed me, while still sound and vigorous, from a disgusting slavery which had always been hateful to me. But let us turn to other matters.

I have taken pride in others, never in myself, and however insignificant I may have been, I have always been still less important in my own judgment. My anger has very often injured myself, but never others. I have always been most desirous of honourable friendships, and have faithfully cherished them. I make this boast without fear, since I am confident that I speak truly. While I am very prone to take offence, I am equally quick to forget injuries, and have a memory tenacious of benefits. In my familiar associations with kings and princes, and in my friendship with noble personages, my good fortune has been such as to excite envy. But it is the cruel fate of those who are growing old that they can commonly only weep for friends who have passed away. The greatest kings of this age have loved and courted me. They may know why; I certainly do not. With some of them I was on such terms that they seemed in a certain sense my guests rather than I theirs; their lofty position in no way embarrassing me, but, on the contrary, bringing with it many advantages. I fled, however, from many of those to whom I was greatly attached; and such was my innate longing for liberty, that I studiously avoided those whose very name seemed incompatible with the freedom that I loved.

I possessed a well-balanced rather than a keen intellect, one prone to all kinds of good and wholesome study, but especially inclined to moral philosophy and the art of poetry. The latter, indeed, I neglected as time went on, and took delight in sacred literature. Finding in that a hidden sweetness which I had once esteemed but lightly, I came to regard the works of the poets as only amenities. Among the many subjects which interested me, I dwelt especially upon antiquity, for our own age has always repelled me, so that, had it not been for the love of those dear to me, I should have preferred to have been born in any other period than our own. In order to forget my own time, I have constantly striven to place myself in spirit in other ages, and consequently I delighted in history; not that the conflicting statements did not offend me, but when in doubt I accepted what appeared to me most probable, or yielded to the authority of the writer.

My style, as many claimed, was clear and forcible; but to me it seemed weak and obscure. In ordinary conversation with friends, or with those about me, I never gave any thought to my language, and I have always wondered that Augustus Caesar should have taken such pains in this respect. When, however, the subject itself, or the place or listener, seemed to demand it, I gave some attention to style, with what success I cannot pretend to say; let them judge in whose presence I spoke. If only I have lived well, it matters little to me how I talked. Mere elegance of language can produce at best but an empty renown.

My life up to the present has, either through fate or my own choice, fallen into the following divisions. A part only of my first year was spent at Arezzo, where I first saw the light. The six following years were, owing to the recall of my mother from exile, spent upon my father's estate at Ancisa, about fourteen miles above Florence. I passed my eighth year at Pisa, the ninth and following years in Farther Gaul, at Avignon, on the left bank of the Rhone, where the Roman Pontiff holds and has long held the Church of Christ in shameful exile. It seemed a few years ago as if Urban V. was on the point of restoring the Church to its ancient seat, but it is clear that nothing is coming of this effort, and, what is to me the worst of all, the Pope seems to have repented him of his good work, for failure came while he was still living. Had he lived but a little longer, he would certainly have learned how I regarded his retreat. My pen was in my hand when he abruptly surrendered at once his exalted office and his life. Unhappy man, who might have died before the altar of Saint Peter and in his own habitation! Had his successors remained in their capital he would have been looked upon as the cause of this benign change, while, had they left Rome, his virtue would have been all the more conspicuous in contrast with their fault.

But such laments are somewhat remote from my subject. On the windy banks of the river Rhone I spent my boyhood, guided by my parents, and then, guided by my own fancies, the whole of my youth. Yet there were long intervals spent elsewhere, for I first passed four years at the little town of Carpentras, somewhat to the east of Avignon: in these two places I learned as much of grammar, logic, and rhetoric as my age permitted, or rather, as much as it is customary to teach in school: how little that is, dear reader, thou knowest. I then set out for Montpellier to study law, and spent four years there, then three at Bologna. I heard the whole body of the civil law, and would, as many thought, have distinguished myself later, had I but continued my studies. I gave up the subject altogether, however, so soon as it was no longer necessary to consult the wishes of my parents. My reason was that, although the dignity of the law, which is doubtless very great, and especially the numerous references it contains to Roman antiquity, did not fail to delight me, I felt it to be habitually degraded by those who practise it. It went against me painfully to acquire an art which I would not practise dishonestly, and could hardly hope to exercise otherwise. Had I made the latter attempt, my scrupulousness would doubtless have been ascribed to simplicity.

So at the age of two and twenty I returned home. I call my place of exile home, Avignon, where I had been since childhood; for habit has almost the potency of nature itself. I had already begun to be known there, and my friendship was sought by prominent men; wherefore I cannot say. I confess this is now a source of surprise to me, although it seemed natural enough at an age when we are used to regard ourselves as worthy of the highest respect. I was courted first and foremost by that very distinguished and noble family, the Colonnesi, who, at that period, adorned the Roman Curia with their presence. However it might be now, I was at that time certainly quite unworthy of the esteem in which I was held by them. I was especially honoured by the incomparable Giacomo Colonna, then Bishop of Lombez, whose peer I know not whether I have ever seen or ever shall see, and was taken by him to Gascony; there I spent such a divine summer among the foot-hills of the Pyrenees, in happy intercourse with my master and the members of our company, that I can never recall the experience without a sigh of regret.

Returning thence, I passed many years in the house of Giacomo's brother, Cardinal Giovanni Colonna, not as if he were my lord and master, but rather my father, or better, a most affectionate brother —nay, it was as if I were in my own home. About this time, a youthful desire impelled me to visit France and Germany. While I invented certain reasons to satisfy my elders of the propriety of the journey, the real explanation was a great inclination and longing to see new sights. I first visited Paris, as I was anxious to discover what was true and what fabulous in the accounts I had heard of that city. On my return from this journey I went to Rome, which I had since my infancy ardently desired to visit. There I soon came to venerate Stephano, the noble head of the family of the Colonnesi, like some ancient hero, and was in turn treated by him in every respect like a son. The love and good-will of this excellent man toward me remained constant to the end of his life, and lives in me still, nor will it cease until I myself pass away.

On my return, since I experienced a deep-seated and innate repugnance to town life, especially in that disgusting city of Avignon which I heartily abhorred, I sought some means of escape. I fortunately discovered, about fifteen miles from Avignon, a delightful valley, narrow and secluded, called Vaucluse, where the Sorgue, the prince of streams, takes its rise. Captivated by the charms of the place, I transferred thither myself and my books. Were I to describe what I did there during many years, it would prove a long story. Indeed, almost every bit of writing which I have put forth was either accomplished or begun, or at least conceived, there, and my undertakings have been so numerous that they still continue to vex and weary me. My mind, like my body, is characterised by a certain versatility and readiness, rather than by strength, so that many tasks that were easy of conception have been given up by reason of the difficulty of their execution. The character of my surroundings suggested the composition of a sylvan or bucolic song. I also dedicated a work in two books upon *The Life of Solitude,* to Philip, now exalted to the Cardinal-bishopric of Sabina. Although always a great man, he was, at the time of which I speak, only the humble Bishop of Cavaillon. He is the only one of my old friends who is still left to me, and he has always loved and treated me not as a bishop (as Ambrose did Augustine), but as a brother.

While I was wandering in those mountains upon a Friday in Holy Week, the strong desire seized me to write an epic in an heroic strain, taking as my theme Scipio Africanus the Great, who had, strange to say, been dear to me from my childhood. But although I began the execution of this project with enthusiasm, I straightway abandoned it, owing to a variety of distractions. The poem was, however, christened *Africa,* from the name of its hero, and, whether from his fortunes or mine, it did not fail to arouse the interest of many before they had seen it.

While leading a leisurely existence in this region, I received, remarkable as it may seem, upon one and the same day, letters both from the Senate at Rome and the Chancellor of the University of Paris, pressing me to appear in Rome and Paris, respectively, to receive the poet's crown of laurel. In my youthful elation I convinced myself that I was quite worthy of this honour; the recognition came from eminent judges, and I accepted their verdict rather than that of my own better judgment. I hesitated for a time which I should give ear to, and sent a letter to Cardinal Giovanni Colonna, of whom I have already spoken, asking his opinion. He was so near that, although I wrote late in the day, I received his reply before the third hour on the morrow. I followed his advice, and recognised the claims of Rome as superior to all others. My acceptance of his counsel is shown by my twofold letter to him on that occasion, which I still keep. I set off accordingly; but although, after the fashion of youth, I was a most indulgent judge of my own work, I still blushed to accept in my own case the verdict even of such men as those who summoned me, despite the fact that they would certainly not have honoured me in this way, had they not believed me worthy.

So I decided, first to visit Naples, and that celebrated king and philosopher, Robert, who was not more distinguished as a ruler than as a man of culture. He was, indeed, the only monarch of our age who was the friend at once of learning and of virtue, and I trusted that he might correct such things as he found to criticise in my work. The way in which he received and welcomed me is a source of astonishment to me now, and, I doubt not, to the reader also, if he happens to know anything of the matter. Having learned the reason of my coming, the King seemed mightily pleased. He was gratified, doubtless, by my youthful faith in him, and felt, perhaps, that he shared in a way the glory of my coronation, since I had chosen him from all others as the only suitable critic. After talking over a great many things, I showed him my *Africa,* which so delighted him that he asked that it might be dedicated to him in consideration of a handsome reward. This was a request that I could not well refuse, nor, indeed, would I have wished to refuse it, had it been in my power. He then fixed a day upon which we could consider the object of my visit. This occupied us from noon until evening, and the time proving too short, on account of the many matters which arose for discussion, we passed the two following days in the same manner. Having thus tested my poor attainments for three days, the King at last pronounced me worthy of the laurel. He offered to bestow that honour upon me at Naples, and urged me to consent to receive it there, but my veneration for Rome prevailed over the insistence of even so great a monarch as Robert. At length, seeing that I was inflexible in my purpose, he sent me on my way accompanied by royal messengers and letters to the Roman Senate, in which he gave enthusiastic expression to his flattering opinion of me. This royal estimate was, indeed, quite in accord with that of many others, and especially with my own, but to-day I cannot approve either his or my own verdict. In his case, affection and the natural partiality to youth were stronger than his devotion to truth.

On arriving at Rome, I continued, in spite of my unworthiness, to rely upon the judgment of so eminent a critic, and, to the great delight of the Romans who were present, I who had been hitherto a simple student received the laurel crown. This occasion is described elsewhere in my letters, both in prose and verse. The laurel, however, in no way increased my wisdom, although it did arouse some jealousy—but this is too long a story to be told here.

On leaving Rome, I went to Parma, and spent some time with the members of the house of Correggio, who, while they were most kind and generous towards me, agreed but ill among themselves. They governed Parma, however, in a way unknown to that city within the memory of man, and the like of which it will hardly again enjoy in this present age.

I was conscious of the honour which I had but just received, and fearful lest it might seem to have been granted to one unworthy of the distinction; consequently, as I was walking one day in the mountains, and chanced to cross the river Enza to a place called Selva Piana, in the territory of Reggio, struck by the beauty of the spot, I began to write again upon the *Africa,* which I had laid aside. In my enthusiasm, which had seemed quite dead, I wrote some lines that very day, and some each day until I returned to Parma. Here I happened upon a quiet and retired house, which I afterwards bought, and which still belongs to me. I continued my task with such ardour, and completed the work in so short a space of time, that I cannot but marvel now at my despatch. I had already passed my thirty-fourth year when I returned thence to the Fountain of the Sorgue, and to my Transalpine solitude. I had made a long stay both in Parma and Verona, and everywhere I had, I am thankful to say, been treated with much greater esteem than I merited.

Some time after this, my growing reputation procured for me the good-will of a most excellent man, Giacomo the Younger, of Carrara, whose equal I do not know among the rulers of his time. For years he wearied me with messengers and letters when I was beyond the Alps, and with his petitions whenever I happened to be in Italy, urging me to accept his friendship. At last, although I anticipated little satisfaction from the venture, I determined to go to him and see what this insistence on the part of a person so eminent, and at the same time a stranger to me, might really mean. I appeared, though tardily, at Padua, where I was received by him of illustrious memory, not as a mortal, but as the blessed are greeted in heaven—with such delight and such unspeakable affection and esteem, that I cannot adequately describe my welcome in words, and must, therefore, be silent. Among other things, learning that I had led a clerical life from boyhood, he had me made a canon of Padua, in order to bind me the closer to himself and his city. In fine, had his life been spared, I should have found there an end to all my wanderings. But alas! nothing mortal is enduring, and there is nothing sweet which does not presently end in bitterness. Scarcely two years was he spared to me, to his country, and to the world. God, who had given him to us, took him again. Without being blinded by my love for him, I feel that neither I, nor his country, nor the world was worthy of him. Although his son, who succeeded him, was in every way a prudent and distinguished man, who, following his father's example, always loved and honoured me, I could not remain after the death of him with whom, by reason especially of the similarity of our ages, I had been much more closely united.

I returned to Gaul, not so much from a desire to see again what I had already beheld a thousand times, as from the hope, common to the afflicted, of coming to terms with my misfortunes by a change of scene.

Giovanni Boccaccio

══════════ 13 ══════════

The Decameron

Dante's masterpiece, *The Divine Comedy,* is for the most part a medieval poem. Giovanni Boccaccio (1313–1375), Dante's admirer and biographer, was the first to lecture on *The Divine Comedy* under the auspices of the city of Florence, which had banished Dante and then, some years after his death, had endowed a lectureship in his honor. But Boccaccio's own work is usually thought of as belonging to the Renaissance period. His best-known work, *The Decameron,* exemplifies narrative realism, has racy wit and humor, and is to be enjoyed for itself and not primarily for high moral or religious truth. Whereas Dante's universe was based upon the Ptolemaic system of spheres with earth at its center, and had St. Thomas Aquinas's *Summa Theologica* as its philosophical guide, Boccaccio's *Decameron* frees itself from all obligations save that of telling a series of cleverly concocted stories. Boccaccio, who knew the classics and was a serious humanist scholar and writer of Latin treatises, is remembered now only for his Italian works, chiefly *The Decameron.*

Most of the one hundred stories of *The Decameron,* written between 1348 and 1358, were well known, and Boccaccio exhibits his virtuosity in the superior ease with which he tells them. In Boccaccio's time, a writer was supposed to show skill in handling conventional material rather than originality or novelty in inventing plots. The stories are supposedly narrated by a group of gay, witty, and worldly young people who enjoy telling tales; some of the stories are mocking, some are sad, and some are outrageously bawdy. The following selection contains the opening pages from *The Decameron;* it is a description of the plague-stricken city from which the group of young men and women flee to take refuge in a villa overlooking Florence. The narrative included here was a favorite in Boccaccio's time, when stories involving honor, pride, and love were especially popular.

The Decameron of Giovanni Boccaccio, ed. Henry Morley (London: Routledge, 1895), 10–13, 102–10. (This is an adaptation.)

In the year of our blessed Savior's Incarnation, 1348, that memorable plague ravaged the excellent city, far beyond all the rest in Italy; which plague, by operation of the heavenly bodies, or rather for our enormous iniquities, by the just anger of God was sent upon us mortals. Some few years before, it began in the East, sweeping thence an innumerable quantity of living souls, extending itself afterward from place to place westward, until it seized on the said city, where neither human skill nor Providence could find any prevention, even though the city was cleansed of many impurities by the diligent officers ordered to that task. Besides the prevention of all sick persons' entrance, all possible precautions were daily used for the preservation of health. There were also incessant prayers and the supplications of devout people for the abatement of so dangerous a sickness.

About the beginning of the year it also began in a very strange manner, yet not as it had done in the eastern countries where anyone afflicted with the ailment would show signs of inevitable death by bleeding at the nose. But here it began either under the armpits or in the groin with certain swellings, in some to the bigness of an apple, in others like an egg, which in the vulgar speech was termed a botch or a boil. In very short time after, the deadly boils would spread to all parts of the body; whereupon the disease showed itself by black or blue spots, which would appear on the arms of many, or on their thighs, and every part of the body—in some, great and few; in others, small and thick.

Now, as the boil at the beginning was an assured sign of near approaching death, so the spots proved likewise. It seemed that the physician's advice, medicines, or any other remedy, were all useless. It plainly appeared that because of the nature of the illness and the ignorance of the physicians no cure was to be found. Moreover, besides the number of those who were skilled in medicine, there were a great many, both men and women, who without any knowledge of medicine at all became physicians; so that not only few were healed, but well-near all died within three days after the aforementioned signs were seen, some sooner, and others later—commonly without fever or any other complications.

This pestilence was of great power and violence. For not only healthful persons speaking to the sick, or coming to see them, or airing clothes to comfort them were taken ill; but even those who touched their garments or any food upon which a sick person had fed, or anything else he had used contracted the disease in what seemed a miraculous way. Among which marvels let me tell you one thing, which if others had not seen it as well as I, I could hardly be persuaded to write down: the quality of this contagion was of such virulence that the clothes or anything else touched by a dying person proved deadly to any beast or animal, dog or cat, that lay upon or even touched them.

My own eyes saw, among many others, proof of this one day. Some rags of linen and wool torn from a wretched person dead of that disease lay in the open street, and two swine searching for food tossed and tumbled the clothes with their snouts. Whereupon they turned about twice or thrice and fell down dead. This occurrence and other similar ones caused fears and imaginings in those who looked on, often causing them to fly away from the sick and from touching anything that had been near an ill person, for they thought that thus their health could be preserved.

There were some who thought that living soberly and in abstinence would be sufficient protection; so, joining together, they lived apart from all other company, shut up in houses where none had been sick. And there, for their greater security, they used delicate foods and excellent wines, avoiding luxury and refusing to speak to one another, not looking out of the windows or heeding the cries of the dying or watching the corpses being carried to burial. But with their music and pleasure, they lived in hope. Others were of a contrary opinion. They said that there was no medicine for such a dangerous ailment better than to drink hard and be merry. So they sang continually, went everywhere, satisfied their every appetite, laughing at and mocking every sad spectacle. They vowed to spend day and night thus, and they went from tavern to tavern, living without any restraint and abandoning all of their possessions. Most of the houses of the city became common, and strangers entered and did what they pleased without any let or hindrance.

Yet in all of this mean behavior they were wise enough to shun as much as possible the weak and sickly. In the misery and affliction of our city, the authority of the laws, both human and divine, was destroyed through the death of the lawful ministers and officers.

For they all died, or lay so sick or in want of servants and attendants, that they could not carry out any duty. Hence everyone did as he pleased.

Between these two extremities of behavior there were others of more moderate temperament, not being so careful as the first, nor drinking so heedlessly as the second, but using all things sufficient for their appetites, and not shutting themselves up. They walked in the streets, some carrying nosegays of flowers, others odiferous herbs and spiceries, holding them to their noses in the belief that they could protect the brain against the noisome stench of dead carcases. Some others there were of even more inhuman mind (though perhaps they had the surest remedy) who said that the best medicine for the pestilence was to be away from it. Caring for nobody but themselves, many men and women forsook the city, their own houses, their parents, kindred, and friends, and fled. They seemed to believe that the wrath of God, punishing men with this plague, would fall on none save those inside the city. Or else they believed that the ending of all things had come.

Now these people, with their diversity of opinions, did not all die, nor did they all escape. Many among them, falling sick and having set an example by their own flight, died altogether forsaken. So it was that one citizen fled after another, and one neighbor had no care of another. The terror of the time so afflicted the hearts of men that brother forsook brother, uncle abandoned nephew, and wife left husband. Incredible as it seems, fathers and mothers fled away from their own children. As a result a countless number of men and women fell sick and, finding no charity among their friends, became dependent upon untrustworthy servants, who served them only for extravagant wages. Yet even that kind of help was hard to find and consisted mostly of men or women unskilled and ignorant, unfit for anything except to bring the sick person what he called for, or to sit by and await the hour of his death. Even so, the desire for gain which led many to undertake this service often caused their own death.

In this calamity, when the sick were forsaken by neighbors, kindred, and friends, there arose a custom never heard of before. A woman, young, fair, or noble, falling sick, often had to depend upon a man's help. Without any shame she would show any part of her body, just as she would to another woman. If the woman recovered, it sometimes happened that this occasioned further dishonest behavior. Many, being more modest, refused such disgraceful help, choosing rather to die than by such help to be cured.

Because of the lack of effective remedies and the violence of the contagion the multitude of them that died night and day was so great that it was a dreadful sight to behold or even to hear about. Necessity caused behavior quite different from that of former times when it was the custom (as it is now again) for women, relatives, neighbors, and friends to meet at the deceased's house and there express their sorrow for their loss. Or they would assemble before the door and with the priests conduct the dead body with funereal pomp of torchlight and singing to the church chosen by the deceased. But these decent customs, after the fury of the pestilence began to increase, were ignored, and other new customs came in their place. People died without having any women about them, but multitudes also perished without any witness as to how, when, or in what manner they departed. There were few women mourners, or none, to exhibit the outward shows of grief; but there were many who lived only in idleness, like immodest women heedless of their own welfare.

Very few would accompany the body to the grave, not even the neighbors, even though the deceased had been an honorable citizen. Only the meanest kind of people, grave-diggers, coffin-bearers, and the like, who served only for money, made up the procession. The coffin being mounted on their shoulders, they would run with it hastily to the nearest church with four or six poor priests following, sometimes without lights, and, a short service being said, the body would be irreverently thrown into the first open grave they found.

[Toward the end of the third day of the young people's stay in the villa outside Florence, it becomes the turn of one of the young ladies to tell a story. She chooses the tale of Giletta of Narbonne. *Ed.*]

There lived some time ago in the kingdom of France a gentleman named Isnarde, Count of Roussillon. Because he was continually ill, he kept a physician in his house, a Master Gerard of Narbonne. Count Isnarde had only one son, very young and fair, named Bertram, with whom the children of the retainers had their education. Among them was Giletta, daughter of the physician. Her affection for young Bertram was most unusual in so young a maiden. Old Count Isnarde dying, young Bertram became a ward of the

King and was sent to Paris to remain under the royal protection.
Young Giletta grieved long and hard at the loss of her dear Bertram.

A few years after, her father also died, and then her desire became set on visiting Paris herself to see the young Count. She
awaited only time and opportunity to start her journey. But her
friends to whose care she had been committed, because of her rich
dowry, watched closely her walks and behavior, so she could not
by any means escape. She was old enough for marriage, which increased her love for the Count and at the same time led her to
refuse without any explanation the matches proposed by her friends.
By this time the Count had become a gallant young gentleman,
able to choose his own wife. Hence her affections were all the more
aroused by fear that he would choose someone else.

It was widely known that the King of France was in a very dangerous condition because of a strange tumor on his stomach, which,
being ill-tended, became a fistula. It afflicted him daily with extraordinary pain. No physician being found that could offer any hope
of a cure, but instead only increased his suffering, the King de-
spaired of all help and listened to no further advice. Giletta was
very joyful at this, for she hoped that this could be a reason for
her journey. If the disease were no more than she believed it to be,
she could easily cure it, and then she could win Bertram as her husband. Therefore, recalling the rules of medicine which by long
practice and experience she had learned of her father, she com-
pounded certain herbs together into a powder and set off for Paris.

Having arrived there, she first sought for a glimpse of Bertram,
the saint that had caused her pilgrimage. Next, she gained access
to the King, humbly asking his majesty to grant her sight of his
fistula. When the King saw her modest looks he knew her for a
discreet young gentlewoman. He therefore laid the fistula open to
her inspection. When she had seen and felt it, she assured the
King that she knew herself able to cure it. "Sire," she said, "if your
Highness will trust me, I hope, without any peril to your life or
even the least pain, to make you whole and sound within eight
days' time."

The King began to smile at this, saying, "How is it possible for
you, being a young maiden, to do that which the best physicians
in Europe are not able to do? I praise your kindness and will not

be unthankful for your willingness, but I am fully determined to use no more counsel or to try any more medicines."

Giletta replied, "Great King, let not my skill and experience be despised because I am young and a maiden, for I do not depend on my own knowledge, but upon the gracious assistance of Heaven and some rules of skilled observation which I learned of the reverend Gerard of Narbonne, who was my father and a physician of great fame during the whole of his life."

Hearing these words, the King began to admire her gracious demeanor and said to himself, "How do I know whether this young woman is sent to me by the direction of Heaven or not? Why should I not make proof of her skill? Her promise is to cure me in a short time and without any pain or affliction. She shall not have come so far just to return again with only the loss of her labor. I am resolved to try her skill." He then spoke to her: "Fair maiden, if you cause me to break my determination and then fail to cure me, what can you expect to follow?"

"Whatsoever, great King," said she, "shall please you. Let me be strongly guarded, yet not hindered when I am carrying on the cure. And then if I do not perfectly heal you within eight days, let a good fire be made and consume my body to ashes. But if I accomplish the cure and set your Highness free from all further trouble, what recompense shall come to me?"

The King praised the confidence she had in her own skill, and replied, "Fair maiden, because you are a maid and unmarried, if you succeed and I find myself fully cured, I will match you with some gentleman in marriage who shall be honorable and of good reputation. And I shall furnish you with a good dowry as well."

"My gracious sovereign," she said, "I am most heartily thankful that your Highness will procure a marriage for me, but I desire to have the husband I shall choose, by your gracious favor. But I shall not choose any of your sons or any member of the royal house."

This the King gladly granted, and young Giletta began to minister the cure. Within fewer days than her limited time, the King was sound and perfectly cured. When he perceived this, he said to her, "Believe me, gracious maid, most worthily have you won yourself a husband. Name him, and you shall have him."

She replied, "Then I have won Count Bertram of Roussillon, whom I have loved from my infancy, and cannot love any other."

The King was not eager to grant the young Count's hand to her, but his solemn promise and his royal word, which he would not by any means break, had been given. He therefore commanded that the Count be sent for and spoke to him thus: "Noble Count, it is not unknown to us that you are a gentleman of great honor, and it is our royal pleasure to free you from your wardship so that you may return home and arrange matters for the reception of the wife whom we have decided to give you."

The Count answered the King with most humble thanks, but wanted to know who his wife was to be.

"She is the young gentlewoman," replied the King, "who by the grace of Heaven has saved my life."

The Count knew her, of course, and thought that although she was fair, her humble birth made her unworthy of him. He disdainfully answered the King thus: "Would your Highness give me a quack doctor for my wife, one that deals in powders and pills? I hope I am able to do much better for myself."

"Would you have us break our oath which we have given to this virtuous maid for the recovery of our health? She will have no other reward but Count Bertram for her husband."

"Sir," replied the Count, "you may dispossess me of all that is mine, because I am your ward and subject. And you may choose whom you will for my wife. But allow me to tell you that this marriage will be over my objection and I will never agree willingly to it."

"Sir," said the King, "it is our will that it should be so. She is virtuous, fair and wise. She loves you most affectionately. With her you will lead a more happy life than with the greatest lady in our kingdom."

The Count stood silent and discontented, but the King commanded preparations for the wedding, and when the appointed time had arrived, the Count, against his will, received his wife from the King.

When all of this was done, the Count requested permission of the King to leave for his own home for the consummation of the marriage there. But instead of riding home, the Count went to Tuscany, where he heard of a war between the Florentines and Siennese. The Florentines welcomed him and made him captain of a company.

The poor, forsaken, newly-married Countess was hardly pleased with such dishonorable treatment, yet, discreetly hiding her disappointment and hoping by her virtuous demeanor to induce him to return, she rode to Roussillon where all of the people received her very lovingly. Now because of the Count's long absence, all things were disordered: mutinies, quarrels, civil dissensions, had even caused much bloodshed. But she, like the wise and provident lady she was, brought order again. The Count's vassals came to admire her so much that they greatly condemned the Count's unkindness toward her.

When the whole county of Roussillon, by her policy and wisdom, was fully pacified, she chose two knights, whom she sent to the Count, her husband, to let him know that if it was because of her that he stayed away from his home, she would gladly leave and no longer trouble him. He replied harshly, "Let her do as she wants. I'll not live with her or anywhere near her. Tell her from me that when she gets this ring from my finger to wear on hers, and when she holds in her arms a child that I have begotten on her, then I'll come to live with her." The ring that he meant was the dearest thing he possessed, and he was never known to take it from his finger because he believed it had special powers.

The two knights knew that these conditions were impossible, but they got nothing more from the Count and sorrowfully took his reply back to their lady. She was, of course, dismayed at the severity of his rejection, but nevertheless began to scheme how she could satisfy these conditions and have her husband and his love. Having decided what to do, she called together all of the Count's vassals and told them how she had attempted to persuade the Count to return and how he had spurned her. She then revealed that rather than force the Count to live in exile, she herself would leave and spend the rest of her life on pilgrimages and in deeds of charity, praying always for the Count's soul and her own. She urged them then to undertake the government of the Count's domain and to let him know of her leaving and her decision never to return to Roussillon. Everyone wept on hearing her and tried, in vain, to dissuade her.

Having bade farewell to everyone, but not telling where she was going, she left, accompanied by only her maid and one kinsman. She wore a pilgrim's habit, yet she provided herself with plenty of money and jewels.

She went directly to Florence, where she took lodging with a poor widow and pretended to live contentedly as a pilgrim (though she was impatiently longing for news of the Count). The very next day she saw him ride past the house at the head of his company. She recognized him, of course, but asked the widow who he was.

"A stranger who calls himself Count of Roussillon," replied the widow. "He is well thought of in the city and is in love with a neighbor of mine, a young gentlewoman who lives with her mother, a worthy and honest woman. She is unmarried only because of her poverty."

The Countess listened carefully and debated with herself what to do. Having learned the name of the lady and her daughter and where they lived, she, still wearing her pilgrim's clothes, visited them. She found mother and daughter living in poverty, and asked the mother for a few words in private. When they were alone, the Countess said, "We have both suffered from bad fortune. But you can, if you will, help us both and bring comfort to us both."

"Believe me," answered the lady, "I would do anything within the limits of honesty."

The Countess then said, "I must rely on your trust and fidelity, for if I do not have them, both of us may be ruined."

"Tell me anything you want," replied the old lady, "and be assured that I shall never deceive you."

The Countess then told the whole story of her love from the beginning to the present moment, revealing her true identity and the purpose of her coming to Florence. So well did she speak that the old lady believed her altogether, especially since she had heard from others some of the Countess's story of misfortune. All of this made her more compassionate for the Countess's plight.

When the Countess had told all of her past history, she went on: "Among my miseries and misfortunes, which have almost broken my heart to retell, there are two things that I must overcome if I am ever to have my husband and his love. Yet these two things I can accomplish with your help, if what I have heard is true. You can tell if this is so. Since my arrival in this city, it has been told me that my husband, the Count, is deeply in love with your daughter."

"If the Count," replied the lady, "loves my daughter and already has a wife, he will find that his greatness will not help him to dishonor her just because she is poor. It is true that there may be some love on the part of the Count, but I shall do whatever I can for you, for I prize my daughter's honesty as highly as he does his proud honor."

"Madam," said the Countess, "I thank you for your offer. But before I ask you to do anything more, let me tell you what I intend to do for you. Your daughter is beautiful and ready for marriage, but, I hear, is prevented from doing so for want of a dowry. In recompense of the favor I am going to ask of you, I shall give you as much as you think necessary for her dowry."

Poverty made the poor lady's agreement quick. Moreover, she had a noble heart, and said, "Countess, how can I serve you so as to deserve such a generous offer? If the act is honest and I can preserve my reputation, I would gladly help you. You may then do as you see fit about a reward."

"Then, Madam," replied the Countess, "tell the Count, by some trustworthy messenger, that your daughter is ready to give herself to him if she receives, as his pledge of honor, the ring he wears on his little finger, which, as she has no doubt heard, he treasures very much. If he sends the ring, you shall give it to me and then send word to him that your daughter is ready to receive him. Then let him come secretly at night to your house where I, instead of your daughter, shall go to bed with him. Thus, unknown to him, I may with luck conceive his child. At the proper time, with his child in my arms and his ring on my finger, I may gain his love and live thereafter with him as a good wife should with her husband. And you will have been the cause of this good fortune."

The old lady thought that all of this would be difficult to achieve and might cause scandal about her daughter. Nevertheless, considering that she could be the means to a good end by enabling the virtuous Countess to reform an erring husband, she promised to help. Within a few days, she very cleverly saw to it that the ring was obtained, despite the Count's reluctance to part with it; and she succeeded in putting the Countess in her daughter's bed, where the Count, by God's grace, ardently begat two fine sons whom the Countess bore in due time.

Thus the old lady gave the Countess full possession of her husband many times, but always secretly and in the dark, so that the Count never suspected that he lay with his own wife and was being cheated of the woman whom he thought he possessed. Moreover, when he left in the mornings, always before daybreak so as to avoid suspicion, he often gave her jewels and other gifts which the Countess carefully treasured.

Perceiving definitely that she was with child, she at last told the old lady that she would no longer trouble her. "Madam," she said, "I thank Heaven and you because my desire has been so well satisfied. It is time for me to reward you and take my leave. You may make any demand of me you please, but not as a wage, because that would seem base and mercenary. What you receive of me is an honorable recompense for honorable and virtuous assistance, such as any honest lady in similar distress should be able to expect."

Although poverty might well have urged the lady to demand an extravagant sum, she asked for only a hundred pounds as friendly assistance toward her daughter's wedding. And she asked for that with a becoming hesitancy. But the Countess gave her five hundred pounds and many costly jewels besides.

Then the Countess returned to her lodgings at the widow's house. The old lady and her daughter left Florence. The Count was distressed, but never heard any further word of her or her daughter, who was married happily and honorably.

Not long after, Count Bertram was recalled to Roussillon, where he willingly went, having heard that his wife was no longer there. The Countess remained in Florence until the birth of her twin sons, who greatly resembled their father. She was most careful of their nursing, and when they were old enough to travel, went to Montpellier where she rested for a time. Learning that the Count was to hold his court on All Saints Day, she joined there the throng of lords and knights and ladies. Clad in her pilgrim's habit, she entered the great hall where all the tables were spread for the feast. Pushing through the crowd, with her two children in her arms, she kneeled at last before the Count and, weeping copiously, spoke to him: "Worthy lord, I am your poor, despised, and unfortunate wife who, in order to allow you to return to your own home, have gone begging through the world. And now I hope that you will honorably live up to your own strict conditions, stated to the two knights whom I sent to you. These conditions I was commanded to obey. Behold, here in my arms, not one son begotten by you, but two, and your ring on my finger besides. If you are a man of honor, now is the time, after my long and tedious journey, for you to welcome me as your own true wife."

The Count was astonished, for he knew his ring quite well, and both children were so perfectly like him that everyone agreed that he must be their father. Upon his asking how all this could have happened, the Countess told the whole assembly the entire story. Moreover, she repeated their talk abed and showed the jewels that he had given her. All of these proofs of his shame and her devotion to her husband compelled him to acknowledge that she told the whole truth.

Therefore, commending her constancy, wit, and courage, he kissed the two sweet little boys and, to keep his promises, as he was urged to do by all, especially the ladies, he accepted the Countess as his lawful wife. Folding her in his arms and tenderly kissing her, he bade her welcome as his virtuous, loyal, and loving wife, as she would be for him forever. He knew that she had more becoming dresses in the house, and he requested several ladies of the court to accompany her to her chamber and help her rid herself of the pilgrim's garb and put on her most becoming dress, her wedding dress. He termed her his wife indeed and gave thanks to the King for having forced him to wed. Now was Count Bertram of Roussillon truly married to the fair Giletta of Narbonne.

Giovanni Pico della Mirandola

14

Oration on the Dignity of Man

Giovanni Pico, Count of Mirandola (1463–1494), was the perfect example of the brilliant, young, restless intellectual of the Renaissance. Repelled by the traditional curriculum of the University of Bologna, Pico spent several years wandering through Italy and France, collecting a library, acquiring a remarkable miscellaneous knowledge of the Greek and Latin classics, and studying Hebrew, Chaldee, and Arabic. He was especially interested in the occult and in Neoplatonism. These studies seemed to him to promise some kind of supersensory knowledge of the divine mysteries of all religions.

As a youth of twenty-four, Pico confidently offered to defend in public disputation nine hundred propositions, which represented his own conclusions in philosophy and theology. Despite the interest aroused by his audacity, the disputation was never held, for some of the theses suggested by Pico aroused suspicions of heresy.

Pico took all knowledge as his province and attempted to show the truth of Christianity as both a religion and a philosophy by bringing together into an intellectual harmony the traditional classics and the philosophy of Hebraism and Islam. With his handsome appearance, keen intelligence, and restless and quick perceptions, Pico made a vivid impression upon his contemporaries—a living proof of the Platonic "Ideal Youth," as one of his philosophically minded admirers termed him. The *Oration on the Dignity of Man,* originally intended as an introductory speech for his proposed disputation of 1487, is an excellent reflection of the aspirations of Renaissance humanism.

Giovanni Pico della Mirandola, *Oration on the Dignity of Man,* trans. Elizabeth L. Forbes. Reprinted from *The Renaissance Philosophy of Man,* edited by Ernst Cassirer, Paul O. Kristeller, and John H. Randall, Jr., by permission of The University of Chicago Press. Copyright 1948 by The University of Chicago. All rights reserved. [Pp. 223–27, 229–35.]

I have read in the records of the Arabians, reverend Fathers, that Abdala the Saracen, when questioned as to what on this stage of the world, as it were, could be seen most worthy of wonder, replied: "There is nothing to be seen more wonderful than man." In agreement with this opinion is the saying of Hermes Trismegistus: "A great miracle, Asclepius, is man." But when I weighed the reason for these maxims, the many grounds for the excellence of human nature reported by many men failed to satisfy me—that man is the intermediary between creatures, the intimate of the gods, the king of the lower beings, by the acuteness of his senses, by the discernment of his reason, and by the light of his intelligence the interpreter of nature, the interval between fixed eternity and fleeting time, and (as the Persians say) the bond, nay, rather, the marriage song of the world, on David's testimony but little lower than the angels. Admittedly great though these reasons be, they are not the principal grounds, that is, those which may rightfully claim for themselves the privilege of the highest admiration. For why should we not admire more the angels themselves and the blessed choirs of heaven? At last it seems to me I have come to understand why man is the most fortunate of creatures and consequently worthy of all admiration and what precisely is that rank which is his lot in the universal chain of Being—a rank to be envied not only by brutes but even by the stars and by minds beyond this world. It is a matter past faith and a wondrous one. Why should it not be? For it is on this very account that man is rightly called and judged a great miracle and a wonderful creature indeed.

But hear, Fathers, exactly what this rank is and, as friendly auditors, conformably to your kindness, do me this favor. God the Father, the supreme Architect, had already built this cosmic home we behold, the most sacred temple of His godhead, by the laws of His mysterious wisdom. The region above the heavens He had adorned with Intelligences, the heavenly spheres He had quickened with eternal souls, and the excrementary and filthy parts of the lower world He had filled with a multitude of animals of every kind. But, when the work was finished, the Craftsman kept wishing that there were someone to ponder the plan of so great a work, to love its beauty, and to wonder at its vastness. Therefore, when everything was done (as Moses and Timaeus bear witness), He finally took thought concerning the creation of man. But there was not among His archetypes that from which He could fashion a new offspring, nor was there in His treasure-houses anything which He might bestow on His new son as an inheritance, nor was there in the seats of all the world a place where the latter might sit to contemplate the universe. All was now complete; all things had been assigned to the highest, the middle, and the lowest orders. But in its final creation it was not the part of the Father's power to fail as though exhausted. It was not the part of His wisdom to waver in a needful matter through poverty of counsel. It was not the part of His kindly love that he who was to praise God's divine generosity in regard to others should be compelled to condemn it in regard to himself.

At last the best of artisans ordained that that creature to whom He had been able to give nothing proper to himself should have joint possession of whatever had been peculiar to each of the different kinds of being. He therefore took man as a creature of indeterminate nature and, assigning him a place in the middle of the world, addressed him thus: "Neither a fixed abode nor a form that is thine alone nor any function peculiar to thyself have we given thee, Adam, to the end that according to thy longing and according to thy judgment thou mayest have and possess what abode, what form, and what functions thou thyself shalt desire. The nature of all other beings is limited and constrained within the bounds of laws prescribed by Us. Thou, constrained by no limits, in accordance with thine own free will, in whose hand We have placed thee, shalt ordain for thyself the limits of thy nature. We have set thee at the world's center that thou mayest from thence more easily observe whatever is in the world. We have made thee neither of heaven nor of earth, neither mortal nor immortal, so that with freedom of choice and with honor, as though the maker and molder of thyself, thou mayest fashion thyself in whatever shape thou shalt prefer. Thou shalt have the power to degenerate into the lower forms of life, which are brutish. Thou shalt have the power, out of thy soul's judgment, to be reborn into the higher forms, which are divine."

O supreme generosity of God the Father, O highest and most marvelous felicity of man! To him it is granted to have whatever he chooses, to be whatever he wills. Beasts as soon as they are born (so says Lucilius) bring with them from their mother's womb all they will ever possess. Spiritual beings, either from the beginning or soon thereafter, become what they are to be for ever and ever. On man when he came into life the Father conferred the seeds of all kinds and the germs of every way of life. Whatever seeds each man cultivates will grow to maturity and bear in him their own fruit. If they be vegetative, he will be like a plant. If sensitive, he will become brutish. If rational, he will grow into a heavenly being. If intellectual, he will be an angel and the son of God. And if, happy in the lot of no created thing, he withdraws into the center of his own unity, his spirit, made one with God, in the solitary darkness of God, who is set above all things, shall surpass them all. Who would not admire this our chameleon? Or who could more greatly admire aught else whatever? It is man who Asclepius of Athens, arguing from his mutability of character and from his self-transforming nature, on just grounds says was symbolized by Proteus in the mysteries. Hence those metamorphoses renowned among the Hebrews and the Pythagoreans.

For the occult theology of the Hebrews sometimes transforms the holy Enoch into an angel of divinity whom they call "Mal'akh Adonay Shebaoth," and sometimes transforms others into other divinities. The Pythagoreans degrade impious men into brutes and, if one is to believe Empedocles, even into plants. Mohammed, in imitation, often had this saying on his tongue: "They who have deviated from divine law become beasts," and surely he spoke justly. For it is not the bark that makes the plant but its senseless and insentient nature; neither is it the hide that makes the beast of burden but its irrational, sensitive soul; neither is it the orbed form that makes the heavens but their undeviating order; nor is it the sundering from body but his spiritual intelligence that makes the angel. For if you see one abandoned to his appetites crawling on the ground, it is a plant and not a man you see; if you see one blinded by the vain illusions of imagery, as it were of Calypso, and, softened by their gnawing allurement, delivered over to his senses, it is a beast and not a man you see. If you see a philosopher determining all things by means of right reason, him you shall reverence: he is a heavenly being and not of this earth. If you see a pure contemplator, one unaware of the body and confined to the inner reaches of the mind, he is neither an earthly nor a heavenly being; he is a more reverend divinity vested with human flesh.

Are there any who would not admire man, who is, in the sacred writings of Moses and the Christians, not without reason described sometimes by the name of "all flesh," sometimes by that of "every creature," inasmuch as he himself molds, fashions, and changes himself into the form of all flesh and into the character of every creature? For this reason the Persian Euanthes, in describing the Chaldaean theology, writes that man has no semblance that is inborn and his very own but many that are external and foreign to him; whence this saying of the Chaldaeans: "Hanorish tharah sharinas," that is, "Man is a being of varied, manifold, and inconstant nature." But why do we emphasize this? To the end that after we have been born to this condition—that we can become what we will—we should understand that we ought to have especial care to this, that it should never be said against us that, although born to a privileged position, we failed to recognize it and became like unto wild animals and senseless beasts of burden, but that rather the saying of Asaph the prophet should apply: "Ye are all angels and sons of the Most High," and that we may not, by abusing the most indulgent generosity of the Father, make for ourselves that freedom of choice He has given into something harmful instead of salutary. Let a certain holy ambition invade our souls, so that, not content with the mediocre, we shall pant after the highest and (since we may if we wish) toil with all our strength to obtain it.

Let us disdain earthly things, despise heavenly things, and, finally, esteeming less whatever is of the world, hasten to that court which is beyond the world and nearest to the Godhead. There, as the sacred mysteries relate, Seraphim, Cherubim, and Thrones hold the first places; let us, incapable of yielding to them, and intolerant of a lower place, emulate their dignity and their glory. If we have willed it, we shall be second to them in nothing.

• • •

Then let us fill our well-prepared and purified soul with the light of natural philosophy, so that we may at last perfect her in the knowledge of things divine. And lest we be satisfied with those of our faith, let us consult the patriarch Jacob, whose form gleams carved on the throne of glory. Sleeping in the lower world but keeping watch in the upper, the wisest of fathers will advise us. But he will advise us through a figure (in this way everything was wont to come to those men) that there is a ladder extending from

the lowest earth to the highest heaven, divided in a series of many
steps, with the Lord seated at the top, and angels in contemplation ascending and descending over them alternately by turns.

If this is what we must practice in our aspiration to the angelic
way of life, I ask: "Who will touch the ladder of the Lord either
with fouled foot or with unclean hands?" As the sacred mysteries
have it, it is impious for the impure to touch the pure. But what
are these feet? What these hands? Surely the foot of the soul is that
most contemptible part by which the soul rests on matter as on the
soil of the earth, I mean the nourishing and feeding power, the
tinder of lust, and the teacher of pleasurable weakness. Why should
we not call the hands of the soul its irascible power, which strug-
gles on its behalf as the champion of desire and as plunderer seizes
in the dust and sun what desire will devour slumbering in the
shade? These hands, these feet, that is, all the sentient part whereon
resides the attraction of the body which, as they say, by wrench-
ing the neck holds the soul in check, lest we be hurled down from
the ladder as impious and unclean, let us bathe in moral philosophy as if in a living river. Yet this will not be enough if we wish
to be companions of the angels going up and down on Jacob's
ladder, unless we have first been well fitted and instructed to be
promoted duly from step to step, to stray nowhere from the stairway, and to engage in the alternate comings and goings. Once we
have achieved this by the art of discourse or reasoning, then, inspired by the Cherubic spirit, using philosophy through the steps
of the ladder, that is, of nature, and penetrating all things from
center to center, we shall sometimes descend, with titanic force
rending the unity like Osiris into many parts, and we shall sometimes ascend, with the force of Phoebus collecting the parts like
the limbs of Osiris into a unity, until, resting at last in the bosom
of the Father who is above the ladder, we shall be made perfect
with the felicity of theology.

Let us also inquire of the just Job, who entered into a life-
covenant with God before he himself was brought forth into life,
what the most high God requires above all in those tens of hundreds of thousands who attend him. He will answer that it is peace,
in accord with what we read in him: "He maketh peace in his
high places." And since the middle order expounds to the lower
orders the counsel of the highest order, let Empedocles the philosopher expound to us the words of Job the theologian. He indi-

cates to us a twofold nature present in our souls, by one side of
which we are raised on high to the heavenly regions, and by the
other side plunged downward into the lower, through strife and
friendship or through war and peace, as he witnesses in the verses
in which he makes complaint that he is being driven into the sea,
himself goaded by strife and discord into the semblance of a madman and a fugitive from the gods.

Surely, Fathers, there is in us a discord many times as great;
we have at hand wars grievous and more than civil, wars of the
spirit which, if we dislike them, if we aspire to that peace which
may so raise us to the sublime that we shall be established among
the exalted of the Lord, only philosophy will entirely allay and
subdue in us. In the first place, if our man but ask a truce of his
enemies, moral philosophy will check the unbridled inroads of
the many-sided beast and the leonine passions of wrath and violence. If we then take wiser counsel with ourselves and learn to
desire the security of everlasting peace, it will be at hand and will
generously fulfil our prayers. After both beasts are felled like a
sacrificed sow, it will confirm an inviolable compact of holiest
peace between flesh and spirit. Dialectic will appease the tumults
of reason made confused and anxious by inconsistencies of statement and sophisms of syllogisms. Natural philosophy will allay the
strife and differences of opinion which vex, distract, and wound
the spirit from all sides. But she will so assuage them as to compel us to remember that, according to Heraclitus, nature was begotten from war, that it was on this account repeatedly called
"strife" by Homer, and that it is not, therefore, in the power of
natural philosophy to give us in nature a true quiet and unshaken
peace but that this is the function and privilege of her mistress,
that is, of holiest theology. She will show us the way and as comrade lead us to her who, seeing us hastening from afar, will ex-
claim "Come to me, ye who have labored. Come and I will restore
you. Come to me, and I will give you peace, which the world and
nature cannot give you."

When we have been so soothingly called, so kindly urged, we
shall fly up with winged feet, like earthly Mercuries, to the em-
braces of our blessed mother and enjoy that wished-for peace, most
holy peace, indivisible bond, of one accord in the friendship
through which all rational souls not only shall come into harmony
in the one mind which is above all minds but shall in some in-

effable way become altogether one. This is that friendship which the Pythagoreans say is the end of all philosophy. This is that peace which God creates in his heavens, which the angels descending to earth proclaimed to men of good will, that through it men might ascend to heaven and become angels. Let us wish this peace for our friends, for our century. Let us wish it for every home into which we go; let us wish it for our own soul, that through it she shall herself be made the house of God, and to the end that as soon as she has cast out her uncleanness through moral philosophy and dialectic, adorned herself with manifold philosophy as with the splendor of a courtier, and crowned the pediments of her doors with the garlands of theology, the King of Glory may descend and, coming with his Father, make his stay with her. If she show herself worthy of so great a guest, she shall, by the boundless mercy which is his, in golden raiment like a wedding gown, and surrounded by a varied throng of sciences, receive her beautiful guest not merely as a guest but as a spouse from whom she will never be parted. She will desire rather to be parted from her own people and, forgetting her father's house and herself, will desire to die in herself in order to live in her spouse, in whose sight surely the death of his saints is precious—death, I say, if we must call death that fulness of life, the consideration of which wise men have asserted to be the aim of philosophy.

Let us also cite Moses himself, but little removed from the springing abundance of the holy and unspeakable wisdom by whose nectar the angels are made drunk. Let us hearken to the venerable judge in these words proclaiming laws to us who are dwellers in the desert loneliness of this body: "Let those who, as yet unclean, still need moral philosophy, live with the people outside the tabernacle under the sky, meanwhile purifying themselves like the priests of Thessaly. Let those who have already ordered their conduct be received into the sanctuary but not quite yet touch the holy vessels; let them first like zealous Levites in the service of dialectic minister to the holy things of philosophy. Then when they have been admitted even to these, let them now behold the many-colored robe of the higher palace of the Lord, that is to say, the stars; let them now behold the heavenly candlestick divided into seven lights; let them now behold the fur tent, that is, the elements, in the priesthood of philosophy, so that when they are in the end, through the favor of theological sublimity, granted entrance into the inner part of the temple, they may rejoice in the glory of the Godhead with no veil before his image." This of a surety Moses commands us and, in commanding, summons, urges, and encourages us by means of philosophy to prepare ourselves a way, while we can, to the heavenly glory to come.

But indeed not only the Mosaic and Christian mysteries but also the theology of the ancients show us the benefits and value of the liberal arts, the discussion of which I am about to undertake. For what else did the degrees of the initiates observed in the mysteries of the Greeks mean? For they arrived at a perception of the mysteries when they had first been purified through those expiatory sciences, as it were, moral philosophy and dialectic. What else can that perception possibly be than an interpretation of occult nature by means of philosophy? Then at length to those who were so disposed came that ΕΠΟΠΤΕΙΑ [Initiation in the Eleusinian mysteries], that is to say, the observation of things divine by the light of theology. Who would not long to be initiated into such sacred rites? Who would not desire, by neglecting all human concerns, by despising the goods of fortune, and by disregarding those of the body, to become the guest of the gods while yet living on earth, and, made drunk by the nectar of eternity, to be endowed with the gifts of immortality though still a mortal being? Who would not wish to be so inflamed with those Socratic frenzies sung by Plato in the *Phaedrus,* that, by the oarage of feet and wings escaping speedily from hence, that is, from a world set on evil, he might be borne on the fastest of courses to the heavenly Jerusalem? Let us be driven, Fathers, let us be driven by the frenzies of Socrates, that they may so throw us into ecstasy as to put our mind and ourselves in God. Let us be driven by them, if we have first done what is in our power. For if through moral philosophy the forces of our passions have by a fitting agreement become so intent on harmony that they can sing together in undisturbed concord, and if through dialectic our reason has moved progressively in a rhythmical measure, then we shall be stirred by the frenzy of the Muses and drink the heavenly harmony with our inmost hearing. Thereupon Bacchus, the leader of the Muses, by showing in his mysteries, that is, in the visible signs of nature, the invisible things of God to us who study philosophy, will intoxicate us with the fulness of God's house, in which, if we prove faithful, like Moses, hallowed theology shall come and inspire us with a doubled frenzy.

For, exalted to her lofty height, we shall measure therefrom all things that are and shall be and have been in indivisible eternity; and, admiring their original beauty, like the seers of Phoebus, we shall become her own winged lovers. And at last, roused by ineffable love as by a sting, like burning Seraphim rapt from ourselves, full of divine power we shall no longer be ourselves but shall become He Himself Who made us.

If anyone investigates the holy names of Apollo, their meanings and hidden mysteries, these amply show that that god is no less a philosopher than a seer; but, since Ammonius has sufficiently examined this subject, there is no reason why I should now treat it otherwise. But, Fathers, three Delphic precepts may suggest themselves to your minds, which are very necessary to those who are to go into the most sacred and revered temple, not of the false but of the true Apollo, who lights every soul as it enters this world. You will see that they give us no other advice than that we should with all our strength embrace this threefold philosophy which is the concern of our present debate. For the saying μηδὲν ἄγαν, that is, "Nothing too much," prescribes a standard and rule for all the virtues through the doctrine of the Mean, with which moral philosophy duly deals. Then the saying γνῶθι σεαυτόν, that is, "Know thyself," urges and encourages us to the investigation of all nature, of which the nature of man is both the connecting link and, so to speak, the "mixed bowl." For he who knows himself in himself knows all things, as Zoroaster first wrote, and then Plato in his *Alcibiades*. When we are finally lighted in this knowledge by natural philosophy, and nearest to God are uttering the theological greeting, εἶ, that is, "Thou art," we shall likewise in bliss be addressing the true Apollo on intimate terms.

Desiderius Erasmus

═══ 15 ═══

The Praise of Folly

Desiderius Erasmus of Rotterdam (*ca.* 1466–1536) dominated the European world of letters in the early sixteenth century. Under pressure from his guardians, he became an Augustinian monk and was ordained a priest; he was, however, permitted to leave the monastery and to travel extensively. Although he remained a loyal Christian all his life, he lived more as a scholar than as a priest. Wherever men were interested in learning, there Erasmus went. He journeyed to England, for instance, to lecture on Greek at Cambridge and became fast friends with English scholars, especially Sir Thomas More, at whose suggestion Erasmus wrote *The Praise of Folly* (1509). His life was one of indefatigable scholarly industry. He has been called the "Prince of Humanists" and "Schoolmaster to the Renaissance."

Erasmus, keenly aware of the corrupt practices of the Church, was a strong proponent of reform. His edition of the Greek New Testament gave a scholarly impetus to reform, while his forthright criticism of abuses encouraged critical examination of traditional practices and beliefs. Religion for Erasmus was both a personal matter and a question of scholarship and doctrine. Revolt against religious authority, however, seemed to him to lead only to religious anarchy; instead, he advocated gradual reform from within. Erasmus therefore appealed to men's reason and sense of humor, refusing to take up the defense of the rebel Luther at the Diet of Worms, but, on the other hand, refusing to be merely a spokesman for the orthodox views of the Church. Neither a servant of reform nor a slave of reaction, he was disliked by both parties.

Erasmus's *Praise of Folly* is an ironical survey of sixteenth-century European society. Folly—presented in the guise of a goddess of ancient mythology—is the speaker; she describes the vanities and nonsense of those who, in their ignorance, greed, and envy, are—in effect—her wor-

Desiderius Erasmus, *The Praise of Folly* (London: Reeves and Turner, 1876), 82–86, 121–23, 127–28, 134–36, 138–40, 156–60.

shipers. Some of her followers are easily recognized: the vain and proud merchant, the angry and jealous husband, the silly rich woman. But Folly (as is shown in the following selection) also finds her devotees in unexpected places: in the Church and among the scholastic philosophers in the universities, where Erasmus's wit delights in searching them out.

What shall I say of such as cry up and maintain the cheat of pardons and indulgences and by these compute the time of each soul's residence in purgatory, and assign them a longer or shorter continuance, according as they purchase more or fewer of these paltry pardons and saleable exemptions? Or what can be said bad enough of others, who pretend that by the force of such magical charms, or by the fumbling over their beads in the rehearsal of such and such petitions (which some religious impostors invented, either for diversion, or what is more likely, for advantage), they shall procure riches, honour, pleasure, health, long life, a lusty old age, nay, after death a sitting at the right hand of our Saviour in His kingdom; though as to this last part of their happiness, they care not how long it be deferred, having scarce any appetite toward tasting the joys of heaven, till they are surfeited, glutted with, and can no longer relish their enjoyments on earth. By this easy way of purchasing pardons, any notorious highwayman, any plundering soldier, or any bribe-taking judge, shall disburse some part of their unjust gains, and so think all their grossest impieties sufficiently atoned for; so many perjuries, lusts, drunkenness, quarrels, bloodsheds, cheats, treacheries, and all sorts of debaucheries, shall all be, as it were, struck a bargain for, and such a contract made, as if they had paid off all arrears, and might now begin upon a new score.

And what can be more ridiculous, than for some others to be confident of going to heaven by repeating daily those seven verses out of the Psalms, which the devil taught St. Bernard, thinking thereby to have put a trick upon him, but that he was over-reached in his cunning.

Several of these fooleries, which are so gross and absurd, as I myself am even ashamed to own, are practised and admired, not

only by the vulgar, but by such proficients in religion as one might
well expect should have more wit.

From the same principles of folly proceeds the custom of each
country's challenging their particular guardian-saint; nay, each
saint has his distinct office allotted to him, and is accordingly addressed to upon the respective occasions: as one for the tooth-ache,
a second to grant an easy delivery in child-birth, a third to help
persons to lost goods, another to protect seamen in a long voyage,
a fifth to guard the farmer's cows and sheep, and so on; for to
rehearse all instances would be extremely tedious.

There are some more catholic saints petitioned to upon all occasions, as more especially the Virgin Mary, whose blind devotees
think it manners now to place the mother before the Son.

And of all the prayers and intercessions that are made to these
respective saints the substance of them is no more than downright
Folly. Among all the trophies that for tokens of gratitude are
hung upon the walls and ceilings of churches, you shall find no
relics presented as a memorandum of any that were ever cured of
Folly, or had been made one dram the wiser. One perhaps after
shipwreck got safe to shore; another recovered when he had been
run through by an enemy; one, when all his fellow-soldiers were
killed upon the spot, as cunningly perhaps as cowardly, made his
escape from the field; another, while he was a hanging, the rope
broke, and so he saved his neck, and renewed his licence for practising his old trade of thieving; another broke gaol, and got loose;
a patient, against his physician's will, recovered of a dangerous
fever; another drank poison, which putting him into a violent
looseness, did his body more good than hurt, to the great grief of
his wife, who hoped upon this occasion to have become a joyful
widow; another had his waggon overturned, and yet none of his
horses lamed; another had caught a grievous fall, and yet recovered from the bruise; another had been tampering with his neighbour's wife, and escaped very narrowly from being caught by the
enraged cuckold in the very act. After all these acknowledgments
of escapes from such singular dangers, there is none (as I have before intimated) that return thanks for being freed from Folly; Folly
being so sweet and luscious, that it is rather sued for as a happiness,
than deprecated as a punishment. But why should I launch out
into so wide a sea of superstitions?

. . .

The divines present themselves next; but it may perhaps be most safe to pass them by, and not to touch upon so harsh a string as this subject would afford. Beside, the undertaking may be very hazardous; for they are a sort of men generally very hot and passionate; and should I provoke them, I doubt not would set upon me with a full cry, and force me with shame to recant, which if I stubbornly refuse to do, they will presently brand me for a heretic, and thunder out an excommunication, which is their spiritual weapon to wound such as lift up a hand against them. It is true, no men own a less dependence on me, yet have they reason to confess themselves indebted for no small obligations. For it is by one of my properties, self-love, that they fancy themselves, with their elder brother Paul, caught up into the third heaven, from whence, like shepherds indeed, they look down upon their flock, the laity, grazing as it were, in the vales of the world below. They fence themselves in with so many surrounders of magisterial definitions, conclusions, corollaries, propositions explicit and implicit, that there is no falling in with them; or if they do chance to be urged to a seeming non-plus, yet they find out so many evasions, that all the art of man can never bind them so fast, but that an easy distinction shall give them a starting-hole to escape the scandal of being baffled. They will cut asunder the toughest argument with as much ease as Alexander did the gordian knot; they will thunder out so many rattling terms as shall fright an adversary into conviction. They are exquisitely dexterous in unfolding the most intricate mysteries; they will tell you to a tittle all the successive proceedings of Omnipotence in the creation of the universe; they will explain the precise manner of original sin being derived from our first parents; they will satisfy you in what manner, by what degrees, and in how long a time, our Saviour was conceived in the Virgin's womb, and demonstrate in the consecrated wafer how accidents may subsist without a subject. Nay, these are accounted trivial, easy questions; they have yet far greater difficulties behind, which notwithstanding they solve with as much expedition as the former; as namely, whether supernatural generation requires any instant of time for its acting? whether Christ, as a son, bears a double specifically distinct relation to God the Father, and his virgin mother? whether this proposition is possible to be true, the first person of the Trinity hated the second? whether God, who took our nature upon him in the form of a man, could as well have be-

come a woman, a devil, a beast, a herb, or a stone? and were it so
possible that the Godhead had appeared in any shape of an inani-
mate substance, how he should then have preached his gospel? or
how have been nailed to the cross? whether if St. Peter had celebrated the eucharist at the same time our Saviour was hanging on
the cross, the consecrated bread would have been transubstantiated
into the same body that remained on the tree?

.   .   .

Farther, the apostles often mention *Grace,* yet never distinguish
between *gratia, gratis data,* and *gratia gratificans.* They earnestly
exhort us likewise to good works, yet never explain the difference
between *Opus operans,* and *Opus operatum.* They very frequently
press and invite us to seek after charity, without dividing it into
infused and acquired, or determining whether it be a substance or
an accident, a created or an uncreated being. They detested sin
themselves, and warned others from the commission of it; and yet
I am sure they could never have defined so dogmatically, as the
Scotists have since done. St. Paul, who in other's judgment is no
less the chief of the apostles, than he was in his own the chief
of sinners, who being bred at the feet of Gamaliel, was certainly
more eminently a scholar than any of the rest, yet he often exclaims
against vain philosophy, warns us from doting about questions and
strifes of words, and charges us to avoid profane and vain babblings,
and oppositions of science falsely so called; which he would not
have done, if he had thought it worth his while to have become
acquainted with them, which he might soon have been, the dis-
putes of that age being but small, and more intelligible sophisms,
in reference to the vastly greater intricacies they are now improved
to. But yet, however, our scholastic divines are so modest, that if
they meet with any passage in St. Paul, or any other penman of
holy writ, which is not so well modelled, or critically disposed of, as
they could wish, they will not roughly condemn it, but bend it
rather to a favorable interpretation, out of reverence to antiquity,
and respect to the holy scriptures; though indeed it were unreasonable to expect anything of this nature from the apostles, whose
lord and master had given unto them to know the mysteries of God,
but not those of philosophy.

.   .   .

The next to these are another sort of brainsick fools, who style themselves monks and of religious orders, though they assume both titles very unjustly: for as to the last, they have very little religion in them; and as to the former, the etymology of the word monk implies a solitariness, or being alone; whereas they are so thick abroad that we cannot pass any street or alley without meeting them. Now I cannot imagine what one degree of men would be more hopelessly wretched, if I did not stand their friend, and buoy them up in that lake of misery, which by the engagements of a holy vow they have voluntarily immerged themselves in. But when these sort of men are so unwelcome to others, as that the very sight of them is thought ominous, I yet make them highly in love with themselves, and fond admirers of their own happiness. The first step whereunto they esteem a profound ignorance, thinking carnal knowledge a great enemy to their spiritual welfare, and seem confident of becoming greater proficients in divine mysteries the less they are poisoned with any human learning. They imagine that they bear a sweet consort with the heavenly choir, when they tone out their daily tally of psalms, which they rehearse only by rote, without permitting their understanding or affections to go along with their voice. Among these some make a good profitable trade of beggary, going about from house to house, not like the apostles, to break, but to beg, their bread; nay, thrust into all public-houses, come aboard the passage-boats, get into the travelling waggons, and omit no opportunity of time or place for the craving people's charity; doing a great deal of injury to common highway beggars by interloping in their traffic of alms. And when they are thus voluntarily poor, destitute, not provided with two coats, nor with any money in their purse, they have the impudence to pretend that they imitate the first disciples, whom their master expressly sent out in such an equipage. It is pretty to observe how they regulate all their actions as it were by weight and measure to so exact a proportion, as if the whole loss of their religion depended upon the omission of the least punctilio. Thus they must be very critical in the precise number of knots to the tying on of their sandals; what distinct colours their respective habits, and what stuff made of; how broad and long their girdles; how big, and in what fashion, their hoods; whether their bald crowns be to a hair's-breadth of the right cut; how many hours they must sleep, at what minute rise to prayers, &c. And these several customs are altered according to the humours of different persons and places.

. . .

[They] place their greatest stress for salvation on a strict conformity to their foppish ceremonies, and a belief of their legendary traditions; wherein they fancy to have acquitted themselves with so much of supererogation, that one heaven can never be a condign reward for their meritorious life; little thinking that the Judge of all the earth at the last day shall put them off, with a who hath required these things at your hands; and call them to account only for the stewardship of his legacy, which was the precept of love and charity. It will be pretty to hear their pleas before the great tribunal: one will brag how he mortified his carnal appetite by feeding only upon fish: another will urge that he spent most of his time on earth in the divine exercise of singing psalms: a third will tell how many days he fasted, and what severe penance he imposed on himself for the bringing his body into subjection: another shall produce in his own behalf as many ceremonies as would load a fleet of merchant-men: a fifth shall plead that in threescore years he never so much as touched a piece of money, except he fingered it through a thick pair of gloves: a sixth, to testify his former humility, shall bring along with him his sacred hood, so old and nasty, that any seaman had rather stand bare headed on the deck, than put it on to defend his ears in the sharpest storms: the next that comes to answer for himself shall plead, that for fifty years together, he had lived like a sponge upon the same place, and was content never to change his homely habitation: another shall whisper softly, and tell the Judge he has lost his voice by a continual singing of holy hymns and anthems: the next shall confess how he fell into a lethargy by a strict, reserved, and sedentary life: and the last shall intimate that he has forgot to speak, by having always kept silence, in obedience to the injunction of taking heed lest he should have offended with his tongue. But amidst all their fine excuses our Saviour shall interrupt them with this answer, "Woe unto you, scribes and pharisees, hypocrites. Verily I know you not. I left you but one precept, of loving one another, which I do not hear any one plead he has faithfully discharged. I told you plainly in my gospel, without any parable, that my father's kingdom was prepared not for such as should lay claim to it by austerities, prayers, or fastings, but for those who should render themselves worthy of it by the exercise of faith, and the offices of charity. I cannot own such as depend on their own merits without a reliance on my mercy. As many of you, therefore, as trust to the broken reeds of your own deserts may even go search out a new heaven, for you shall never enter into that, which from the foundations of the world was prepared only for such as are true of heart."

When these monks and friars shall meet with such a shameful repulse, and see that ploughmen and mechanics are admitted into that kingdom, from which they themselves are shut out, how sneakingly will they look, and how pitifully slink away? Yet till this last trial they had more comfort of a future happiness, because more hopes of it than any other men. And these persons are not only great in their own eyes, but highly esteemed and respected by others, especially those of the order of mendicants, whom none dare to offer any affront to, because as confessors they are intrusted with all the secrets of particular intrigues, which they are bound by oath not to discover; yet many times, when they are almost drunk, they cannot but reflect a little on their habit, and thus reason with themselves, what means this white upper garment, but only an unspotted innocence? What signifies my inner purple, but only an ardent love and zeal to God? What imports my outermost pall, so wide and long that it covers the whole mule when I ride, nay, should be big enough to cover a camel, but only a diffusive charity, that should spread itself for a succour and protection to all, by teaching, exhorting, comforting, reproving, admonishing, composing of differences, courageously withstanding wicked princes, and sacrificing for the safety of our flock our life and blood, as well as our wealth and riches; though indeed riches ought not to be at all possessed by such as boast themselves successors to the apostles, who were poor, needy, and destitute: I say, if they did but lay these considerations to heart they would never be so ambitious of being created to this honour; they would willingly resign it when conferred upon them, or at least would be as industrious, watchful and laborious, as the primitive apostles were.

Now as to the popes of Rome, who pretend themselves Christ's vicars, if they would but imitate his exemplary life, in the being employed in an unintermitted course of preaching; in the being attended with poverty, nakedness, hunger, and a contempt of this world; if they did but consider the import of the word pope, which

signifies a father; or if they did but practise their surname of most
holy, what order or degrees of men would be in a worse condition?
There would be then no such vigorous making of parties, and buying of votes, in the conclave upon a vacancy of that see: and those
who by bribery, or other indirect courses, should get themselves
elected, would never secure their sitting firm in the chair by pistol,
poison, force, and violence. How much of their pleasure would be
abated if they were but endowed with one dram of wisdom? Wisdom, did I say? Nay, with one grain of that salt which our Saviour
bid them not lose the savour of. All their riches, all their honour,
their jurisdictions, their Peter's patrimony, their offices, their dispensations, their licences, their indulgences, their long train and
attendants (see in how short a compass I have abbreviated all
their marketing of religion); in a word, all their perquisites would
be forfeited and lost; and in their room would succeed watchings,
fastings, tears, prayers, sermons, hard studies, repenting sighs, and
a thousand such like severe penalties: nay, what's yet more deplor-
able, it would then follow, that all their clerks, amanuenses, nota-
ries, advocates, proctors, secretaries, the offices of grooms, ostlers,
serving-men, pimps (and somewhat else, which for modesty's sake
I shall not mention); in short, all these troops of attendants, which
depend on his holiness, would all lose their several employments.
This indeed would be hard, but what yet remains would be more
dreadful: the very Head of the Church, the spiritual prince, would
then be brought from all his splendour to the poor equipage of a
scrip and staff. But all this is upon the supposition only that they
understood what circumstances they are placed in; whereas now,
by a wholesome neglect of thinking, they live as well as heart can
wish: whatever of toil and drudgery belongs to their office that they
assign over to St. Peter, or St. Paul, who have time enough to mind
it; but if there be any thing of pleasure and grandeur, that they
assume to themselves, as being hereunto called: so that by my influence no sort of people live more to their own ease and content.
They think to satisfy that Master they pretend to serve, our Lord
and Saviour, with their great state and magnificence, with the ceremonies of instalments, with the titles of reverence and holiness, and
with exercising their episcopal function only in blessing and cursing. The working of miracles is old and out-dated; to teach the people is too laborious; to interpret scripture is to invade the prerogative of the schoolmen; to pray is too idle; to shed tears is cowardly

and unmanly; to fast is too mean and sordid; to be easy and familiar is beneath the grandeur of him, who, without being sued to and intreated, will scarce give princes the honour of kissing his toe; finally, to die for religion is too self-denying; and to be crucified as their Lord of Life, is base and ignominious. Their only weapons ought to be those of the Spirit; and of these indeed they are mighty liberal, as of their interdicts, their suspensions, their denunciations, their aggravations, their greater and lesser excommunications, and their roaring bulls, that fright whomever they are thundered against; and these most holy fathers never issue them out more frequently than against those, who, at the instigation of the devil, and not having the fear of God before their eyes, do feloniously and maliciously attempt to lessen and impair St. Peter's patrimony: and though that apostle tells our Saviour in the gospel, in the name of all the other disciples, we have left all, and followed you, yet they challenge as his inheritance, fields, towns, treasures, and large dominions; for the defending whereof, inflamed with a holy zeal, they fight with fire and sword, to the great loss and effusion of Christian blood, thinking they are apostolical maintainers of Christ's spouse, the church, when they have murdered all such as they call her enemies; though indeed the church has no enemies more bloody and tyrannical than such impious popes, who give dispensations for the not preaching of Christ; evacuate the main effect and design of our redemption by their pecuniary bribes and sales; adulterate the gospel by their forced interpretations, and undermining traditions; and lastly, by their lusts and wickedness grieve the Holy Spirit, and make their Saviour's wounds to bleed anew.

Niccolò Machiavelli

16

The Prince

Niccolò Machiavelli (1469–1527), for a time an ambassador and secretary of the Republic of Florence, was exiled when the Medicis returned to power in 1512. During his exile he wrote *The Prince* (1513), which was circulated in manuscript form but not published until 1532, five years after his death. In his later years, Machiavelli was permitted to return to Florence and was commissioned by the Medicis to write *The History of Florence*. He was not, however, entrusted by them with any other important official post.

Machiavelli's influence was profound in his own day and has continued so down to our own. He departed from conventional medieval political theory, with its endless comparisons of the body politic to the human body—where the king or prince represented the head and the people represented the body and limbs, and so on. Nor did Machiavelli regard the prince as the divinely appointed ruler; in his treatise, *The Prince,* the state is considered entirely secular, and nothing happens to a state save by the application of power. The ruler's whole duty is to maintain order and to keep the state strong. In order to do this, the prince must gain and retain power by whatever means are available. The Romans, Machiavelli felt, were the best practitioners of this policy, and his writings are full of his admiration for them.

Unfortunately for his reputation, Machiavelli is remembered chiefly for his *Prince,* which is, in the opinion of many, a lesser work than his *Discourses on Livy.* Machiavelli was attacked bitterly by those who regarded him as an embodiment of evil ("Old Nick himself"—the name coined for him by English mockers) and by more astute practitioners of tyranny who, according to Voltaire, disliked him because he gave away their trade secrets. In literature and legend Machiavelli's name became

Niccolò Machiavelli, *The Prince,* in *The Historical, Political, and Diplomatic Writings of Niccolò Machiavelli,* trans. Christian E. Detmold (Boston: Osgood, 1882), II, 3–4, 48–61, 84–88.

synonymous with the villain who, excusing his actions with the doctrine that the end justifies the means, uses any method to gain power and enjoys crime for its own sake. In his defense one can cite Machiavelli's hope of uniting Italy so that the ceaseless wars and invasions would end. He can also be viewed as merely an objective reporter of the actual state of affairs in the Italy of his time.

To the Magnificent Lorenzo, Son of Piero De' Medici

Those who desire to win the favor of princes generally endeavor to do so by offering them those things which they themselves prize most, or such as they observe the prince to delight in most. Thence it is that princes have very often presented to them horses, arms, cloth of gold, precious stones, and similar ornaments worthy of their greatness. Wishing now myself to offer to your Magnificence some proof of my devotion, I have found nothing amongst all I possess that I hold more dear or esteem more highly than the knowledge of the actions of great men, which I have acquired by long experience of modern affairs, and a continued study of ancient history.

These I have meditated upon for a long time, and examined with great care and diligence; and having now written them out in a small volume, I send this to your Magnificence. And although I judge this work unworthy of you, yet I trust that your kindness of heart may induce you to accept it, considering that I cannot offer you anything better than the means of understanding in the briefest time all that which I have learnt by so many years of study, and with so much trouble and danger to myself.

. . .

A prince . . . should have no other thought or object so much at heart, and make no other thing so much his especial study, as the art of war and the organization and discipline of his army; for that is the only art that is expected of him who commands. And such is its power, that it not only maintains in their position those who were born princes, but it often enables men born in private station to achieve the rank of princes. And on the other hand, we have seen that princes who thought more of indulgence in pleasure than of arms have thereby lost their states.

Thus the neglect of the art of war is the principal cause of the loss of your state, whilst a proficiency in it often enables you to acquire one. Francesco Sforza, from being skilled in arms, rose from private station to be Duke of Milan; and his descendants, by shunning the labors and fatigue of arms, relapsed into the condition of private citizens.

Amongst the other causes of evil that will befall a prince who is destitute of a proper military force is, that it will make him contemned; which is one of those disgraces against which a prince ought especially to guard, as we shall demonstrate further on. For there is no sort of proportion between one who is well armed and one who is not so; nor is it reasonable that he who is armed should voluntarily obey the unarmed, or that a prince who is without a military force should remain secure amongst his armed subjects. For when there is disdain on the one side and mistrust on the other, it is impossible that the two should work well together. A prince, then, who is not master of the art of war, besides other misfortunes, cannot be respected by his soldiers, nor can he depend upon them. And therefore should the practice of arms ever be uppermost in the prince's thoughts; he should study it in time of peace as much as in actual war, which he can do in two ways, the one by practical exercise, and the other by scientific study. As regards the former, he must not only keep his troops well disciplined and exercised, but he must also frequently follow the chase, whereby his body will become inured to hardships, and he will become familiar with the character of the country, and learn where the mountains rise and the valleys debouch, and how the plains lie; he will learn to know the nature of rivers and of the swamps, to all of which he should give the greatest attention. For this knowledge is valuable in many ways to the prince, who thereby learns to know his own country, and can therefore better understand its defence. Again, by the knowledge of and practical acquaintance with one country, he will with greater facility comprehend the character of others, which it may be necessary for him to understand. For instance, the mountains, valleys, plains, rivers, and swamps of Tuscany bear a certain resemblance to those of other provinces; so that by the knowledge of the character and formation of one country he will readily arrive at that of others. A prince who is wanting in that experience lacks the very first essentials which a commander should possess; for that knowledge teaches him where to find the enemy, to select proper places for intrenchments, to conduct armies, regulate marches, and order battles, and to keep the field with advantage.

Amongst other praises that have been accorded by different writers to Philopoemen, prince of the Achaians, was, that in time of peace he devoted himself constantly to the study of the art of war; and when he walked in the country with friends, he often stopped and argued with them thus: "Suppose the enemy were on yonder mountain, and we should happen to be here with our army, which of the two would have the advantage? How could we go most safely to find the enemy, observing proper order? If we should wish to retreat, how should we proceed? and if the enemy were to retreat, which way had we best pursue him?" And thus in walking he proposed to his friends all the cases that possibly could occur with an army, hearing their opinions, and giving his own, and corroborating them with reasons; so that by these continued discussions no case could ever arise in the conduct of an army for which he had not thought of the proper remedy. As regards the exercise of the mind, the prince should read history, and therein study the actions of eminent men, observe how they bore themselves in war, and examine the causes of their victories and defeats, so that he may imitate the former and avoid the latter. But above all should he follow the example of whatever distinguished man he may have chosen for his model; assuming that some one has been specially praised and held up to him as glorious, whose actions and exploits he should ever bear in mind. Thus it is told of Alexander that he imitated Achilles, and of Caesar that he had taken Alexander for his model, as Scipio had done with Cyrus.

. . .

It remains now to be seen in what manner a prince should conduct himself towards his subjects and his allies; and knowing that this matter has already been treated by many others, I apprehend that my writing upon it also may be deemed presumptuous, especially as in the discussion of the same I shall differ from the rules laid down by others. But as my aim is to write something that may be useful to him for whom it is intended, it seems to me proper to pursue the real truth of the matter, rather than to indulge in mere speculation on the same; for many have imagined republics and principalities such as have never been known to exist in reality. For the manner in which men live is so different from the way in which they ought to live, that he who leaves the common course for that which he ought to follow will find that it leads him to ruin rather than to safety. For a man who, in all respects, will carry out only his professions of good, will be apt to be ruined amongst so many who are evil. A prince therefore who desires to maintain himself must learn to be not always good, but to be so or not as necessity may require. Leaving aside then the imaginary things concerning princes, and confining ourselves only to the realities, I say that all men when they are spoken of, and more especially princes, from being in a more conspicuous position, are noted for some quality that brings them either praise or censure. Thus one is deemed liberal, another miserly (*misero*) to use a Tuscan expression (for avaricious is he who by rapine desires to gain, and miserly we call him who abstains too much from the enjoyment of his own). One man is esteemed generous, another rapacious; one cruel, another merciful; one faithless, and another faithful; one effeminate and pusillanimous, another ferocious and brave; one affable, another haughty; one lascivious, another chaste; one sincere, the other cunning; one facile, another inflexible; one grave, another frivolous; one religious, another sceptical; and so on.

I am well aware that it would be most praiseworthy for a prince to possess all of the above-named qualities that are esteemed good; but as he cannot have them all, nor entirely observe them, because of his human nature which does not permit it, he should at least be prudent enough to know how to avoid the infamy of those vices that would rob him of his state; and if possible also to guard against such as are likely to endanger it. But if that be not possible, then he may with less hesitation follow his natural inclinations. Nor need he care about incurring censure for such vices, without which the preservation of his state may be difficult. For, all things considered, it will be found that some things that seem like virtue will lead you to ruin if you follow them; whilst others, that apparently are vices, will, if followed, result in your safety and well-being.

To begin with the first of the above-named qualities, I say that it is well for a prince to be deemed liberal; and yet liberality, indulged in so that you will no longer be feared, will prove injurious.

For liberality worthily exercised, as it should be, will not be recognized, and may bring upon you the reproach of the very opposite. For if you desire the reputation of being liberal, you must not stop at any degree of sumptuousness; so that a prince will in this way generally consume his entire substance, and may in the end, if he wishes to keep up his reputation for liberality, be obliged to subject his people to extraordinary burdens, and resort to taxation, and employ all sorts of measures that will enable him to procure money. This will soon make him odious with his people; and when he becomes poor, he will be contemned by everybody; so that having by his prodigality injured many and benefited few, he will be the first to suffer every inconvenience, and be exposed to every danger. And when he becomes conscious of this and attempts to retrench, he will at once expose himself to the imputation of being a miser.

A prince then, being unable without injury to himself to practise the virtue of liberality in such manner that it may be generally recognized, should not, when he becomes aware of this and is prudent, mind incurring the charge of parsimoniousness. For after a while, when it is seen that by his prudence and economy he makes his revenues suffice him, and that he is able to provide for his defence in case of war, and engage in enterprises without burdening his people, he will be considered liberal enough by all those from whom he takes nothing, and these are the many; whilst only those to whom he does not give, and which are the few, will look upon him as parsimonious.

In our own times we have not seen any great things accomplished except by those who were regarded as parsimonious; all others have been ruined. Pope Julius II., having been helped by his reputation of liberality to attain the Pontificate, did not afterwards care to keep up that reputation to enable him to engage in war against the king of France; and he carried on ever so many wars without levying any extraordinary taxes. For his long-continued economy enabled him to supply the extraordinary expenses of his wars.

If the present king of Spain had sought the reputation of being liberal, he would not have been able to engage in so many enterprises, nor could he have carried them to a successful issue. A prince, then, who would avoid robbing his own subjects, and be able to defend himself, and who would avoid becoming poor and abject or rapacious, should not mind incurring the reputation of being parsimonious; for that is one of those vices that will enable him to maintain his state. . . .

And were any one to assert that there have been many princes who have achieved great things with their armies, and who were accounted most liberal, I answer that a prince either spends his own substance and that of his subjects, or that of others. Of the first two he should be very sparing, but in spending that of others he ought not to omit any act of liberality. The prince who in person leads his armies into foreign countries, and supports them by plunder, pillage, and exactions, and thus dispenses the substance of others, should do so with the greatest liberality, as otherwise his soldiers would not follow him. For that which belongs neither to him nor to his own subjects, a prince may spend most lavishly, as was done by Cyrus, Caesar, and Alexander. The spending of other people's substance will not diminish, but rather increase, his reputation; it is only the spending of his own that is injurious to a prince.

And there is nothing that consumes itself so quickly as liberality; for the very act of using it causes it to lose the faculty of being used, and will either impoverish and make you contemned, or it will make you rapacious and odious. And of all the things against which a prince should guard most carefully is the incurring the hatred and contempt of his subjects. Now, liberality will bring upon you either the one or the other; there is therefore more wisdom in submitting to be called parsimonious, which may bring you blame without hatred, than, by aiming to be called liberal, to incur unavoidably the reputation of rapacity, which will bring upon you infamy as well as hatred.

Coming down now to the other aforementioned qualities, I say that every prince ought to desire the reputation of being merciful, and not cruel; at the same time, he should be careful not to misuse that mercy. Cesar Borgia was reputed cruel, yet by his cruelty he reunited the Romagna to his states, and restored that province to order, peace, and loyalty; and if we carefully examine his course, we shall find it to have been really much more merciful than the course of the people of Florence, who, to escape the reputation of cruelty, allowed Pistoia to be destroyed. A prince, therefore, should not mind the ill repute of cruelty, when he can thereby keep his subjects united and loyal; for a few displays of severity will really be more merciful than to allow, by an excess of clemency, disorders to occur, which are apt to result in rapine and murder; for these injure a whole community, whilst the executions ordered by the prince fall only upon a few individuals. And, above all others, the new prince will find it almost impossible to avoid the reputation of cruelty, because new states are generally exposed to many dangers. It was on this account that Virgil made Dido to excuse the severity of her government, because it was still new, saying,—

> "My cruel fate,
> And doubts attending an unsettled state,
> Force me to guard my coasts from foreign foes."

A prince, however, should be slow to believe and to act; nor should he be too easily alarmed by his own fears, and should proceed moderately and with prudence and humanity, so that an excess of confidence may not make him incautious, nor too much mistrust make him intolerant. This, then, gives rise to the question "whether it be better to be beloved than feared, or to be feared than beloved." It will naturally be answered that it would be desirable to be both the one and the other; but as it is difficult to be both at the same time, it is much more safe to be feared than to be loved, when you have to choose between the two. For it may be said of men in general that they are ungrateful and fickle, dissemblers, avoiders of danger, and greedy of gain. So long as you shower benefits upon them, they are all yours; they offer you their blood, their substance, their lives, and their children, provided the necessity for it is far off; but when it is near at hand, then they revolt. And the prince who relies upon their words, without having otherwise provided for his security, is ruined; for friendships that are won by rewards, and not by greatness and nobility of soul, although deserved, yet are not real, and cannot be depended upon in time of adversity.

Besides, men have less hesitation in offending one who makes himself beloved than one who makes himself feared; for love holds by a bond of obligation which, as mankind is bad, is broken on every occasion whenever it is for the interest of the obliged party to break it. But fear holds by the apprehension of punishment, which never leaves men. A prince, however, should make himself feared in such a manner that, if he has not won the affections of his people, he shall at least not incur their hatred; for the being feared, and not hated, can go very well together, if the prince abstains from taking the substance of his subjects, and leaves them their women.

And if you should be obliged to inflict capital punishment upon any one, then be sure to do so only when there is manifest cause and proper justification for it; and, above all things, abstain from taking people's property, for men will sooner forget the death of their fathers than the loss of their patrimony. Besides, there will never be any lack of reasons for taking people's property; and a prince who once begins to live by rapine will ever find excuses for seizing other people's property. On the other hand, reasons for taking life are not so easily found, and are more readily exhausted. But when a prince is at the head of his army, with a multitude of soldiers under his command, then it is above all things necessary for him to disregard the reputation of cruelty; for without such severity an army cannot be kept together, nor disposed for any successful feat of arms.

Amongst the many admirable qualities of Hannibal, it is related of him that, having an immense army composed of a very great variety of races of men, which he led to war in foreign countries, no quarrels ever occurred amongst them, nor were there ever any dissensions between them and their chief, either in his good or in his adverse fortunes; which can only be accounted for by his extreme cruelty. This, together with his boundless courage, made him ever venerated and terrible in the eyes of his soldiers; and without that extreme severity all his other virtues would not have sufficed to produce that result.

Inconsiderate writers have, on the one hand, admired his great deeds, and, on the other, condemned the principal cause of the same. And the proof that his other virtues would not have sufficed him may be seen from the case of Scipio, who was one of the most remarkable men, not only of his own time, but in all history. His armies revolted in Spain solely in consequence of his extreme clemency, which allowed his soldiers more license than comports with proper military discipline. This fact was censured in the Roman Senate by Fabius Maximus, who called Scipio the corrupter of the Roman soldiers. The tribe of the Locrians having been wantonly destroyed by one of the lieutenants of Scipio, he neither punished him for that nor for his insolence,—simply because of his own easy nature; so that, when somebody wished to excuse Scipio in the Senate, he said, "that there were many men who knew better how to avoid errors themselves than to punish them in others." This easy nature of Scipio's would in time have dimmed his fame and glory if he had persevered in it under the Empire; but living as he did under the government of the Senate, this dangerous quality of his was not only covered up, but actually redounded to his honor.

To come back now to the question whether it be better to be beloved than feared, I conclude that, as men love of their own free will, but are inspired with fear by the will of the prince, a wise prince should always rely upon himself, and not upon the will of others; but, above all, should he always strive to avoid being hated, as I have already said above.

It must be evident to every one that it is more praiseworthy for a prince always to maintain good faith, and practise integrity rather than craft and deceit. And yet the experience of our own times has shown that those princes have achieved great things who made small account of good faith, and who understood by cunning to circumvent the intelligence of others; and that in the end they got the better of those whose actions were dictated by loyalty and good faith. You must know, therefore, that there are two ways of carrying on a contest; the one by law, and the other by force. The first is practised by men, and the other by animals; and as the first is often insufficient, it becomes necessary to resort to the second.

A prince then should know how to employ the nature of man, and that of the beasts as well. This was figuratively taught by ancient writers, who relate how Achilles and many other princes were given to Chiron the centaur to be nurtured, and how they were trained under his tutorship; which fable means nothing else than that their preceptor combined the qualities of the man and the beast; and that a prince, to succeed, will have to employ both the one and the other nature, as the one without the other cannot produce lasting results.

It being necessary then for a prince to know well how to employ the nature of the beasts, he should be able to assume both that of the fox and that of the lion; for whilst the latter cannot escape the traps laid for him, the former cannot defend himself against the wolves. A prince should be a fox, to know the traps and snares; and a lion, to be able to frighten the wolves; for those who simply hold to the nature of the lion do not understand their business.

A sagacious prince then cannot and should not fulfil his pledges when their observance is contrary to his interest, and when the causes that induced him to pledge his faith no longer exist. If men

were all good, then indeed this precept would be bad; but as men
are naturally bad, and will not observe their faith towards you, you
must, in the same way, not observe yours to them; and no prince
ever yet lacked legitimate reasons with which to color his want of
good faith. Innumerable modern examples could be given of this;
and it could easily be shown how many treaties of peace, and how
many engagements, have been made null and void by the faith-
lessness of princes; and he who has best known how to play the fox
has ever been the most successful.

But it is necessary that the prince should know how to color this
nature well, and how to be a great hypocrite and dissembler. For
men are so simple, and yield so much to immediate necessity, that
the deceiver will never lack dupes. I will mention one of the most
recent examples. Alexander VI. never did nor ever thought of anything but to deceive, and always found a reason for doing so. No
one ever had greater skill in asseverating, or who affirmed his
pledges with greater oaths and observed them less, than Pope Alexander; and yet he was always successful in his deceits, because he
knew the weakness of men in that particular.

It is not necessary, however, for a prince to possess all the above-
mentioned qualities; but it is essential that he should at least seem
to have them. I will even venture to say, that to have and to practise them constantly is pernicious, but to seem to have them is useful. For instance, a prince should seem to be merciful, faithful,
humane, religious, and upright, and should even be so in reality;
but he should have his mind so trained that, when occasion requires it, he may know how to change to the opposite. And it must
be understood that a prince, and especially one who has but recently acquired his state, cannot perform all those things which
cause men to be esteemed as good; he being often obliged, for the
sake of maintaining his state, to act contrary to humanity, charity,
and religion. And therefore is it necessary that he should have a
versatile mind, capable of changing readily, according as the winds
and changes of fortune bid him; and, as has been said above, not
to swerve from the good if possible, but to know how to resort to
evil if necessity demands it.

A prince then should be very careful never to allow anything to
escape his lips that does not abound in the above-named five qualities, so that to see and to hear him he may seem all charity, integrity,
and humanity, all uprightness, and all piety. And more than all

else is it necessary for a prince to seem to possess the last quality; for mankind in general judge more by what they see and hear than by what they feel, every one being capable of the former, and but few of the latter. Everybody sees what you seem to be, but few really feel what you are; and these few dare not oppose the opinion of the many, who are protected by the majesty of the state; for the actions of all men, and especially those of princes, are judged by the result, where there is no other judge to whom to appeal.

A prince then should look mainly to the successful maintenance of his state. The means which he employs for this will always be accounted honorable, and will be praised by everybody; for the common people are always taken by appearances and by results, and it is the vulgar mass that constitutes the world. But a very few have rank and station, whilst the many have nothing to sustain them. A certain prince of our time, whom it is well not to name, never preached anything but peace and good faith; but if he had always observed either the one or the other, it would in most instances have cost him his reputation or his state.

Having thus considered separately the most important of the above-mentioned qualities which a prince should possess, I will now briefly discuss the others under this general maxim: that a prince should endeavor, as has already been said, to avoid everything that would tend to make him odious and contemned. And in proportion as he avoids that will he have performed his part well, and need fear no danger from any other vices. Above all, a prince makes himself odious by rapacity, that is, by taking away from his subjects their property and their women, from which he should carefully abstain. The great mass of men will live quietly and contentedly, provided you do not rob them of their substance and their honor; so that you will have to contend only with the ambition of a few, which is easily restrained in various ways.

A prince becomes despised when he incurs by his acts the reputation of being variable, inconstant, effeminate, pusillanimous, and irresolute; he should therefore guard against this as against a dangerous rock, and should strive to display in all his actions grandeur, courage, gravity, and determination. And in judging the private causes of his subjects, his decisions should be irrevocable. Thus will he maintain himself in such esteem that no one will think of deceiving or betraying him. The prince, who by his habit-

ual conduct gives cause for such an opinion of himself, will acquire
so great a reputation that it will be difficult to conspire against
him, or to attack him; provided that it be generally known that he
is truly excellent, and revered by his subjects. For there are two
things which a prince has to fear: the one, attempts against him
by his own subjects; and the other, attacks from without by powerful foreigners. Against the latter he will be able to defend himself
by good armies and good allies, and whoever has the one will not
lack the other. And so long as his external affairs are kept quiet,
his internal security will not be disturbed, unless it should be by a
conspiracy. And even if he were to be assailed from without, if he
has a well-organized army and has lived as he should have done, he
will always (unless he should give way himself) be able to withstand
any such attacks, as we have related was done by Nabis, tyrant of
Sparta. But even when at peace externally, it nevertheless behooves
the prince to be on his guard, lest his subjects conspire against him
secretly. He will, however, be sufficiently secure against this, if he
avoids being hated and despised, and keeps his subjects well satisfied with himself, which should ever be his aim, as I have already
explained above. Not to be hated nor contemned by the mass of the
people is one of the best safeguards for a prince against conspiracies;
for conspirators always believe that the death of the prince will be
satisfactory to the people; but when they know that it will rather
offend than conciliate the people, they will not venture upon such
a course, for the difficulties that surround conspirators are infinite.

Experience proves that, although there have been many conspiracies, yet but few have come to a good end; for he who conspires
cannot act alone, nor can he take any associates except such as he
believes to be malcontents; and so soon as you divulge your plans
to a malcontent, you furnish him the means wherewith to procure
satisfaction. For by denouncing it he may hope to derive great advantages for himself, seeing that such a course will insure him those
advantages, whilst the other is full of doubts and dangers. He must
indeed be a very rare friend of yours, or an inveterate enemy of
the prince, to observe good faith and not to betray you.

· · ·

Reviewing now all I have said in the foregoing discourses, and
thinking to myself that, if the present time should be favorable
for Italy to receive and honor a new prince, and the opportunity

were given to a prudent and virtuous man to establish a new form of government, that would bring honor to himself and happiness to the mass of the Italian people, so many things would combine for the advantage of such a new prince, that, so far as I know, no previous time was ever more favorable for such a change. And if, as I have said, it was necessary for the purpose of displaying the virtue of Moses that the people of Israel should be held in bondage in Egypt; and that the Persians should be opposed to the Medes, so as to bring to light the greatness and courage of Cyrus; and that the Athenians should be dispersed for the purpose of illustrating the excellence of Theseus; so at present, for the purpose of making manifest the virtues of one Italian spirit, it was necessary that Italy should have been brought to her present condition of being in a worse bondage than that of the Jews, more enslaved than the Persians, more scattered than the Athenians, without a head, without order, vanquished and despoiled, lacerated, overrun by her enemies, and subjected to every kind of devastation.

And although, up to the present time, there may have been some one who may have given a gleam of hope that he was ordained by Heaven to redeem Italy, yet have we seen how, in the very zenith of his career, he was so checked by fortune that poor Italy remained as it were lifeless, and waiting to see who might be chosen to heal her wounds,—to put an end to her devastation, to the sacking of Lombardy, to the spoliation and ruinous taxation of the kingdom of Naples and of Tuscany,—and who should heal her sores that have festered so long. You see how she prays God that he may send some one who shall redeem her from this cruelty and barbarous insolence. You see her eagerly disposed to follow any banner, provided there be some one to bear it aloft. But there is no one at present in whom she could place more hope than in your illustrious house, O magnificent Lorenzo! which, with its virtue and fortune, favored by God and the Church, of which it is now the head, could make an effectual beginning of her deliverance. And this will not be difficult for you, if you will first study carefully the lives and actions of the men whom I have named above. And although these men were rare and wonderful, they were nevertheless but men, and the opportunities which they had were far less favorable than the present; nor were their undertakings more just or more easy than this; neither were they more favored by the Almighty than what you are. Here, then, is great justice; for war is just when it is necessary, and a resort to arm is beneficent when there is no hope in anything else. The opportunity is most favorable, and when that is the case there can be no great difficulties, provided you follow the course of those whom I have held up to you as examples. Although in their case extraordinary things, without parallel, were brought about by the hand of God,—the sea divided for their passage, a pillar of cloud pointed their way through the wilderness, the rock poured forth water to assuage their thirst, and it rained manna to appease their hunger,—yet your greatness combines all, and on your own efforts will depend the result. God will not do everything; for that would deprive us of our free will, and of that share of glory which belongs to us.

Nor should we wonder that not one of the Italians whom I have mentioned has been able to accomplish that which it is to be hoped will be done by your illustrious house; for if in so many revolutions in Italy, and in the conduct of so many wars, it would seem that military capacity and valor have become extinct, it is owing to the fact that the old military system was defective, and no one has come forward capable of establishing a new one. And nothing brings a man who has newly risen so much honor as the establishing of new laws and institutions of his own creation; if they have greatness in them and become well established, they will make the prince admired and revered; and there is no lack of opportunity in Italy for the introduction of every kind of reform. The people have great courage, provided it be not wanting in their leaders. Look but at their single combats, and their encounters when there are but a few on either side, and see how superior the Italians have shown themselves in strength, dexterity, and ability. But when it comes to their armies, then these qualities do not appear, because of the incapacity of the chiefs, who cannot enforce obedience from those who are versed in the art of war, and every one believes himself to be so; for up to the present time there have been none so decidedly superior in valor and good fortune that the others yielded him obedience. Thence it comes that in so great a length of time, and in the many wars that have occurred within the past twenty years, the armies, whenever wholly composed of Italians, have given but poor account of themselves. Witness first Taro, then Alessandria, Capua, Genoa, Vaila, Bologna, and Mestri.

If, then, your illustrious house is willing to follow the examples of those distinguished men who have redeemed their countries, you

will before anything else, and as the very foundation of every enterprise, have to provide yourself with a national army. And you
cannot have more faithful, truer, and better soldiers than the
Italians. And whilst each individual is good, they will become still
better when they are all united, and know that they are commanded
by their own prince, who will honor and support them. It is necessary, therefore, to provide troops of this kind, so as to be able successfully to oppose Italian valor to the attacks of foreigners.

And although the infantry of the Swiss and of the Spaniards is
looked upon as terrible, yet both of them have a defect, which will
permit a third organization not only to resist them, but confidently
hope to vanquish them. For the Spaniards cannot withstand the
shock of cavalry, and the Swiss dread infantry, when they encounter
it in battle as obstinate as themselves. Whence we have seen, what
further experience will prove more fully, that the Spaniards cannot
resist the French cavalry, and that the Swiss succumb to the Spanish infantry. And although we have not yet had a full trial of the
latter, yet have we had a fair specimen of it in the battle of Ravenna, where the Spanish infantry confronted the line of battle of
the Germans, who have adopted the same system as the Swiss; and
where the Spaniards with great agility, and protected by their
bucklers, rushed under the pikes of the Germans, and were thus
able to attack them securely without the Germans being able to
prevent it; and had it not been for the cavalry which fell upon
the Spaniards, they might have destroyed the entire German infantry.

Knowing, then, the defects of the one and the other of these
systems of infantry, you can organize a new one that shall avoid
these defects, and shall be able to resist cavalry as well as infantry.
And this is to be done, not by a change of arms, but by an entirely
different organization and discipline. This is one of the things
which, if successfully introduced, will give fame and greatness to a
new prince.

You must not, then, allow this opportunity to pass, so that Italy,
after waiting so long, may at last see her deliverer appear. Nor can
I possibly express with what affection he would be received in all
those provinces that have suffered so long from this inundation of
foreign foes!—with what thirst for vengeance, with what persistent
faith, with what devotion, and with what tears! What door would
be closed to him? Who would refuse him obedience? What envy

would dare oppose him? What Italian would refuse him homage? This barbarous dominion of the foreigner offends the very nostrils of everybody!

Let your illustrious house, then, assume this task with that courage and hopefulness which every just enterprise inspires; so that under your banner our country may recover its ancient fame, and under your auspices may be verified the words of Petrarch:—

> Virtue against wrath
> Will take up arms, and may the struggle soon begin!
> For the ancient valor
> In Italian hearts is not yet dead.*

* Poem translated by *editor*.

Baldassare Castiglione

========= 17 =========

The Courtier

Baldassare Castiglione (1478–1529) is himself one of the best examples of the ideal Renaissance gentleman described in his prose dialogue, *The Courtier*. A man with a varied career—including man of letters, adviser to princes, and official of the Church—Castiglione was always faithful to his code of gentlemanly honor. For several years he resided at the court of Guidobaldo da Montefeltro, Duke of Urbino. In the Duke's service, Castiglione went on several diplomatic missions, one of which took him to England to the court of Henry VII. Later, Castiglione was involved in one of the major quarrels of the century—between Pope Clement VII and the Holy Roman Emperor, Charles V. Castiglione lived his last years in Spain, where he entered the Church and became Bishop of Avila.

Castiglione's *The Courtier*, written in 1514 and published in 1528, is an expression of the Renaissance at its best. Translated into English in 1561 by Sir Thomas Hoby, the work exerted a great influence upon Shakespeare's contemporaries and stands even now as the classic expression of the aristocratic credo. It purports to be the record of conversations of a group of witty and learned men and women (whose thinking was influenced by the new learning of the Renaissance) who gathered in the evenings in the hall of the ducal palace of Urbino—the most princely residence in Italy, according to contemporary opinion. The discussions deal with the ethical, intellectual, military, sporting, and social gifts and abilities of the ideal gentleman. As the following selection opens, Count Ludovico da Canossa is setting forth what he considers to be the qualifications of the ideal gentleman-courtier. The others then join in with their contributions to this description of the well-born, well-bred ideal aristocrat whose attributes summarize the aristocratic tradition in Western culture.

Baldassare Castiglione, *The Book of the Courtier*, trans. Leonard E. Opdycke (New York: Scribner, 1901), 22–26, 59–66, 86–88, 175–79, 297–99, 308–09.

"I wish, then, that this Courtier of ours should be nobly born and of gentle race; because it is far less unseemly for one of ignoble birth to fail in worthy deeds, than for one of noble birth, who, if he strays from the path of his predecessors, stains his family name, and not only fails to achieve but loses what has been achieved already; for noble birth is like a bright lamp that manifests and makes visible good and evil deeds, and kindles and stimulates to virtue both by fear of shame and by hope of praise. And since this splendour of nobility does not illumine the deeds of the humbly born, they lack that stimulus and fear of shame, nor do they feel any obligation to advance beyond what their predecessors have done; while to the nobly born it seems a reproach not to reach at least the goal set them by their ancestors. And thus it nearly always happens that both in the profession of arms and in other worthy pursuits the most famous men have been of noble birth, because nature has implanted in everything that hidden seed which gives a certain force and quality of its own essence to all things that are derived from it, and makes them like itself: as we see not only in the breeds of horses and of other animals, but also in trees, the shoots of which nearly always resemble the trunk; and if they sometimes degenerate, it arises from poor cultivation. And so it is with men, who if rightly trained are nearly always like those from whom they spring, and often better; but if there be no one to give them proper care, they become like savages and never reach perfection.

"It is true that, by favour of the stars or of nature, some men are endowed at birth with such graces that they seem not to have been born, but rather as if some god had formed them with his very hands and adorned them with every excellence of mind and body. So too there are many men so foolish and rude that one cannot but think that nature brought them into the world out of contempt or mockery. Just as these can usually accomplish little even with constant diligence and good training, so with slight pains those others reach the highest summit of excellence. And to give you an instance: you see my lord Don Ippolito d'Este, Cardinal of Ferrara, who has enjoyed such fortune from his birth, that his person, his aspect, his words and all his movements are so disposed and imbued with this grace, that—although he is young—he exhibits among the most aged prelates such weight of character that he seems fitter to teach than to be taught; likewise in conversation with men and women of every rank, in games, in pleasantry and in banter, he has a certain sweetness and manners so gracious, that whoso speaks with him or even sees him, must needs remain attached to him forever.

"But to return to our subject: I say that there is a middle state between perfect grace on the one hand and senseless folly on the other; and those who are not thus perfectly endowed by nature, with study and toil can in great part polish and amend their natural defects. Besides his noble birth, then, I would have the Courtier favoured in this regard also, and endowed by nature not only with talent and beauty of person and feature, but with a certain grace and (as we say) air that shall make him at first sight pleasing and agreeable to all who see him; and I would have this an ornament that should dispose and unite all his actions, and in his outward aspect give promise of whatever is worthy the society and favour of every great lord."

Here, without waiting longer, my lord Gaspar Pallavicino said:

"In order that our game may have the form prescribed, and that we may not seem to slight the privilege given us to contradict, I say that this nobility of birth does not appear to me so essential in the Courtier; and if I thought I were saying what was new to any of us, I should cite instances of many men born of the noblest blood who have been full of vices; and on the other hand, of many men among the humbly born who by their virtue have made their posterity illustrious. And if what you just said to be true, namely that there is in everything this occult influence of the original seed, then we should all be in the same case, because we had the same origin, nor would any man be more noble than another. But as to our differences and grades of eminence and obscurity, I believe there are many other causes: among which I rate fortune to be chief; for we see her holding sway in all mundane affairs, often amusing herself by lifting to heaven whom she pleases (although wholly without merit), and burying in the depths those most worthy to be exalted.

"I quite agree with what you say as to the good fortune of those endowed from birth with advantages of mind and body: but this is seen as well among the humbly born as among the nobly born, since nature has no such subtle distinctions as these; and often, as

I said, the highest gifts of nature are found among the most obscure. Therefore, since this nobility of birth is won neither by talent nor by strength nor by craft, and is rather the merit of our predecessors than our own, it seems to me too extravagant to maintain that if our Courtier's parents be humbly born, all his good qualities are spoiled, and that all those other qualifications that you mentioned do not avail to raise him to the summit of perfection; I mean talent, beauty of feature, comeliness of person, and that grace which makes him always charming to everyone at first sight."

Then Count Ludovico replied:

"I do not deny that the same virtues may rule the low-born and the noble: but (not to repeat what we have said already or the many other arguments that could be adduced in praise of noble birth, which is honoured always and by everyone, it being reasonable that good should beget good), since we have to form a Courtier without flaw and endowed with every praiseworthy quality, it seems to me necessary to make him nobly born, as well for many other reasons as for universal opinion, which is at once disposed in favour of noble birth. For if there be two Courtiers who have as yet given no impression of themselves by good or evil acts, as soon as the one is known to have been born a gentleman and the other not, he who is low-born will be far less esteemed by everyone than he who is high-born, and will need much effort and time to make upon men's minds that good impression which the other will have achieved in a moment and merely by being a gentleman.

. . .

"But to come to some details, I am of opinion that the principal and true profession of the Courtier ought to be that of arms; which I would have him follow actively above all else, and be known among others as bold and strong, and loyal to whomsoever he serves. And he will win a reputation for these good qualities by exercising them at all times and in all places, since one may never fail in this without severest censure. And just as among women, their fair fame once sullied never recovers its first lustre, so the reputation of a gentleman who bears arms, if once it be in the least tarnished with cowardice or other disgrace, remains forever infamous before the world and full of ignominy. Therefore the more our Courtier excels in this art, the more he will be worthy of praise; and yet I do not deem essential in him that perfect knowledge of things and those other qualities that befit a commander; since this would be too wide a sea, let us be content, as we have said, with perfect loyalty and unconquered courage, and that he be always seen to possess them. For the courageous are often recognized even more in small things than in great; and frequently in perils of importance and where there are many spectators, some men are to be found, who, although their hearts be dead within them, yet, moved by shame or by the presence of others, press forward almost with their eyes shut, and do their duty God knows how. While on occasions of little moment, when they think they can avoid putting themselves in danger without being detected, they are glad to keep safe. But those who, even when they do not expect to be observed or seen or recognized by anyone, show their ardour and neglect nothing, however paltry, that may be laid to their charge,—they have that strength of mind which we seek in our Courtier.

"Not that we would have him look so fierce, or go about blustering, or say that he has taken his cuirass to wife, or threaten with those grim scowls that we have often seen in Berto; because to such men as this, one might justly say that which a brave lady jestingly said in gentle company to one whom I will not name at present; who, being invited by her out of compliment to dance, refused not only that, but to listen to the music, and many other entertainments proposed to him,—saying always that such silly trifles were not his business; so that at last the lady said, 'What is your business, then?' He replied with a sour look, 'To fight.' Then the lady at once said, 'Now that you are in no war and out of fighting trim, I should think it were a good thing to have yourself well oiled, and to stow yourself with all your battle harness in a closet until you be needed, lest you grow more rusty than you are'; and so, amid much laughter from the bystanders, she left the discomfited fellow to his silly presumption.

"Therefore let the man we are seeking, be very bold, stern, and always among the first, where the enemy are to be seen; and in every other place, gentle, modest, reserved, above all things avoiding ostentation and that impudent self-praise by which men ever excite hatred and disgust in all who hear them.

· · ·

"I would have him more than passably accomplished in letters, at least in those studies that are called the humanities, and conversant not only with the Latin language but with the Greek, for the sake of the many different things that have been admirably written therein. Let him be well versed in the poets, and not less in the orators and historians, and also proficient in writing verse and prose, especially in this vulgar tongue of ours; for besides the enjoyment he will find in it, he will by this means never lack agreeable entertainment with ladies, who are usually fond of such things. And if other occupations or want of study prevent his reaching such perfection as to render his writings worthy of great praise, let him be careful to suppress them so that others may not laugh at him, and let him show them only to a friend whom he can trust: because they will at least be of this service to him, that the exercise will enable him to judge the work of others. For it very rarely happens that a man who is not accustomed to write, however learned he may be, can ever quite appreciate the toil and industry of writers, or taste the sweetness and excellence of style, and those latent niceties that are often found in the ancients.

"Moreover these studies will also make him fluent and, as Aristippus said to the tyrant, confident and assured in speaking with everyone. Hence I would have our Courtier keep one precept fixed in mind; which is that in this and everything else he should be always on his guard, and diffident rather than forward, and that he should keep from falsely persuading himself that he knows that which he does not know. For by nature we all are fonder of praise than we ought to be, and our ears love the melody of words that praise us more than any other sweet song or sound; and thus, like sirens' voices, they are often the cause of shipwreck to him who does not close his ears to such deceptive harmony. Among the ancient sages this danger was recognized, and books were written showing in what way the true friend may be distinguished from the flatterer. But what does this avail, if there be many, nay a host, of those who clearly perceive that they are flattered, yet love him who flatters them, and hold him in hatred who tells them the truth? And often when they find him who praises them too sparing in his words, they even help him and say such things of themselves, that the flatterer is put to shame, most impudent though he be.

"Let us leave these blind ones to their errour, and have our

Courtier of such good judgment that he will not take black for white, or have more self-confidence than he clearly knows to be well founded; and especially in those peculiarities which (if you remember) messer Cesare in his game said we had often used as an instrument to bring men's folly to light. On the contrary, even if he well knows the praises bestowed upon him to be true, let him not err by accepting them too openly or confirming them without some protest; but rather let him as it were disclaim them modestly, always showing and really esteeming arms as his chief profession, and all other good accomplishments as an ornament thereto. And particularly among soldiers let him not act like those who insist on seeming soldiers in learning, and learned men among soldiers. In this way, for the reasons we have alleged, he will avoid affectation, and even the middling things that he does, shall seem very great."

Messer Pietro Bembo here replied:

"Count, I do not see why you insist that this Courtier, being lettered and endowed with so many other admirable accomplishments, should hold everything as an ornament of arms, and not arms and the rest as an ornament of letters; which without other accompaniment are as superiour in dignity to arms, as the mind is to the body, for the practice of them properly pertains to the mind, as that of arms does to the body."

Then the Count replied:

"Nay, the practice of arms pertains to both mind and body. But I would not have you judge in such a cause, messer Pietro, for you would be too much suspected of bias by one of the two sides: and as the controversy has already been long waged by very wise men, there is no need to renew it; but I regard it as settled in favour of arms, and would have our Courtier so regard it too, since I may form him as I wish. And if you are of contrary mind, wait till you hear of a contest wherein he who defends the cause of arms is allowed to use arms, just as those who defend letters make use of letters in their defence; for if everyone avails himself of his proper weapons, you shall see that men of letters will be worsted."

"Ah," said messer Pietro, "a while ago you blamed the French for prizing letters little, and told what glorious lustre is shed on man by letters and how they make him immortal; and now it seems you have changed your mind. Do you not remember that

Before the famous tomb of brave Achilles
Thus spake the mighty Alexander, sighing:
'O happy youth, who found so clear a trumpet,
And lofty bard to make thy deeds undying!'

And if Alexander envied Achilles not for his deeds, but for the fortune that had granted him the happiness of having his exploits celebrated by Homer, we may conclude that Alexander esteemed Homer's poems above Achilles's arms. For what other judge do you wait then, or for what other sentence upon the dignity of arms and letters, than that pronounced by one of the greatest commanders that have ever been?"

Then the Count replied:

"I blame the French for thinking that letters are a hindrance to the profession of arms, and I hold that learning is more proper to no one than to a warrior; and in our Courtier I would have these two accomplishments joined and each aided by the other, as is most proper: nor do I think I have changed my mind in this. But as I said, I do not wish to discuss which of the two is more worthy of praise. It is enough that men of letters almost never select for praise any but great men and glorious deeds, which in themselves merit praise for the mere essential quality from which they spring; besides this they are very noble material for writers: which is a great ornament, and in part the cause of perpetuating writings, which perhaps would not be so much read and appreciated if they lacked their noble theme, but vain and of little moment.

"And if Alexander was envious that Achilles should be praised by Homer, it does not therefore follow that he esteemed letters above arms; wherein if he had felt himself as far behind Achilles as he deemed all those who wrote of him were behind Homer, I am sure he would far rather have desired fine acts on his part than fine speeches on the part of others. Hence I believe that saying of his to have been a tacit eulogy of himself, and that he was expressing a desire for what he thought he did not possess (that is, the supreme excellence of a writer), and not for what he believed he already had attained (that is, prowess in arms, wherein he did not deem Achilles at all his superior). Thus he called Achilles happy, as if hinting that although his own fame had hitherto not been so celebrated in the world as Achilles's, which was made bright and illustrious by that poem so divine,—it was not because his valour and merits were less or deserving of less praise, but because fortune bestowed upon Achilles that miracle of nature as a glorious trumpet for his achievements. Perhaps also he wished to incite some noble genius to write about him, by showing that this must be as pleasing to him as were his love and veneration for the sacred monuments of letters: whereof we have spoken long enough for the present."

"Nay, too long," replied my lord Ludovico Pio; "for I believe that in the whole world it would be impossible to find a receptacle large enough to hold all the things you would have in our Courtier."

Then the Count said:

"Wait a little, for there are many more that he must have."

"In that case," replied Pietro da Napoli, "Grasso de' Medici would have a great advantage over messer Pietro Bembo."

Here everyone laughed, and the Count began anew and said:

"My lords, you must know that I am not content with the Courtier unless he be also a musician and unless, besides understanding and being able to read notes, he can play upon divers instruments. For if we consider rightly, there is to be found no rest from toil or medicine for the troubled spirit more becoming and praiseworthy in time of leisure, than this; and especially in courts, where besides the relief from tedium that music affords us all, many things are done to please the ladies, whose tender and gentle spirit is easily penetrated by harmony and filled with sweetness. Thus it is no marvel that in both ancient and modern times they have always been inclined to favour musicians, and have found refreshing spiritual food in music."

Then my lord Gaspar said:

"I admit that music as well as many other vanities may be proper to women and perhaps to some that have the semblance of men, but not to those who really are men; for these ought not to enervate their mind with delights and thus induce therein a fear of death."

"Say not so," replied the Count; "for I shall enter upon a vast sea in praise of music. And I shall call to mind how it was always celebrated and held sacred among the ancients, and how very sage philosophers were of opinion that the world is composed of music, that the heavens make harmony in their moving, and that the soul, being ordered in like fashion, awakes and as it were revives its powers through music.

"Thus it is written that Alexander was sometimes excited by it so passionately, that he was forced almost against his will to leave the banquet table and rush to arms; and when the musician changed the temper of the tune, he grew calm again, lay aside his arms, and returned to the banquet table. Moreover I will tell you that grave Socrates learned to play the cithern at a very advanced age. And I remember having once heard that Plato and Aristotle would have the man of culture a musician also; and they show by a host of arguments that the power of music over us is very great, and (for many reasons which would be too long to tell now) that it must needs be taught from childhood, not so much for the mere melody that we hear, but for the power it has to induce in us a fresh and good habit of mind and an habitual tendency to virtue, which renders the soul more capable of happiness, just as bodily exercise renders the body more robust; and that music is not only no hindrance in the pursuits of peace and war, but is very helpful therein.

"Again, Lycurgus approved of music in his harsh laws. And we read that in their battles the very warlike Lacedemonians and Cretans used the cithern and other dulcet instruments; that many very excellent commanders of antiquity, like Epaminondas, practised music; and that those who were ignorant of it, like Themistocles, were far less esteemed. Have you not read that music was among the first accomplishments which the worthy old Chiron taught Achilles in tender youth, whom he reared from the age of nurse and cradle? and that the sage preceptor insisted that the hands which were to shed so much Trojan blood, should be often busied with the cithern? Where is the soldier who would be ashamed to imitate Achilles,—to say nothing of many other famous commanders whom I could cite?

"Therefore seek not to deprive our Courtier of music, which not only soothes men's minds, but often tames wild beasts; and he who enjoys it not, may be sure that his spirit is ill attuned. See what power it has, to make (as once it did) a fish submit to be ridden by a man upon the boisterous sea. We find it used in holy temples to render praise and thanks to God; and we must believe that it is pleasing to Him and that He has given it to us as most sweet alleviation for our fatigues and troubles. Wherefore rough toilers of the field under a burning sun often cheat their weariness with crude and rustic song. With music the rude peasant lass, who is up before the day to spin or weave, wards off her drowsiness and makes her toil a pleasure; music is very cheering pastime for poor sailors after rain, wind and tempest: a solace to tired pilgrims on their long and weary journeys, and often to sorrowing captives in their chains and fetters. Thus, as stronger proof that melody even if rude is very great relief from every human toil and care, nature seems to have taught it to the nurse as chief remedy for the continual wailing of frail children, who by the sound of her voice are brought restful and placid sleep, forgetful of the tears so proper to them and given us in that age by nature as a presage of our after life."

As the Count now remained silent for a little, the Magnifico Giuliano said:

"I do not at all agree with my lord Gaspar. Nay I think, for the reasons you give and for many others, that music is not only an ornament but a necessity to the Courtier. Yet I would have you declare in what way this and the other accomplishments that you prescribe for him, are to be practised, and at what time and in what manner. For many things that are praiseworthy in themselves often become very inappropriate when practised out of season, and on the other hand, some that seem of little moment are highly esteemed when made use of opportunely."

Then the Count said:

"Before we enter upon that subject, I wish to discuss another matter, which I deem of great importance and therefore think our Courtier ought by no means to omit: and this is to know how to draw and to have acquaintance with the very art of painting.

"And do not marvel that I desire this art, which to-day may seem to savour of the artisan and little to befit a gentleman; for I remember having read that the ancients, especially throughout Greece, had their boys of gentle birth study painting in school as an honourable and necessary thing, and it was admitted to the first rank of liberal arts; while by public edict they forbade that it be taught to slaves. Among the Romans too, it was held in highest honour, and the very noble family of the Fabii took their name from it; for the first Fabius was given the name *Pictor*, because,— being indeed a most excellent painter, and so devoted to painting that when he painted the walls of the temple of Health,—he inscribed his own name thereon; for although he was born of a family thus renowned and honoured with so many consular titles, triumphs and other dignities, and although he was a man of letters and learned in the law, and numbered among the orators,—yet he thought to add splendour and ornament to his fame by leaving a memorial that he had been a painter. Nor is there lack of many other men of illustrious family, celebrated in this art; which besides being very noble and worthy in itself, is of great utility, and especially in war for drawing places, sites, rivers, bridges, rocks, fortresses, and the like; since however well we may keep them in memory (which is very difficult), we cannot show them to others.

"And truly he who does not esteem this art, seems to me very unreasonable; for this universal fabric that we see,—with the vast heaven so richly adorned with shining stars, and in the midst the earth girdled by the seas, varied with mountains, valleys and rivers, and bedecked with so many divers trees, beautiful flowers and grasses,—may be said to be a great and noble picture, composed by the hand of nature and of God; and whoever is able to imitate it, seems to me deserving of great praise: nor can it be imitated without knowledge of many things, as he knows well who tries. Hence the ancients greatly prized both the art and the artist, which thus attained the summit of highest excellence; very sure proof of which may be found in the antique marble and bronze statues that yet are seen."

[The conversation turns to the courtier's ability in sports. Lord Federico speaks. *Ed.*]

"This dancing of yours in the sun pleases me not in any way, nor do I see what gain there is in it. But in my opinion whoever cares to wrestle or run or leap with peasants, ought to do so as a matter of practice and out of courtesy as we say, not in rivalry with them. And a man ought to be almost sure of winning; else let him not engage, because it is too unseemly and shameful a thing, and beneath his dignity, to see a gentleman vanquished by a peasant, and especially at wrestling. Hence I think it is well to abstain, at least in the presence of many, for the gain of beating is very small and the loss of being beaten is very great.

"The game of tennis also is nearly always played in public, and is one of those sports to which a crowd lends much distinction. Therefore I would have our Courtier practise this, and all the others except the handling of arms, as something that is not his profession, and let him show that he does not seek or expect praise for it, nor let him seem to devote much care or time to it, although he may do it admirably. Nor let him be like some men who delight in music, and in speaking with anyone always begin to sing under their breath whenever there is a pause in the conversation. Others always go dancing as they pass through streets and churches. Others, when they meet a friend in the piazza or anywhere else, at once put themselves in posture as if for fencing or wrestling, according to their favourite humour."

Here messer Cesare Gonzaga said:

"A young cardinal we have in Rome does better than that; for out of pride in his fine bodily frame, he conducts into his garden all who come to visit him (even although he has never seen them before), and urgently presses them to strip to the doublet and try a turn with him at leaping."

Messer Federico laughed; then he went on:

"There are certain other exercises that can be practised in public and in private, like dancing; and in this I think the Courtier ought to have a care, for when dancing in the presence of many and in a place full of people, it seems to me that he should preserve a certain dignity, albeit tempered with a lithe and airy grace of movement; and although he may feel himself to be very nimble and a master of time and measure, let him not attempt those agilities of foot and double steps which we find very becoming in our friend Barletta, but which perhaps would be little suited to a gentleman. Yet in a room privately, as we are now, I think he may try both, and may dance morris-dances and brawls; but not in public unless he be masked, when it is not displeasing even though he be recognized by all.

"Indeed there is no better way of displaying oneself in such matters at public sports, either armed or unarmed; because disguise carries with it a certain freedom and licence, which among other things enable a man to choose a part for which he feels himself qualified, and to use care and elaboration upon the chief point of the thing wherein he would display himself, and a certain nonchalance as to that which does not count,—which greatly enhances the charm: as for a youth to array himself like an old man, yet in easy dress so as to be able to show his vigour; a cavalier in the guise of a rustic shepherd or some other like costume, but with a perfect horse and gracefully bedecked in character;—because the mind of the spectators is quick to fill out the image of that which is presented to the eyes at first glance; and then seeing the thing turn out much better than the costume promised, they are amused and delighted.

"But in these sports and shows where masks are worn, it would not be seemly for a prince to try to enact the part of a prince, because that pleasure which the spectators find in novelty would be in great measure lacking, since it is news to no one that the prince is the prince; and he, conscious that besides being the prince he is trying to play the prince, loses the freedom to do all those things that are beneath a prince's dignity. And if there were any contest in these sports, especially with arms, he might even make men think that he chose to impersonate a prince in order not to be beaten but spared by others; moreover were he to do in sport the same that it behooves him to do in earnest upon occasion, he would deprive his own proper action of dignity, and make it almost seem as if that too were sport. But at such times, if the prince lays aside his character of prince, and mingles equally with his inferiors yet in such fashion as to be recognizable, by renouncing his own rank he attains a higher one, in that he prefers to excel the rest not by authority but by merit, and to show that his worth is not enhanced by the fact that he is a prince.

"I say then that in these martial sports the Courtier ought to use the like discretion, according to his rank. In horseback vaulting too, in wrestling, running and leaping, I should be well pleased to have him shun the vulgar crowd, or at most let himself be very rarely seen; for there is not on earth a thing so excellent but the ignorant will tire of it and hold it of small account, if they see it often.

"As to music I hold the same opinion: hence I would not have our Courtier behave like many, who are no sooner come anywhere (even into the presence of gentlemen with whom they have no acquaintance), than without waiting to be urged they set about doing what they know and often what they do not know; so that it seems as if they had come only for the purpose of showing themselves, and had that for their chief profession. Therefore let the Courtier resort to music as a pastime and almost unwillingly, and not before vulgar people nor very many. And although he may know and understand that which he is doing, in this too I would have him hide the study and pains that are necessary in everything one would do well, and seem to value this accomplishment lightly in himself, but by practising it admirably make others value it highly."

[The ladies demand that the gentlemen tell what qualities they would attribute to a lady worthy of the attention of the ideal courtier. *Ed.*]

Then my lady Duchess said:

"Do not wander from your subject, my lord Magnifico, but hold to the order given you and describe the Court Lady, to the end that so noble a Lady as this may have someone competent to serve her worthily."

The Magnifico continued:

"Then, my Lady, to show that your commands have power to induce me to essay even that which I know not how to do, I will speak of this excellent Lady as I would have her; and when I have fashioned her to my liking, not being able then to have another such, like Pygmalion I will take her for my own.

"And although my lord Gaspar has said that the same rules which are set the Courtier, serve also for the Lady, I am of another mind; for while some qualities are common to both and as necessary to man as to woman, there are nevertheless some others that befit woman more than man, and some are befitting man to which she ought to be wholly a stranger. The same I say of bodily exercises; but above all, methinks that in her ways, manners, words, gestures and bearing, a woman ought to be very unlike a man; for just as it befits him to show a certain stout and sturdy manliness, so it is becoming in a woman to have a soft and dainty tenderness with an air of womanly sweetness in her every movement, which, in her going or staying or saying what you will, shall always make her seem the woman, without any likeness of a man.

"Now, if this precept be added to the rules that these gentlemen have taught the Courtier, I certainly think she ought to be able to profit by many of them, and to adorn herself with admirable accomplishments, as my lord Gaspar says. For I believe that many faculties of the mind are as necessary to woman as to man; likewise gentle birth, to avoid affectation, to be naturally graceful in all her doings, to be mannerly, clever, prudent, not arrogant, not envious, not slanderous, not vain, not quarrelsome, not silly, to know how to win and keep the favour of her mistress and of all others, to practise well and gracefully the exercises that befit women.

I am quite of the opinion, too, that beauty is more necessary to her than to the Courtier, for in truth that woman lacks much who lacks beauty. Then, too, she ought to be more circumspect and take greater care not to give occasion for evil being said of her, and so to act that she may not only escape a stain of guilt but even of suspicion, for a woman has not so many ways of defending herself against false imputations as has a man.

"But as Count Ludovico has explained very minutely the chief profession of the Courtier, and has insisted it be that of arms, methinks it is also fitting to tell what in my judgment is that of the Court Lady: and when I have done this, I shall think myself quit of the greater part of my duty.

"Laying aside, then, those faculties of the mind that she ought to have in common with the Courtier (such as prudence, magnanimity, continence, and many others), and likewise those qualities that befit all women (such as kindness, discretion, ability to manage her husband's property and her house and children if she be married, and all those capacities that are requisite in a good housewife), I say that in a lady who lives at court methinks above all else a certain pleasant affability is befitting, whereby she may be able to entertain politely every sort of man with agreeable and seemly converse, suited to the time and place, and to the rank of the person with whom she may speak, uniting with calm and modest manners, and with that seemliness which should ever dispose all her actions, a quick vivacity of spirit whereby she may show herself alien to all indelicacy; but with such a kindly manner as shall make us think her no less chaste, prudent and benign, than agreeable, witty and discreet: and so she must preserve a certain mean (difficult and composed almost of contraries), and must barely touch certain limits but not pass them.

"Thus, in her wish to be thought good and pure, the Lady ought not to be so coy and seem so to abhor company and talk that are a little free, as to take her leave as soon as she finds herself therein; for it might easily be thought that she was pretending to be thus austere in order to hide something about herself which she feared others might come to know; and such prudish manners are always odious. Nor ought she, on the other hand, for the sake of showing herself free and agreeable, to utter unseemly words or practise a certain wild and unbridled familiarity and ways likely to make that believed of her which perhaps is not true; but when she is present at such talk, she ought to listen with a little blush and shame.

"Likewise she ought to avoid an errour into which I have seen many women fall, which is that of saying and of willingly listening to evil about other women. For those women who, on hearing the unseemly ways of other women described, grow angry thereat and seem to disbelieve it and to regard it almost monstrous that a woman should be immodest,—they, by accounting the offence so heinous, give reason to think that they do not commit it. But those who go about continually prying into other women's intrigues, and narrate them so minutely and with such zest, seem to be envious of them and to wish that everyone may know it, to the end that like matters may not be reckoned as a fault in their own case; and thus they fall into certain laughs and ways that show they then feel greatest pleasure. And hence it comes that men, while seeming to listen gladly, usually hold such women in small respect and have very little regard for them, and think these ways of theirs are an invitation to advance farther, and thus often go such lengths with them as bring them deserved reproach, and finally esteem them so lightly as to despise their company and even find them tedious."

. . .

Having so far spoken, the Magnifico was silent and sat quiet, as if he had ended his discourse. Then my lord Gaspar said:

"Verily, my lord Magnifico, you have adorned this Lady well and given her excellent qualities. Yet methinks you have kept much to generalities, and mentioned some things in her so great that I think you were ashamed to explain them, and have rather desired than taught them, after the manner of those who sometimes wish for things impossible and beyond nature. Therefore I would have you declare to us a little better what are the bodily exercises proper to a Court Lady, and in what way she ought to converse, and what those many things are whereof you say it befits her to have knowledge; and whether you mean that she should use the prudence, the magnanimity, the continence, and the many other virtues you have named, merely to aid her in the government of her house, children and family (which however you would not have her chief profession), or indeed in her conversation and graceful practice of those bodily exercises; and, by your faith, guard against setting these poor virtues to such menial duty that they must needs be ashamed of it."

The Magnifico laughed, and said:

"My lord Gaspar, you cannot help showing your ill will towards women. But in truth I thought I had said enough, and especially before such hearers; for I am quite sure there is no one here who does not perceive that in the matter of bodily exercises it does not befit women to handle weapons, to ride, to play tennis, to wrestle, and to do many other things that befit men."

Then the Unico Aretino said:

"Among the ancients it was the custom for women to wrestle unclothed with men; but we have lost this good custom, along with many others."

Messer Cesare Gonzaga added:

"And in my time I have seen women play tennis, handle weapons, ride, go hunting, and perform nearly all the exercises that a cavalier can."

The Magnifico replied:

"Since I may fashion this Lady as I wish, not only am I unwilling to have her practise such vigourous and rugged manly exercises, but I would have her practise even those that are becoming to women, circumspectly and with that gentle daintiness which we have said befits her; and thus in dancing I would not see her use too active and violent movements, nor in singing or playing those abrupt and oft-repeated diminutions which show more skill than sweetness; likewise the musical instruments that she uses ought, in my opinion, to be appropriate to this intent. Imagine how unlovely it would be to see a women play drums, fifes or trumpets, or other like instruments; and this because their harshness hides and destroys that mild gentleness which so much adorns every act a woman does. Therefore when she starts to dance or make music of any kind, she ought to bring herself to it by letting herself be urged a little, and with a touch of shyness which shall show that noble shame which is the opposite of effrontery."

[Cardinal Bembo praises the Platonic notion of ideal beauty. *Ed.*]

Messer Pietro Bembo was silent, and those gentlemen still urged him to speak further of this love and of the mode of enjoying beauty truly; and he at last said:

"Methinks I have shown clearly enough that old men can love more happily than young, which was my thesis; therefore it does not become me to go further."

Count Ludovico replied:

"You have better shown the unhappiness of youths than the happiness of old men, whom as yet you have not taught what road to follow in this love of theirs, but have only told them to be guided by reason; and by many it is thought impossible for love to abide with reason."

Bembo still sought to put an end to his discourse, but my lady Duchess begged him to speak; and he began anew thus:

"Too unhappy would human nature be, if our soul (wherein such ardent desire can spring up easily) were forced to feed it solely upon that which is common to her with the beasts, and could not direct it to that other nobler part which is peculiar to herself. Therefore, since so indeed it pleases you, I have no wish to avoid discoursing upon this noble subject. And as I feel myself unworthy to speak of Love's most sacred mysteries, I pray him so to inspire my thought and tongue that I may be able to show this excellent Courtier how to love beyond the manner of the vulgar crowd; and since from boyhood up I have dedicated my whole life to him, so now also may my words comport with this intent and with his praise.

"I say, then, that as in youth human nature is so greatly prone to sense, the Courtier may be allowed to love sensually while he is young. But if afterwards in maturer years he chances still to be kindled with this amourous desire, he must be very wary and take care not to deceive himself by allowing himself to be led into those calamities which in the young merit more compassion than blame, and, on the contrary, in the old more blame than compassion.

. . .

"Therefore let him shun the blind judgment of sense, and with his eyes enjoy the splendour of his lady, her grace, her amourous sparkle, the laughs, the ways and all the other pleasant ornaments of her beauty. Likewise with his hearing let him enjoy the sweetness of her voice, the concord of her words, the harmony of her music (if his beloved be a musician). Thus will he feed his soul on sweetest food by means of these two senses—which have little of the corporeal and are ministers of reason—without passing in his desire for the body to any appetite less than seemly.

"Next let him obey, please and honour his lady with all reverence, and hold her dearer than himself, and prefer her convenience and pleasures to his own, and love in her not less the beauty of mind than that of body. Therefore let him take care not to leave her to fall into any kind of errour, but by admonition and good advice let him always seek to lead her on to modesty, to temperance, to true chastity, and see to it that no thoughts find place in her except those that are pure and free from every stain of vice; and by thus sowing virtue in the garden of her fair mind, he will gather fruits of fairest behaviour too, and will taste them with wonderful delight. And this will be the true engendering and manifesting of beauty in beauty, which by some is said to be the end of love.

"In such fashion will our Courtier be most acceptable to his lady, and she will always show herself obedient, sweet and affable to him, and as desirous of pleasing him as of being loved by him; and the wishes of both will be most virtuous and harmonious, and they themselves will thus be very happy."

Here my lord Morello said:

"To engender beauty in beauty, forsooth, would be to beget a beautiful child in a beautiful woman; and pleasing him in this would seem to me a much clearer token that she loved her lover than treating him with the affability of which you speak."

Bembo laughed, and said:

"You must not go beyond bounds, my lord Morello; nor does a woman give small token of her love when she gives her lover her beauty, which is so precious a thing, and by the ways that are the avenues to her soul (that is, sight and hearing) sends the glances of her eyes, the image of her face, her voice, her words, which strike home to the lover's heart and give him proof of her love."

[Lady Emilia jestingly reproves one of the gentlemen for his doubting that women are capable of Platonic love. *Ed.*]

My lady Emilia laughed, and said:

"My lord Gaspar, if you return to wronging us so often, I promise you that you will not be pardoned again."

My lord Gaspar replied:

"No wrong is done you by saying that women's souls are not so purged of passion as those of men, nor given to contemplation, as messer Pietro said those must be who would taste divine love. Thus we do not read that any woman has had this grace, but that many men have had it, like Plato, Socrates and Plotinus, and many others; and so many of our holy Fathers, like St. Francis, upon whom an ardent spirit of love impressed the most holy seal of the five wounds: nor could aught but the power of love lift St. Paul to the vision of those mysteries whereof man is not allowed to speak; nor show St. Stephen the opened heavens."

Here the Magnifico Giuliano replied:

"In this, women will by no means be outdone by men; for Socrates himself confesses that all the mysteries of love which he knew were revealed to him by a woman, who was the famous Diotima; and the angel who wounded St. Francis with the fire of love, has also made several women of our age worthy of the same seal. You must remember, too, that St. Mary Magdalen had many sins forgiven her because she loved much, and perhaps with no less grace than St. Paul was she many times lifted to the third heaven by angelic love; and so many others, who (as I narrated yesterday more at large) for the love of Christ's name took no heed of life, nor were afraid of torments or any manner of death however horrible and cruel it might be; and they were not old, as messer Pietro would have our Courtier, but tender and delicate girls, and of that age wherein he says that sensual love ought to be allowed in men."

My lord Gaspar began making ready to reply, but my lady Duchess said:

"Of this let messer Pietro Bembo be the judge, and let us abide by his decision whether or not women are as capable of divine love as men are. But as the controversy between you might be too long, it will be well to postpone it until tomorrow."

"Nay, until this evening," said messer Cesare Gonzaga.

"How until this evening?" said my lady Duchess.

Messer Cesare replied:

"Because it is already day"; and he showed her the light that was beginning to come in through the cracks at the windows.

Then everyone rose to his feet in great surprise, for the discussion did not seem to have lasted longer than usual; but by reason of having been begun much later, and by its pleasantness, it had so beguiled the company that they had not perceived the flight of hours; nor was there anyone who felt the heaviness of sleep upon his eyes, which nearly always happens when the accustomed hour of sleep is passed in watching. The windows having then been opened on that side of the palace which looks towards the lofty crest of Mount Catria, they saw that a beautiful dawn of rosy hue was already born in the east, and that all the stars had vanished save Venus, sweet mistress of the sky, who holds the bonds of night and day; from which there seemed to breathe a gentle wind that filled the air with crisp coolness and began to waken sweet choruses of joyous birds in the murmuring forests of the hills hard by.

So, having reverently taken leave of my lady Duchess, they all started towards their chambers without light of torches, that of day being enough for them; and as they were about to quit the room, my lord Prefect turned to my lady Duchess, and said:

"My Lady, to finish the controversy between my lord Gaspar and my lord Magnifico, we will come with our judge this evening earlier than we did yesterday."

My lady Emilia replied:

"On condition that if my lord Gaspar wishes to accuse women and put some fresh imputation upon them, as is his wont, he shall also give bond to sustain his charge, for I account him a shifty disputant."

Sir Thomas More

═══ 18 ═══

Utopia

Sir Thomas More (1478–1535) was the leading English humanist of his generation. Successful in the profession of law, More was also known as a man of keen wit and learning. Entering King Henry VIII's service, he became Lord Chancellor, the most important of the royal offices. More resigned this position in 1532, however, thus hoping to avoid having to take part in the political and religious quarrels that accompanied Henry's dynastic ambitions and his break with the papacy. So important a man, however, was not allowed to remain in obscurity. On his refusal to take any oath of loyalty to the king that would involve rejection of the pope's authority, More was tried, found guilty of high treason, and beheaded in 1535.

Like his friend Erasmus, More injected a religious tone into his humanism. Scholarship, a sense of humor, and the intention of reforming society and the Church were common to the work of both men.

More's *Utopia* (1516) is an imaginary discourse by a fictional traveler to the New World. The narrator, Raphael Hythloday, tells of the land of Utopia, a name coined by More from the Greek word meaning "nowhere." Hythloday describes the Utopians' socialized economy, their system of compulsory and universal education for both men and women, and their austere life under the firm discipline of a wise and benevolent prince, who is completely tolerant of all religious views save atheism. More thus presents a picture of a society completely different from his own—one that is free from corruption in politics and law, and, more significantly, free from the poverty and crime resulting from selfish misuse of private property by the rich and powerful. Together with Plato's *Republic,* More's *Utopia* has been taken as a model by those social reformers who like to envisage an ideal society founded on perfect order and justice.

Sir Thomas More, *Utopia,* trans. Ralph Robinson (1556), reprinted (Cambridge: Cambridge University Press, 1888), 78–99, 143–47. (This is an adaptation.)

Farming is a science common to all, both men and women, and they are all expert. They are instructed from their youth, partly in school with lessons and precepts, and partly in the country near the city, where they learn not only by seeing agriculture practised but engaging in it also as a kind of play. Besides farming, which is common to all, everyone learns another craft as his own. Most commonly this is clothworking in wool or flax, or masonry, or blacksmithing, or carpentry. There are no other trades followed there by any great number. Their garments are of one fashion throughout the island (except that men and women wear different garments, and there is a difference between the married and unmarried). The style stays the same always, is handsome in appearance, allows free movement of the body, and is fit for both winter and summer. Every family makes its own clothes. But of other crafts every man learns one, as do the women. But the women, being weaker, are put to the easier crafts like working wool or flax. The more laborious tasks are entrusted to the men. For the most part, every man is brought up in his father's craft. They are naturally inclined to it; but if a youth wants to learn another, he is adopted by a family engaged in the occupation he wants to learn. His own father and the magistrate take care that he is given to an honest and worthy householder. Yes, and if any person, after he has learned one craft, wants to learn still another, he is permitted to do so.

When he has learned both, he follows the one he prefers, unless the city needs one more than the other. The chief, and almost the only duty of the officers is to see that no man is idle but that everyone works diligently at his own craft, yet not all day from early morning to late at night like beasts of burden. For this would be worse than the fate of slaves, which is, nevertheless, the life of workmen almost everywhere except in Utopia. For they divide the day and night into twenty-four equal hours and devote only six hours to work, three before noon. Then they go straight to dinner, and after dinner, when they have rested two hours, they work three hours and then have supper. About eight in the evening (counting one o'clock as the first hour after noon) they go to bed. Eight hours they give to sleep. In the hours not devoted to work, sleep, or meals, every man spends his time as he wishes. This is not intended to permit waste of time, however, but that, being free from their own occupations, they can devote some time to some other branch of learning. For it is a custom there to have daily lectures early in the mornings. Although only those who are specifically designated as students are forced to be present, a great number of all kinds of people, both men and women, attend. However, if any man would rather spend this time on his own occupation (for there are many whose minds are unsuited to liberal studies), he is not blamed but praised and commended as helping the common welfare.

After supper they spend an hour in play: in summer in their gardens, in winter in their common halls, where they dine and sup. There they practice music or engage in pleasant conversation. Dice and other such foolish and pernicious games are unknown. But they have some games not much unlike chess. One is the battle of numbers, in which one number wins over another. In another, the vices fight against virtues, as if in battle array. In this game, there is clearly shown the strife and discord that vices have among themselves, but also their unity and concord against the virtues; what vices are opposed to what virtues; how they assail virtues openly with power and strength; how they operate secretly with wiles and subtlety; what the virtues need for help and aid in overcoming the power of the vices; how they too can use craft; and finally by what means victory can be achieved.

One thing you must consider more clearly here, lest you be mistaken: seeing that they spend only six hours in work, you may perhaps think that they may lack many necessary things. But this is not so. For that small time is not only sufficient but even too much for the provision of an abundant supply of all things necessary to life. You will understand this if you consider how many people in other countries live idly: almost all women, who are half the population, or, if the women be employed, the men are idle. Besides this, there is a great and idle company of priests and religious men, as they call them. Add to them all rich men, especially landowners commonly called gentlemen, and noblemen. Take in this number also their servants. I mean all that gang of vain swaggerers. Join to them also sturdy and ingenious beggars, disguising the idleness of their lives with some pretended deformity or disease. Truly, you shall find the goods used in daily life are produced by the labor of fewer than you thought.

Now, consider with yourself how few of those who do labor are

employed in necessary work. For where money is the most important reward, many superfluous and vain occupations will flourish to
cater to idle wants and foolish pleasures. But if the same multitude
that now is occupied in such work were divided into the few occupations necessary to supply basic wants, there would be such a
quantity of necessary goods produced that undoubtedly prices
would be too little to support the workmen and artificers. If, however, all those now busy in worthless occupations and the whole
flock of those that live in idleness and sloth, consuming and wasting
more of the things produced by other men's labor than the laborers
themselves do—if all these, I say, were engaged in worthwhile occupations, you can easily see how little time would be sufficient to
provide us with everything necessary, either to supply basic commodities or to provide a certain amount of modest and natural
pleasures.

The truth of this is demonstrated in Utopia, for there in the
whole city and the adjoining countryside, there are scarcely five
hundred (in addition to the sick and aged) of the entire population
who are excused from labor. Among these are the officers who, although they are by law exempt from labor, nevertheless set a good
example by their voluntary work. The same freedom from labor is
also granted those who, recommended by the priests and elected by
the officers, are given a permanent excuse from labor so that they
may engage in learning. But if any of these does not live up to
expectations, he is sent back to the rank of artificers. On the other
hand, it often happens that a laborer spends all of his free time
in learning and makes such progress that he is taken from his trade
and promoted to the company of the learned. From this class of
learned people are chosen the ambassadors, the priests, magistrates
and finally the prince himself, whom they call, in their old tongue,
Barzanes, and also by a newer name, Adamus.

The rest of the people are neither idle nor occupied in worthless
tasks. It is easily seen, therefore, that in only a few hours much productive work is accomplished. Moreover, they do not need to spend
as much work in the necessary occupations as other nations. In
other places, the building and repairing of houses takes up many
men's continual labor because unthrifty persons allow their houses
to fall into decay, so that what might have been repaired with little
cost must be entirely rebuilt with great cost by their successors. It

often happens, too, that a house that cost one man a great sum does not please another, who neglects it and lets it fall into ruin. Then he builds another just as costly somewhere else. Among the Utopians, however, where everything is well managed and the commonwealth well ordered, it very seldom happens that a new plot is chosen for building. Not only do they find quick remedies for present faults, but also repair houses that are ready to fall. In this way their houses last long, with so little labor and few repairs needed that men engaged in this occupation sometimes have almost nothing to do and are ordered to hew lumber at home and square and trim stone so that if any work becomes necessary it can be more speedily done.

Now, sir, notice, I pray, how few workmen they need for their clothing. First of all, while they are at work they wear simple garments of leather or skins that will last seven years. When they go outdoors, they put on a cloak which hides the coarser apparel. These cloaks, throughout the entire island, are all of one color, that is, the natural color of the wool. Hence, they use much less woolen cloth than other countries, and at much less cost. Linen cloth is made with less labor and is, therefore, used more. But in linen only whiteness is prized; in wool only cleanliness. As for the smallness or fineness of the thread, it is unimportant. This is the reason that in other places four or five cloth gowns of different colors, and as many silk coats are not enough for one man. If he is a particular man, he may think ten too few, whereas there one garment will serve a man four years. Why should he want more? If he had them, he would not be better off or more protected from cold, nor handsomer in apparel.

Since they are all occupied in worthwhile occupations and a few workmen are sufficient in any one trade (this is the reason there is a plentiful supply of everything), they sometimes turn out a numerous company of people to mend the highways, if need be. Often, when they have no such work, a proclamation is made decreeing fewer hours of work. For the magistrates do not compel the citizens to engage unwillingly in unnecessary labor. In that commonwealth the chief and only aim is to spend as much time as possible in the free exercise and training of the mind, for in this they believe the chief felicity of life to consist.

* * *

Now I will tell how the citizens behave toward each other, how the people entertain and amuse themselves, and how they distribute their goods. First, the city consists of families, the families being made up of kindred. For women, when they are married at the legal age, become part of their husband's family. But the male children and all the male offspring continue in their own family, being governed by the eldest man, unless he is senile, in which case he is replaced by the next oldest. But in order to prevent the number of citizens from increasing or decreasing, it is ordained that no family (there are 6,000 families in each city and nearby countryside) shall have fewer than ten children between the ages of thirteen and sixteen. Of children under this age, no number is set. This number is easily maintained by putting the children of larger families into smaller families. If by chance a city has more than can be accommodated, the excess is used in other cities. If the population of the entire island exceeds the set number, they choose citizens from every city to build up a town under their own laws in a neighboring land where there is waste land, accepting also natives of that country if they want to join and dwell with them. Thus joining and dwelling together, they easily agree in one way of life, to the great wealth of both peoples. For they manage things so by their laws that ground which was before neither good nor profitable for anyone becomes fruitful enough for both. If the natives will not dwell with them and accept their laws, they drive them out of the land they have taken for themselves. If the natives resist or rebel, they make war upon them. For they consider it a just war that is fought to dispossess people from land which they do not use and keep others from using.

If by chance the number in any city is so diminished that it cannot be filled up without reducing the proper number in the other cities (which they say happened only twice, by the plague, since the beginning of the island), they replenish the number with citizens brought from their own foreign towns. They would rather see these foreign towns decay and perish than any city of the island diminish.

But to return to the behavior of the citizens toward each other: the eldest, as I have said, rules the family, the wives and their husbands; the children help their parents, and, in short, all younger people assist their elders.

Every city is divided into four equal parts or quarters. In the midst of each quarter there is a market place for all kinds of things. There the products of every family's labor are brought into certain houses, and all kinds of commodities are stored in several barns or storehouses. From thence the father of every family, or every householder, takes whatever he needs and carries it with him without money, exchange, pawn, or pledge. Why should anything be denied him—seeing that there is abundance of everything and that no one will ask for more than he needs? Why should it be thought that men who know they will never be in want would ask for more than is merely enough? Certainly, fear of want causes covetousness and greed, but only in man does it cause pride, because man thinks it a glorious thing to excel in ostentatious and vain display of possessions. This vice has no place among the Utopians.

Next to the market places that I spoke of stand meat markets where herbs, fruits, bread, fish, and all sorts of four-footed beasts and wild fowl that furnish meat for humans are stored and offered. First, the filth is washed away in the clear running river outside the city at properly appointed places. Then the beasts are killed and washed by the bondmen. For they do not permit free citizens to become accustomed to killing beasts. They consider it kindness to let animals grow old and die naturally. Nor do they allow any unclean or filthy thing to be brought into the city lest stench infect the air and cause pestilence.

Moreover, every street has great halls equidistant from each other and each has its own name. In these halls dwell the officers, and every hall has thirty families assigned to it, fifteen on each side. The stewards of these halls come at a certain time to the meat markets where they receive meat according to the number of families in their hall. The first care of all, however, is the sick in the hospitals. For around the city, a little outside the walls, they have four hospitals, so large that they seem like four little towns. They are made so spacious that the sick will not be crowded and uncomfortable or those with contagious diseases so close to others as to endanger them with infection. These hospitals are so well built and furnished with everything necessary to health, and the attendants and physicians so diligent and skillful that, although no man is sent there against his will, sick persons would rather go to them than remain home.

After the hospital steward has received the kinds of meat prescribed by the physician, the best is equally divided among the

halls. . . . To these halls at the dinner hour come all the inhabitants of the ward, summoned by trumpet. No one, however, is forbidden to get his own meat and take it home, for they know that
no one will do so without reason. No man is forbidden to dine at
home, but no one does so willingly. It would be foolish to take the
trouble to prepare a bad dinner at home when they are welcome
to good fare at the nearby hall.

In the hall, all menial service and drudgery are performed by
bondmen. But the women of every family have charge of the cook-
ing and dressing the meat. They sit at three tables or more, according to their number. The men sit on the bench next the wall; the
women opposite, so that if any sudden illness should affect them,
as often happens to women with child, they may leave quickly and
go to the nursery.

The nurses stay with the infants in a special room, which always
has a fire lit and a supply of clean water. Cradles are provided so
they may lay the children down or take them out of their swaddling
clothes and warm them before the fire and refresh them with play.
Every mother nurses her own child unless death or sickness prevents.
If that happens, the officers' wives quickly provide a nurse, which
is not difficult, for those who can perform this service are glad to
volunteer. This kind act is much praised, and the child that is
nursed always regards his nurse as his natural mother.

Children under five are cared for by the nurses. All other children, both boys and girls, up to the age of marriage either serve at
the tables or, if still too young, stand quietly by. Whatever is given
them they eat, and they have no separate dinner time. . . . Their
dinners are very short, but their suppers longer because a working
period follows dinner, but after supper come sleep and rest. No
supper is passed without music . . . and they burn gums and spices,
and sprinkle perfume about, leaving nothing undone that affords
pleasure. For they incline to the opinion that no harmless pleasure
should be forbidden.

                              .   .   .

If anyone wants to visit friends in another city or to see the place
itself, he can easily get permission from the officers or magistrates
unless there is some good reason for refusal. No one journeys alone,
but a group is sent, carrying letters from the prince showing that
they have permission for the journey and setting the day of their
required return. They have a wagon given them, with a bondman

to drive the oxen. Unless they have women along, they send the wagon home because it is an impediment. Though they carry nothing with them, they never lack for anything during the whole trip. For wherever they stop, they are at home. If they stop at a place for more than a day, everyone falls to his own occupation and is welcomed by the workmen and companies of the same craft.

If any man on his own and without permission leaves his precinct, and does not have the prince's letters, he is apprehended as a fugitive or runaway and is rebuked, shamed, and punished. If he is caught again in that fault, he is punished with bondage.

If anyone wants to walk in the fields and countryside belonging to his own city, he is not forbidden, provided that he has obtained the consent of his father and wife. But no matter in what part of the country he chances to be, he is given no food until he has worked his forenoon's stint or done as much as is required before supper. Observing this law and its conditions, he may go wherever he wants within the territory of his own city. He shall thus be no less profitable to his city than if he were always within the limits.

You can see how little time they have for loitering; how they have no way of disguising idleness. There are no taverns, alehouses, brothels, nor any occasion for vice or wickedness, no corners for lurking, no places for evil councils or unlawful assembly. For everyone is always in plain sight; so of necessity he must apply himself to his customary labors or else engage in honest and laudable pastimes.

This fashion of life and work being common to all, they must of necessity have plenty of everything. And since they are all equal partners, no one is poor or needy. The national council where, as I have said, every city sends three men every year, as soon as it knows in what places there is abundance and where there is scarcity, immediately allocates the abundance of one place to make up the lack of another place. This they do freely without any payment, taking nothing from them to whom things are given; but those cities that have given their supplies to cities in need do receive at another time what they need from the cities they aided. So, the whole island is, as it were, one family or household.

When they have made sufficient provision for themselves, which they think must consist of two years' supply because of the uncertainty of the next year's harvest, they send the superfluous goods and crops to other countries: grain, honey, wool, flax, wood, dyestuffs, skins, wax, tallow, leather, and livestock. A seventh of these things they give freely to the poor of the country to which they export, the rest they sell at a reasonable price. By this trade they bring into their own country not only a great deal of gold and silver, but also whatever they lack at home, which is chiefly iron. Because they have practised this trade for a long time, they have more of these things than anyone will readily believe. Therefore, they now do not care whether they sell for cash or for credit. If for credit, they never accept the word of private individuals but the warranty of the whole city set forth in contracts.

· · ·

They keep most of their treasure at home to use for extreme danger, especially to hire at great wages foreign soldiers. For they prefer to endanger mercenaries rather than their own citizens. They know that their enemies can be bribed, and weakened by hired traitors set to fight among themselves. For this purpose they keep a great treasure on hand. This treasure is not for hoarding but for use. I am almost afraid to say this, lest I not be believed, for I would hardly believe another man's telling this, if I had not seen it myself.

It usually happens that if a thing is strange and not familiar in our experience, it is difficult to believe. However, a wise and judicious judge of matters will not be surprised, since all of their laws and customs are so different from ours, if their use of gold and silver is interpreted by their customs, not ours. I mean that they use these not as money, but keep them in case of emergency. In the meantime they are used in such a way that no one prizes them as money.

Anyone can plainly see that money is less important than iron, for men cannot live without iron any more than without fire and water. Nature has given no utility to gold and silver that we cannot do without. Only the folly of men sets them in higher esteem because of their scarcity. But nature, a most kind and loving nurse, has placed the most necessary things ready to our use, as air, water, and earth, and has hidden farthest from us all vain and unprofitable things. Therefore, if these metals should be locked up in some tower, it might be suspected that the prince and council (as the populace is always foolishly imagining) intended by some device to deceive the commons and profit themselves. Furthermore, if they should make plate of the gold and silver and other finely and cunningly wrought stuff, and if at any time they should have to melt it down again to pay their soldiers, they see that men would be loath to part from those things that they took delight in.

To remedy all of this, they have found a means which, since it conforms to all of their other laws and customs (and so different from ours, which set so much store on gold, that it is incredible except to those who are very wise) renders gold worthless. For they eat and drink of vessels of earthenware and glass, beautifully made but of small value. Of gold and silver they commonly make chamber pots and other vessels that serve for the vilest uses not only in the common halls but in every man's private house. Furthermore, of the same metals they make great chains and fetters and gyves in which they chain their bondmen. Finally, some condemned persons must wear earrings of gold, finger rings of gold, and collars of gold, and circlets of gold around their heads. Thus, by all possible means, they make gold and silver a badge of reproach and infamy. These metals, which in other nations are valued as life itself, would, if taken from the Utopians, not be missed any more than one penny.

They also gather pearls by the seashore, and diamonds and garnets from certain rocks; yet they do not seek them out, but find them by chance and cut and polish them. They give them to their children, for they make much of young children and like to dress and ornament them so that when they grow up and see that only little children wear jewels and ornaments, they put aside their own voluntarily, without being counselled to do so by their parents, even as our own children, when grown, throw away their dolls and nuts and toys.

．　．　．

There are several kinds of religion, not only in different parts of the island but also within the same city. Some worship the sun as their god; some, the moon; some, other planets. There are those who worship a man, once excellently virtuous and gloriously famous, not only as god but also as the chiefest and highest god. But the majority of wise people, rejecting all of these creeds, believes that there is a certain divine power, unknown, everlasting, inexplicable, far above the capacity and reach of man's knowledge, dispersed throughout the universe, not in size but in virtue. Him they call the father of all. To him alone they attribute the beginning, growth, processes, changes, and endings of all things. Nor do they worship any deity save him. All the other sects, though they differ, agree on this one point with the wisest—that there is one chief and principal god, maker and ruler of the whole world, whom they all, in their language, term Mythra.

There is some disagreement, however, for some identify this god in one way, some in another fashion. For everyone takes his own god to be the one to whose divine might and majesty the power over all things is commonly attributed. However, they are beginning little by little to forsake these various superstitions and to agree in the religion which seems reasonably to excel the others. There is no doubt that the others would have been abolished long since if it had not been for their habit of ascribing any mischance befalling one who had changed his religion to the enmity of the god whom he was forsaking, as if the god were seeking revenge.

After they heard us speak of Christ, of his doctrine, laws, miracles, and the wonderful constancy of martyrs whose blood was willingly shed to bring the nations of the world into the faith, you would hardly believe how glad they were to accept the Word, either by the secret inspiration of God or because it came closest to that opinion which they already thought of among themselves as the best. I do think, however, that it helped when they heard us say that Christ bade his followers to have all things in common, and that the same communalism still exists among the best Christian groups.

Whatever the cause, many of them accepted our religion and were washed with the holy waters of baptism. Because among us four (no more of us were left alive, two having died) there was no priest, which I heartily regret, they could be instructed in all the points of our religion but lacked those sacraments which only priests can administer. They nevertheless understand them and earnestly desire them, even disputing among themselves whether, without the sending of a Christian bishop, one of their own people might receive the order of priesthood. Truly, they were intending to choose one, but at my departure had not yet done so.

Those who do not agree with Christianity fear no one who has been converted, nor do they speak against any one who has received Christianity. There was one exception, however. One of our company was severely punished. As soon as he was baptised he began, against our will, and with more earnestness than wisdom, to talk about Christ's religion, and became so vehement that he not only preferred our religion before all others but utterly despised and condemned all others, calling them profane and their followers wicked, devilish, and children of everlasting damnation. When he had argued this way for a long time, they seized him, accused and condemned him to exile, not as a despiser of religion but as a stirrer up of sedition among the people. For it is one of the most ancient laws among them that no one shall be blamed for arguing in defense of his own religion. For King Utopus, at the very beginning, heard that the inhabitants of the land were, before his coming there, in continual strife and dissension among themselves because of their religion. He also perceived that this dissension (in which several sects fought only for their own part of the country) was the only reason he was able to conquer the land. Therefore, when he had gained victory, his first decree was that it should be lawful for every man to favor and follow whatever religion he wished, and to do the best he could to bring others to his opinion so long as he did it peaceably, gently, quietly and soberly, without hasty and contentious rebuking and inveighing against others. If he could not by fair and gentle words induce others to his opinion, he must nevertheless refrain from violence and unpleasant and seditious language. He who was guilty of vehemence and strife was banished or placed in bondage.

King Utopus made this law not only for the maintenance of peace, which he saw threatened by continual strife and mortal hatred, but also because he thought this decree would help religion. Of religion he did not define or determine anything, not knowing whether God, desiring many different kinds of respect and worship, might not inspire different men with different kinds of religious beliefs. He thought it an unwise and foolish thing, and arrogant presumption, to compel all others, by threats of violence, to agree to the same belief as yourself. Furthermore, though there may be only one true religion, and all others superstition, he foresaw that (if the matter were handled with reason and restraint) the truth of the right doctrine would at last come to light. If contention and debate were continually used, however, the worst and most stubborn and obstinate men, who uphold their evil opinions most constantly, would win. The holiest and best religion would thus be trodden down and destroyed by violent superstition, as good corn is overgrown and choked by weeds and thorns. Therefore, he left all this matter unprescribed and gave to every man liberty and free choice to believe as he wished.

Benvenuto Cellini

19

Autobiography

Benvenuto Cellini (1500–1571) was, by his own account, master of all arts and of all occasions. Early in life, in his native city of Florence, Cellini was apprenticed, in the time-honored guild custom, to a goldsmith. After a series of troubles resulting from his too-vigorous participation in brawling, he went to Rome and set himself up as an independent craftsman and artist, enjoying the patronage of rich merchants, nobles, and churchmen of high rank. There was no limit to Cellini's ambition nor, it seems, to his success. He enjoyed the favor of King Francis I, Pope Clement VII, and many of the famous and influential men of his time. Forever asserting his individualism, having confidence in himself and his talent, and engaging in physical combat almost as often as in art, Cellini was one of the most memorable (though hardly most admirable) figures of the Renaissance.

His *Autobiography,* in addition to revealing the self-assertive artist, gives a fascinating picture of the era and its personalities: the worldly papal court, which Cellini observes but does not judge; the rivalries of petty princes; the efforts of the nobles, merchants, and prelates to achieve splendor and dignity in their homes and palaces; and the importance of taste and connoisseurship in the life of the wealthy and cultured. How reliable the *Autobiography* is can perhaps be judged by the comment of the English translator, J. A. Symonds, who said that Cellini "was not deliberately untruthful." In the latter part of this selection, Cellini gives a dramatic account of the arduous molding and casting of the "Perseus"; this statue, probably his sculptural masterpiece, still stands today in Florence.

Benvenuto Cellini, *The Life of Benvenuto Cellini,* trans. John Addington Symonds (New York: Brentano's, 1906), I, 71–74, 113–26; II, 253–69.

All men of whatsoever quality they be, who have done anything of excellence, or which may properly resemble excellence, ought, if they are persons of truth and honesty, to describe their life with their own hand; but they ought not to attempt so fine an enterprise till they have passed the age of forty. This duty occurs to my own mind, now that I am travelling beyond the term of fifty-eight years, and am in Florence, the city of my birth. Many untoward things can I remember, such as happen to all who live upon our earth; and from those adversities I am now more free than at any previous period of my career—nay, it seems to me that I enjoy greater content of soul and health of body than ever I did in bygone years. I can also bring to mind some pleasant goods and some inestimable evils, which, when I turn my thoughts backward, strike terror in me, and astonishment that I should have reached this age of fifty-eight, wherein, thanks be to God, I am still travelling prosperously forward.

It is true that men who have laboured with some show of excellence, have already given knowledge of themselves to the world; and this alone ought to suffice them; I mean the fact that they have proved their manhood and achieved renown. Yet one must needs live like others; and so in a work like this there will always be found occasion for natural bragging, which is of divers kinds, and the first is that a man should let others know he draws his lineage from persons of worth and most ancient origin. I am called Benvenuto Cellini, son of Maestro Giovanni, son of Andrea, son of Cristofano Cellini; my mother was Madonna Elisabetta, daughter to Stefano Granacci; both parents citizens of Florence. It is found written in chronicles made by our ancestors of Florence, men of old time and of credibility, even as Giovanni Villani writes, that the city of Florence was evidently built in imitation of the fair city of Rome; and certain remnants of the Coliseum and the Baths can yet be traced. These things are near Santa Croce. The Capitol was where is now the Old Market. The Rotonda is entire, which was made of the temple of Mars, and is now dedicated to our Saint John. That thus it was, can very well be seen, and cannot be denied, but the said buildings are much smaller than those of Rome. He who caused them to be built, they say, was Julius Caesar, in concert with some noble Romans, who, when Fiesole had been stormed and taken, raised a city in this place, and each of them took in hand to erect one of these notable edifices.

Julius Caesar had among his captains a man of highest rank and valour, who was called Fiorino of Cellino, which is a village about two miles distant from Monte Fiascone. Now this Fiorino took up his quarters under the hill of Fiesole, on the ground where Florence now stands, in order to be near the river Arno, and for the convenience of the troops. All those soldiers and others who had to do with the said captain, used then to say: "Let us go to Fiorenze"; as well because the said captain was called Fiorino, as also because the place he had chosen for his quarters was by nature very rich in flowers. Upon the foundation of the city, therefore, since this name struck Julius Caesar as being fair and apt, and given by circumstance, and seeing furthermore that flowers themselves bring good augury, he appointed the name of Florence for the town. He wished besides to pay his valiant captain this compliment; and he loved him all the more for having drawn him from a very humble place, and for the reason that so excellent a man was a creature of his own. The name that learned inventors and investigators of such etymologies adduce, as that Florence is flowing at the Arno, cannot hold; seeing that Rome is flowing at the Tiber, Ferrara is flowing at the Po, Lyons is flowing at the Saone, Paris is flowing at the Seine, and yet the names of all these towns are different, and have come to them by other ways.

Thus then we find; and thus we believe that we are descended from a man of worth. Furthermore, we find that there are Cellinis of our stock in Ravenna, that most ancient town of Italy, where too are plenty of gentle folk. In Pisa also there are some, and I have discovered them in many parts of Christendom; and in this state also the breed exists, men devoted to the profession of arms; for not many years ago a young man, called Luca Cellini, a beardless youth, fought with a soldier of experience and a most valorous man, named Francesco da Vicorti, who had frequently fought before in single combat. This Luca, by his own valour, with sword in hand, overcame and slew him, with such bravery and stoutness that he moved the folk to wonder, who were expecting quite the contrary issue; so that I glory in tracing my descent from men of valour.

As for the trifling honours which I have gained for my house, under the well-known conditions of our present ways of living, and by means of my art, albeit the same are matters of no great moment, I will relate these in their proper time and place, taking much more pride in having been born humble and having had some honourable foundation for my family, than if I had been born of great lineage and had stained or overclouded that by my base qualities. So then I will make a beginning by saying how it pleased God I should be born.

• • •

At Siena I waited for the mail to Rome, which I afterwards joined; and when we passed the Pagha, we met a courier carrying news of the new Pope, Clement VII. Upon my arrival in Rome, I went to work in the shop of the master-goldsmith Santi. He was dead; but a son of his carried on the business. He did not work himself, but entrusted all his commissions to a young man named Lucagnolo from Iesi, a country fellow, who while yet a child had come into Santi's service. This man was short but well proportioned, and was a more skilful craftsman than any one whom I had met with up to that time; remarkable for facility and excellent in design. He executed large plate only; that is to say, vases of the utmost beauty, basons, and such pieces. Having put myself to work there, I began to make some candelabra for the Bishop of Salamanca, a Spaniard. They were richly chased, so far as that sort of work admits. A pupil of Raffaello da Urbino called Gian Francesco, and commonly known as Il Fattore, was a painter of great ability; and being on terms of friendship with the Bishop, he introduced me to his favour, so that I obtained many commissions from that prelate, and earned considerable sums of money.

During that time I went to draw, sometimes in Michelangelo's chapel, and sometimes in the house of Agostino Chigi of Siena, which contained many incomparable paintings by the hand of that great master Raffaello. This I did on feast-days, because the house was then inhabited by Messer Gismondo, Agostino's brother. They plumed themselves exceedingly when they saw young men of my sort coming to study in their palaces. Gismondo's wife, noticing my frequent presence in that house—she was a lady as courteous as could be, and of surpassing beauty—came up to me one day, looked at my drawings, and asked me if I was a sculptor or a painter; to whom I said I was a goldsmith. She remarked that

I drew too well for a goldsmith; and having made one of her waiting-maids bring a lily of the finest diamonds set in gold, she showed it to me, and bade me value it. I valued it at 800 crowns. Then she said that I had very nearly hit the mark, and asked me whether I felt capable of setting the stones really well. I said that I should much like to do so, and began before her eyes to make a little sketch for it, working all the better because of the pleasure I took in conversing with so lovely and agreeable a gentlewoman. When the sketch was finished, another Roman lady of great beauty joined us; she had been above, and now descending to the ground-floor, asked Madonna Porzia what she was doing there. She answered with a smile: "I am amusing myself by watching this worthy young man at his drawing; he is as good as he is handsome." I had by this time acquired a trifle of assurance, mixed, however, with some honest bashfulness; so I blushed and said: "Such as I am, lady, I shall ever be most ready to serve you." The gentlewoman, also slightly blushing, said: "You know well that I want you to serve me"; and reaching me the lily, told me to take it away; and gave me besides twenty golden crowns which she had in her bag, and added: "Set me the jewel after the fashion you have sketched, and keep for me the old gold in which it is now set." On this the Roman lady observed: "If I were in that young man's body, I should go off without asking leave." Madonna Porzia replied that virtues rarely are at home with vices, and that if I did such a thing, I should strongly belie my good looks of an honest man. Then turning round, she took the Roman lady's hand, and with a pleasant smile said: "Farewell, Benvenuto." I stayed on a short while at the drawing I was making, which was a copy of a Jove by Raffaello. When I had finished it and left the house, I set myself to making a little model of wax, in order to show how the jewel would look when it was completed. This I took to Madonna Porzia, whom I found with the same Roman lady. Both of them were highly satisfied with my work, and treated me so kindly that, being somewhat emboldened, I promised the jewel should be twice as good as the model. Accordingly I set hand to it, and in twelve days I finished it in the form of a fleur-de-lys, as I have said above, ornamenting it with little masks, children, and animals, exquisitely enamelled, whereby the diamonds which formed the lily were more than doubled in effect.

While I was working at this piece, Lucagnolo, of whose ability I have before spoken, showed considerable discontent, telling me over and over again that I might acquire far more profit and honour by helping him to execute large plate, as I had done at first. I made him answer that, whenever I chose, I should always be capable of working at great silver pieces; but that things like that on which I was now engaged were not commissioned every day; and beside their bringing no less honour than large silver plate, there was also more profit to be made by them. He laughed me in the face, and said: "Wait and see, Benvenuto; for by the time that you have finished that work of yours, I will make haste to have finished this vase, which I took in hand when you did the jewel; and then experience shall teach you what profit I shall get from my vase, and what you will get from your ornament." I answered that I was very glad indeed to enter into such a competition with so good a craftsman as he was, because the end would show which of us was mistaken. Accordingly both the one and the other of us, with a scornful smile upon our lips, bent our heads in grim earnest to the work, which both were now desirous of accomplishing; so that after about ten days, each had finished his undertaking with great delicacy and artistic skill.

Lucagnolo's was a huge silver piece, used at the table of Pope Clement, into which he flung away bits of bone and the rind of divers fruits, while eating; an object of ostentation rather than necessity. The vase was adorned with two fine handles, together with many masks, both small and great, and masses of lovely foliage, in as exquisite a style of elegance as could be imagined; on seeing which I said it was the most beautiful vase that ever I set eyes on. Thinking he had convinced me, Lucagnolo replied: "Your work seems to me no less beautiful, but we shall soon perceive the difference between the two." So he took his vase and carried it to the Pope, who was very well pleased with it, and ordered at once that he should be paid at the ordinary rate of such large plate. Meanwhile I carried mine to Madonna Porzia, who looked at it with astonishment, and told me I had far surpassed my promise. Then she bade me ask for my reward whatever I liked; for it seemed to her my desert was so great that if I craved a castle she could hardly recompense me; but since that was not in her hands to bestow, she added laughing that I must beg what lay within her power. I

answered that the greatest reward I could desire for my labour
was to have satisfied her ladyship. Then, smiling in my turn, and
bowing to her, I took my leave, saying I wanted no reward but
that. She turned to the Roman lady and said: "You see that the
qualities we discerned in him are companied by virtues, and not
vices." They both expressed their admiration, and then Madonna
Porzia continued: "Friend Benvenuto, have you never heard it said
that when the poor give to the rich, the devil laughs?" I replied:
"Quite true! and yet, in the midst of all his troubles, I should
like this time to see him laugh"; and as I took my leave, she said
that this time she had no will to bestow on him that favour.

When I came back to the shop, Lucagnolo had the money for
his vase in a paper packet; and on my arrival he cried out: "Come
and compare the price of your jewel with the price of my plate."
I said that he must leave things as they were till the next day,
because I hoped that even as my work in its kind was not less excellent than his, so I should be able to show him quite an equal
price for it.

On the day following, Madonna Porzia sent a majordomo of
hers to my shop, who called me out, and putting into my hands
a paper packet full of money from his lady, told me that she
did not choose the devil should have his whole laugh out: by
which she hinted that the money sent me was not the entire payment merited by my industry, and other messages were added
worthy of so courteous a lady. Lucagnolo, who was burning to
compare his packet with mine, burst into the shop; then in the
presence of twelve journeymen and some neighbours, eager to behold the result of this competition, he seized his packet, scorn-
fully exclaiming "Ou ou!" three or four times, while he poured
his money on the counter with a great noise. They were twenty-
five crowns in giulios; and he fancied that mine would be four
or five crowns *di moneta*. I for my part, stunned and stifled by
his cries, and by the looks and smiles of the bystanders, first peeped
into my packet; then, after seeing that it contained nothing but
gold, I retired to one end of the counter, and, keeping my eyes
lowered and making no noise at all, I lifted it with both hands
suddenly above my head, and emptied it like a mill hopper. My
coin was twice as much as his; which caused the onlookers, who
had fixed their eyes on me with some derision, to turn round sud-

denly to him and say: "Lucagnolo, Benvenuto's pieces, being all of gold and twice as many as yours, make a far finer effect." I thought for certain that, what with jealousy and what with shame, Lucagnolo would have fallen dead upon the spot; and though he took the third part of my gain, since I was a journeyman (for such is the custom of the trade, two-thirds fall to the workman and one-third to the masters of the shop), yet inconsiderate envy had more power in him than avarice: it ought indeed to have worked quite the other way, he being a peasant's son from Iesi. He cursed his art and those who taught it him, vowing that thenceforth he would never work at large plate, but give his whole attention to those whoreson gewgaws, since they were so well paid. Equally enraged on my side, I answered that every bird sang its own note; that he talked after the fashion of the hovels he came from; but that I dared swear that I should succeed with ease in making his lubberly lumber, while he would never be successful in my whoreson gewgaws. Thus I flung off in a passion, telling him that I would soon show him that I spoke truth. The bystanders openly declared against him, holding him for a lout, as indeed he was, and me for a man, as I had proved myself.

Next day, I went to thank Madonna Porzia, and told her that her ladyship had done the opposite of what she said she would; for that while I wanted to make the devil laugh, she had made him once more deny God. We both laughed pleasantly at this, and she gave me other commissions for fine and substantial work.

Meanwhile, I contrived, by means of a pupil of Raffaello da Urbino, to get an order from the Bishop of Salamanca for one of those great water-vessels called *acquereccia,* which are used for ornaments to place on sideboards. He wanted a pair made of equal size; and one of them he intrusted to Lucagnolo, the other to me. Giovan Francesco, the painter I have mentioned, gave us the design. Accordingly I set hand with marvellous good-will to this piece of plate, and was accommodated with a part of his workshop by a Milanese named Maestro Giovan Piero della Tacca. Having made my preparations, I calculated how much money I should need for certain affairs of my own, and sent all the rest to assist my poor father.

It so happened that just when this was being paid to him in Florence, he stumbled upon one of those Radicals who were in the

Eight at the time when I got into that little trouble there. It was the very man who had abused him so rudely, and who swore that I should certainly be sent into the country with the lances. Now this fellow had some sons of very bad morals and repute; wherefore my father said to him: "Misfortunes can happen to anybody, especially to men of choleric humour when they are in the right, even as it happened to my son; but let the rest of his life bear witness how virtuously I have brought him up. Would God, for your well-being, that your sons may act neither worse nor better toward you than mine do to me. God rendered me able to bring them up as I have done; and where my own power could not reach, 'twas He who rescued them, against your expectation, out of your violent hands." On leaving the man, he wrote me all this story, begging me for God's sake to practise music at times, in order that I might not lose the fine accomplishment which he had taught me with such trouble. The letter so overflowed with expressions of the tenderest fatherly affection, that I was moved to tears of filial piety, resolving, before he died, to gratify him amply with regard to music. Thus God grants us those lawful blessings which we ask in prayer, nothing doubting.

While I was pushing forward Salamanca's vase, I had only one little boy as help, whom I had taken at the entreaty of friends, and half against my own will, to be my workman. He was about fourteen years of age, bore the name of Paulino, and was son to a Roman burgess, who lived upon the income of his property. Paulino was the best-mannered, the most honest, and the most beautiful boy I ever saw in my whole life. His modest ways and actions, together with his superlative beauty and his devotion to myself, bred in me as great an affection for him as a man's breast can hold. This passionate love led me oftentimes to delight the lad with music; for I observed that his marvellous features, which by complexion wore a tone of modest melancholy, brightened up, and when I took my cornet, broke into a smile so lovely and so sweet, that I do not marvel at the silly stories which the Greeks have written about the deities of heaven. Indeed, if my boy had lived in those times, he would probably have turned their heads still more. He had a sister, named Faustina, more beautiful, I verily believe, than that Faustina about whom the old books gossip so. Sometimes he took me to their vineyard, and, so far as I could judge, it struck me that Paulino's good father would have welcomed me as a son-in-law. This affair led me to play more than I was used to do.

It happened at that time that one Giangiacomo of Cesena, a musician in the Pope's band, and a very excellent performer, sent word through Lorenzo, the trumpeter of Lucca, who is now in our Duke's service, to inquire whether I was inclined to help them at the Pope's Ferragosto, playing soprano with my cornet in some motets of great beauty selected by them for that occasion. Although I had the greatest desire to finish the vase I had begun, yet, since music has a wondrous charm of its own, and also because I wished to please my old father, I consented to join them. During eight days before the festival we practised two hours a day together; then on the first of August we went to the Belvedere, and while Pope Clement was at table, we played those carefully studied motets so well that his Holiness protested he had never heard music more sweetly executed or with better harmony of parts. He sent for Giangiacomo, and asked him where and how he had procured so excellent a cornet for soprano, and inquired particularly who I was. Giangiacomo told him my name in full. Whereupon the Pope said: "So, then, he is the son of Maestro Giovanni?" On being assured I was, the Pope expressed his wish to have me in his service with the other bandsmen. Giangiacomo replied: "Most blessed Father, I cannot pretend for certain that you will get him, for his profession, to which he devotes himself assiduously, is that of a goldsmith, and he works in it miraculously well, and earns by it far more than he could do by playing." To this the Pope added: "I am the better inclined to him now that I find him possessor of a talent more than I expected. See that he obtains the same salary as the rest of you; and tell him from me to join my service, and that I will find work enough by the day for him to do in his other trade." Then stretching out his hand, he gave him a hundred golden crowns of the Camera in a handkerchief, and said: "Divide these so that he may take his share."

When Giangiacomo left the Pope, he came to us, and related in detail all that the Pope had said; and after dividing the money between the eight of us, and giving me my share, he said to me: "Now I am going to have you inscribed among our company." I replied: "Let the day pass; to-morrow I will give my answer." When I left them, I went meditating whether I ought to accept the invi-

tation, inasmuch as I could not but suffer if I abandoned the noble
studies of my art. The following night my father appeared to me
in a dream, and begged me with tears of tenderest affection, for
God's love and his, to enter upon this engagement. Methought I
answered that nothing would induce me to do so. In an instant he
assumed so horrible an aspect as to frighten me out of my wits, and
cried: "If you do not, you will have a father's curse; but if you do,
may you be ever blessed by me!" When I woke, I ran, for very
fright, to have myself inscribed. Then I wrote to my old father,
telling him the news, which so affected him with extreme joy that
a sudden fit of illness took him, and well-nigh brought him to
death's door. In his answer to my letter, he told me that he too had
dreamed nearly the same as I had.

Knowing now that I had gratified my father's honest wish, I
began to think that everything would prosper with me to a glorious
and honourable end. Accordingly, I set myself with indefatigable
industry to the completion of the vase I had begun for Salamanca.
That prelate was a very extraordinary man, extremely rich, but
difficult to please. He sent daily to learn what I was doing; and
when his messenger did not find me at home, he broke into fury,
saying that he would take the work out of my hands and give it to
others to finish. This came of my slavery to that accursed music.
Still I laboured diligently night and day, until, when I had brought
my work to a point when it could be exhibited, I submitted it to
the inspection of the Bishop. This so increased his desire to see it
finished, that I was sorry I had shown it. At the end of three months
I had it ready, with little animals and foliage and masks, as beautiful as one could hope to see. No sooner was it done than I sent it
by the hand of my workman, Paulino, to show that able artist
Lucagnolo, of whom I have spoken above. Paulino, with the grace
and beauty which belonged to him, spoke as follows: "Messer
Lucagnolo, Benvenuto bids me say that he has sent to show you
his promises and your lumber, expecting in return to see from
you his gew-gaws." This message given, Lucagnolo took up the
vase, and carefully examined it; then he said to Paulino: "Fair boy,
tell your master that he is a great and able artist, and that I beg
him to be willing to have me for a friend, and not to engage in
aught else." The mission of that virtuous and marvellous lad caused
me the greatest joy; and then the vase was carried to Salamanca,

who ordered it to be valued. Lucagnolo took part in the valuation, estimating and praising it far above my own opinion. Salamanca, lifting up the vase, cried like a true Spaniard: "I swear by God that I will take as long in paying him as he has lagged in making it." When I heard this, I was exceedingly put out, and fell to cursing all Spain and every one who wished well to it.

. . .

Having succeeded so well with the cast of the Medusa, I had great hope of bringing my Perseus through; for I had laid the wax on, and felt confident that it would come out in bronze as perfectly as the Medusa. The waxen model produced so fine an effect, that when the Duke saw it and was struck with its beauty— whether somebody had persuaded him it could not be carried out with the same finish in metal, or whether he thought so for himself—he came to visit me more frequently than usual, and on one occasion said: "Benvenuto, this figure cannot succeed in bronze; the laws of art do not admit of it." These words of his Excellency stung me so sharply that I answered: "My lord, I know how very little confidence you have in me; and I believe the reason of this is that your most illustrious Excellency lends too ready an ear to my calumniators, or else indeed that you do not understand my art." He hardly let me close the sentence when he broke in: "I profess myself a connoisseur, and understand it very well indeed." I replied: "Yes, like a prince, not like an artist; for if your Excellency understood my trade as well as you imagine, you would trust me on the proofs I have already given. These are, first, the colossal bronze bust of your Excellency, which is now in Elba; secondly, the restoration of the Ganymede in marble, which offered so many difficulties and cost me so much trouble, that I would rather have made the whole statue new from the beginning; thirdly, the Medusa, cast by me in bronze, here now before your Excellency's eyes, the execution of which was a greater triumph of strength and skill than any of my predecessors in this fiendish art have yet achieved. Look you, my lord! I constructed that furnace anew on principles quite different from those of other founders; in addition to many technical improvements and ingenious devices, I supplied it with two issues for the metal, because this difficult and twisted figure could not otherwise have come out perfect. It is only owing to my intelligent insight into means and appliances

that the statue turned out as it did; a triumph judged impossible
by all the practitioners of this art. I should like you furthermore
to be aware, my lord, for certain, that the sole reason why I succeeded with all those great and arduous works in France under his
most admirable Majesty King Francis, was the high courage which
that good monarch put into my heart by the liberal allowances
he made me, and the multitude of workpeople he left at my dis-
posal. I could have as many as I asked for, and employed at times
above forty, all chosen by myself. These were the causes of my
having there produced so many masterpieces in so short a space
of time. Now then, my lord, put trust in me; supply me with the
aid I need, I am confident of being able to complete a work which
will delight your soul. But if your Excellency goes on disheartening
me, and does not advance me the assistance which is absolutely
required, neither I nor any man alive upon this earth can hope to
achieve the slightest thing of value."

It was as much as the Duke could do to stand by and listen to
my pleadings. He kept turning first this way and then that; while
I, in despair, poor wretched I, was calling up remembrance of the
noble state I held in France, to the great sorrow of my soul. All
at once he cried: "Come, tell me, Benvenuto, how is it possible
that yonder splendid head of Medusa, so high up there in the
grasp of Perseus, should ever come out perfect?" I replied upon
the instant: "Look you now, my lord! If your Excellency possessed
that knowledge of the craft which you affirm you have, you would
not fear one moment for the splendid head you speak of. There
is good reason, on the other hand, to feel uneasy about this right
foot, so far below and at a distance from the rest." When he heard
these words, the Duke turned, half in anger, to some gentlemen in
waiting, and exclaimed: "I verily believe that this Benvenuto
prides himself on contradicting everything one says." Then he
faced round to me with a touch of mockery, upon which his attendants did the like, and began to speak as follows: "I will listen
patiently to any argument you can possibly produce in explanation
of your statement, which may convince me of its probability." I
said in answer: "I will adduce so sound an argument that your
Excellency shall perceive the full force of it." So I began: "You
must know, my lord, that the nature of fire is to ascend, and therefore I promise you that Medusa's head will come out famously;

but since it is not in the nature of fire to descend, and I must force it downwards six cubits by artificial means, I assure your Excellency upon this most convincing ground of proof that the foot cannot possibly come out. It will, however, be quite easy for me to restore it." "Why, then," said the Duke, "did you not devise it so that the foot should come out as well as you affirm the head will?" I answered: "I must have made a much larger furnace, with a conduit as thick as my leg; and so I might have forced the molten metal by its own weight to descend so far. Now, my pipe, which runs six cubits to the statue's foot, as I have said, is not thicker than two fingers. However, it was not worth the trouble and ex-pense to make a larger; for I shall easily be able to mend what is lacking. But when my mould is more than half full, as I expect, from this middle point upwards, the fire ascending by its natural property, then the heads of Perseus and Medusa will come out ad-mirably; you may be quite sure of it." After I had thus expounded these convincing arguments, together with many more of the same kind, which it would be tedious to set down here, the Duke shook his head and departed without further ceremony.

Abandoned thus to my own resources, I took new courage, and banished the sad thoughts which kept recurring to my mind, mak-ing me often weep bitter tears of repentance for having left France; for though I did so only to revisit Florence, my sweet birthplace, in order that I might charitably succour my six nieces, this good action, as I well perceived, had been the beginning of my great misfortune. Nevertheless, I felt convinced that when my Perseus was accomplished, all these trials would be turned to high felicity and glorious well-being.

Accordingly I strengthened my heart, and with all the forces of my body and my purse, employing what little money still re-mained to me, I set to work. First I provided myself with several loads of pinewood from the forests of Serristori, in the neighbour-hood of Montelupo. While these were on their way, I clothed my Perseus with the clay which I had prepared many months before-hand, in order that it might be duly seasoned. After making its clay tunic (for that is the term used in this art) and properly arming it and fencing it with iron girders, I began to draw the wax out by means of a slow fire. This melted and issued through numerous air-vents I had made; for the more there are of these, the better will the mould fill. When I had finished drawing off the wax, I constructed a funnel-shaped furnace all round the model of my Perseus. It was built of bricks, so interlaced, the one above the other, that numerous apertures were left for the fire to exhale at. Then I began to lay on wood by degrees, and kept it burning two whole days and nights. At length, when all the wax was gone, and the mould was well baked, I set to work at digging the pit in which to sink it. This I performed with scrupulous regard to all the rules of art. When I had finished that part of my work, I raised the mould by windlasses and stout ropes to a perpendicular position, and suspending it with the greatest care one cubit above the level of the furnace, so that it hung exactly above the middle of the pit, I next lowered it gently down into the very bottom of the furnace, and had it firmly placed with every possible precaution for its safety. When this delicate operation was accomplished, I began to bank it up with the earth I had excavated; and, ever as the earth grew higher, I introduced its proper air-vents, which were little tubes of earthenware, such as folk use for drains and such-like purposes. At length, I felt sure that it was admirably fixed, and that the filling-in of the pit and the placing of the air-vents had been properly performed. I also could see that my workpeople understood my method, which differed very considerably from that of all the other masters in the trade. Feeling confident, then, that I could rely upon them, I next turned to my furnace, which I had filled with numerous pigs of copper and other bronze stuff. The pieces were piled according to the laws of art, that is to say, so resting one upon the other that the flames could play freely through them, in order that the metal might heat and liquefy the sooner. At last I called out heartily to set the furnace going. The logs of pine were heaped in, and, what with the unctuous resin of the wood and the good draught I had given, my furnace worked so well that I was obliged to rush from side to side to keep it going. The labour was more than I could stand; yet I forced myself to strain every nerve and muscle. To increase my anxieties, the workshop took fire, and we were afraid lest the roof should fall upon our heads; while, from the garden, such a storm of wind and rain kept blowing in, that it perceptibly cooled the furnace.

Battling thus with all these untoward circumstances for several

hours, and exerting myself beyond even the measure of my powerful constitution, I could at last bear up no longer, and a sudden
fever, of the utmost possible intensity, attacked me. I felt absolutely obliged to go and fling myself upon my bed. Sorely against
my will having to drag myself away from the spot, I turned to
my assistants, about ten or more in all, what with master-founders,
hand-workers, country-fellows, and my own special journeymen,
among whom was Bernardino Mannellini of Mugello, my appren-
tice through several years. To him in particular I spoke: "Look,
my dear Bernardino, that you observe the rules which I have
taught you; do your best with all despatch, for the metal will soon
be fused. You cannot go wrong; these honest men will get the
channels ready; you will easily be able to drive back the two plugs
with this pair of iron crooks; and I am sure that my mould will
fill miraculously. I feel more ill than I ever did in all my life,
and verily believe that it will kill me before a few hours are over."
Thus, with despair at heart, I left them, and betook myself to bed.

No sooner had I got to bed, than I ordered my serving-maids to
carry food and wine for all the men into the workshop; at the
same time I cried: "I shall not be alive to-morrow." They tried
to encourage me, arguing that my illness would pass over, since it
came from excessive fatigue. In this way I spent two hours battling
with the fever, which steadily increased, and calling out continually: "I feel that I am dying." My housekeeper, who was named
Mona Fiore da Castel del Rio, a very notable manager and no less
warm-hearted, kept chiding me for my discouragement; but, on
the other hand, she paid me every kind attention which was possible. However, the sight of my physical pain and moral dejection
so affected her, that, in spite of that brave heart of hers, she could
not refrain from shedding tears; and yet, so far as she was able,
she took good care I should not see them. While I was thus terribly afflicted, I beheld the figure of a man enter my chamber,
twisted in his body into the form of a capital S. He raised a
lamentable, doleful voice, like one who announces their last hour
to men condemned to die upon the scaffold, and spoke these
words: "O Benvenuto! your statue is spoiled, and there is no hope
whatever of saving it." No sooner had I heard the shriek of that
wretch than I gave a howl which might have been heard from the

sphere of flame. Jumping from my bed, I seized my clothes and began to dress. The maids, and my lad, and every one who came around to help me, got kicks or blows of the fist, while I kept crying out in lamentation: "Ah! traitors! enviers! This is an act of treason, done by malice prepense! But I swear by God that I will sift it to the bottom, and before I die will leave such witness to the world of what I can do as shall make a score of mortals marvel."

When I had got my clothes on, I strode with soul bent on mischief toward the workshop; there I beheld the men, whom I had left erewhile in such high spirits, standing stupefied and downcast. I began at once and spoke: "Up with you! Attend to me! Since you have not been able or willing to obey the directions I gave you, obey me now that I am with you to conduct my work in person. Let no one contradict me, for in cases like this we need the aid of hand and hearing, not of advice." When I had uttered these words, a certain Maestro Alessandro Lastricati broke silence and said: "Look you, Benvenuto, you are going to attempt an enterprise which the laws of art do not sanction, and which cannot succeed." I turned upon him with such fury and so full of mischief that he and all the rest of them exclaimed with one voice: "On then! Give orders! We will obey your least commands, so long as life is left in us." I believe they spoke thus feelingly because they thought I must fall shortly dead upon the ground. I went immediately to inspect the furnace, and found that the metal was all curdled; an accident which we express by "being caked." I told two of the hands to cross the road, and fetch from the house of the butcher Capretta a load of young oak-wood, which had lain dry for above a year; this wood had been previously offered me by Madame Ginevra, wife of the said Capretta. So soon as the first armfuls arrived, I began to fill the grate beneath the furnace. Now oak-wood of that kind heats more powerfully than any other sort of tree; and for this reason, where a slow fire is wanted, as in the case of gun-foundry, alder or pine is preferred. Accordingly, when the logs took fire, oh! how the cake began to stir beneath that awful heat, to glow and sparkle in a blaze! At the same time I kept stirring up the channels and sent men upon the roof to stop the conflagration, which had gathered force from the increased combustion in the furnace; also I caused boards, carpets, and other hangings to be set up against the garden, in order to protect us from the violence of the rain.

When I had thus provided against these several disasters, I roared out first to one man and then to another: "Bring this thing here! Take that thing there!" At this crisis, when the whole gang saw the cake was on the point of melting, they did my bidding, each fellow working with the strength of three. I then ordered half a pig of pewter to be brought, which weighed about sixty pounds, and flung it into the middle of the cake inside the furnace. By this means, and by piling on wood and stirring now with pokers and now with iron rods, the curdled mass rapidly began to liquefy. Then, knowing I had brought the dead to life again, against the firm opinion of those ignoramuses, I felt such vigour fill my veins, that all those pains of fever, all those fears of death, were quite forgotten.

All of a sudden an explosion took place, attended by a tremendous flash of flame, as though a thunderbolt had formed and been discharged amongst us. Unwonted and appalling terror astonied every one, and me more even than the rest. When the din was over and the dazzling light extinguished, we began to look each other in the face. Then I discovered that the cap of the furnace had blown up, and the bronze was bubbling over from its source beneath. So I had the mouths of my mould immediately opened, and at the same time drove in the two plugs which kept back the molten metal. But I noticed that it did not flow as rapidly as usual, the reason being probably that the fierce heat of the fire we kindled had consumed its base alloy. Accordingly I sent for all my pewter platters, porringers, and dishes, to the number of some two hundred pieces, and had a portion of them cast, one by one, into the channels, the rest into the furnace. This expedient succeeded, and every one could now perceive that my bronze was in most perfect liquefaction, and my mould was filling; whereupon they with all heartiness and happy cheer assisted and obeyed my bidding, while I, now here, now there, gave orders, helped with my own hands, and cried aloud: "O God! Thou that by Thy immeasurable power didst rise from the dead, and in Thy glory didst ascend to heaven!" . . . even thus in a moment my mould was filled; and seeing my work finished, I fell upon my knees, and with all my heart gave thanks to God.

After all was over, I turned to a plate of salad on a bench there, and ate with hearty appetite, and drank together with the whole crew. Afterwards I retired to bed, healthy and happy, for it was

now two hours before morning, and slept as sweetly as though I
had never felt a touch of illness. My good housekeeper, without
my giving any orders, had prepared a fat capon for my repast. So
that, when I rose, about the hour for breaking fast, she presented
herself with a smiling countenance, and said: "Oh! is that the man
who felt that he was dying? Upon my word, I think the blows and
kicks you dealt us last night, when you were so enraged, and had
that demon in your body, as it seemed, must have frightened away
your mortal fever! The fever feared that it might catch it too, as
we did!" All my poor household, relieved in like measure from
anxiety and overwhelming labour, went at once to buy earthen
vessels in order to replace the pewter I had cast away. Then we
dined together joyously; nay, I cannot remember a day in my
whole life when I dined with greater gladness or a better appetite.

After our meal I received visits from the several men who had
assisted me. They exchanged congratulations, and thanked God
for our success, saying they had learned and seen things done
which other masters judged impossible. I too grew somewhat glorious; and deeming I had shown myself a man of talent, indulged in
a boastful humour. So I thrust my hand into my purse, and paid
them all to their full satisfaction.

That evil fellow, my mortal foe, Messer Pier Francesco Ricci,
majordomo of the Duke, took great pains to find out how the
affair had gone. In answer to his questions, the two men whom I
suspected of having caked my metal for me, said I was no man,
but of a certainty some powerful devil, since I had accomplished
what no craft of the art could do; indeed they did not believe a
mere ordinary fiend could work such miracles as I in other ways
had shown. They exaggerated the whole affair so much, possibly
in order to excuse their own part in it, that the majordomo wrote
an account to the Duke, who was then in Pisa, far more marvellous
and full of thrilling incidents than what they had narrated.

After I had let my statue cool for two whole days, I began to
uncover it by slow degrees. The first thing I found was that the
head of Medusa had come out most admirably, thanks to the air-
vents; for, as I had told the Duke, it is the nature of fire to ascend.
Upon advancing farther, I discovered that the other head, that,
namely, of Perseus, had succeeded no less admirably; and this astonished me far more, because it is at a considerably lower level than

that of the Medusa. Now the mouths of the mould were placed above the head of Perseus and behind his shoulders; and I found that all the bronze my furnace contained had been exhausted in the head of this figure. It was a miracle to observe that not one fragment remained in the orifice of the channel, and that nothing was wanting to the statue. In my great astonishment I seemed to see in this the hand of God arranging and controlling all.

I went on uncovering the statue with success, and ascertained that everything had come out in perfect order, until I reached the foot of the right leg on which the statue rests. There the heel itself was formed, and going farther, I found the foot apparently complete. This gave me great joy on the one side, but was half unwelcome to me on the other, merely because I had told the Duke that it could not come out. However, when I reached the end, it appeared that the toes and a little piece above them were unfinished, so that about half the foot was wanting. Although I knew that this would add a trifle to my labour, I was very well pleased, because I could now prove to the Duke how well I understood my business. It is true that far more of the foot than I expected had been perfectly formed; the reason of this was that, from causes I have recently described, the bronze was hotter than our rules of art prescribe; also that I had been obliged to supplement the alloy with my pewter cups and platters, which no one else, I think, had ever done before.

Having now ascertained how successfully my work had been accomplished, I lost no time in hurrying to Pisa, where I found the Duke. He gave me a most gracious reception, as did also the Duchess; and although the majordomo had informed them of the whole proceedings, their Excellencies deemed my performance far more stupendous and astonishing when they heard the tale from my own mouth. When I arrived at the foot of Perseus, and said it had not come out perfect, just as I previously warned his Excellency, I saw an expression of wonder pass over his face, while he related to the Duchess how I had predicted this beforehand. Observing the princes to be so well disposed towards me, I begged leave from the Duke to go to Rome. He granted it in most obliging terms, and bade me return as soon as possible to complete his Perseus; giving me letters of recommendation meanwhile to his ambassador, Averardo Serristori. We were then in the first years of Pope Giulio de Monti.

Montaigne

20

Essays: In Defense of Raymond Sebond

Michel Eyquem, Seigneur de Montaigne (1533–1592), was another of the men of many talents who characterized the Renaissance. He frequented the court of the French kings and served as counselor in the Bordeaux *parlement*. He "retired," however, at the age of thirty-eight to his castle of Montaigne and devoted most of the rest of his life to study and writing. Except for two terms as mayor of Bordeaux (1581–1585), Montaigne's chief occupation during the last years of his life was the composition of his *Essays*.

The *Essays* reflect Montaigne's discursive examination of what he learned from books, acquaintances, and his own experience. They reveal a cool, rational intelligence, and show that he was always patient and humorously observant. "Others fashion man"; he said, "I repeat him."

Not swayed by the new religious doctrines of his time, nor concerned with the defense of the old, Montaigne remarked, "The ancientest evil, if it be known to us, bears always lighter on us than a new one of which we know but little." Even new scientific discoveries seemed to him only possible contributors to further confusion. Nevertheless, Montaigne was sure that there were such qualities as greatness and magnanimity, which he saw demonstrated occasionally by the men of his own time (more often by the humble people than by the rulers) as well as by the ancients. His essays deal with such diverse subjects as the education of children and the true nature of Roman grandeur.

Montaigne's epicureanism links him with the life of contented reason which was the goal of one of his favorite authors, Lucretius, whom he quotes extensively. The greatest influence of Montaigne's essays was upon intellectuals and writers. In England the translation of his essays (by

Montaigne, *In Defense of Raymond Sebond,* trans. Arthur H. Beattie, in *Milestones of Thought in the History of Ideas* series, eds. F. W. Strothmann and F. W. Locke (New York: Ungar, 1959), 7–12, 17–22, 34–41, 60–65, 85–87. Reprinted by permission of the publisher.

John Florio in 1603) became standard reading for anyone with pretensions to wit and learning. The following selection is from *In Defense of Raymond Sebond,* a long essay in which Montaigne presents his skeptical views on religious controversy and on man's aspiration to power, virtue, and wisdom.

Consider if it is not by our hands that we shape religion, drawing as from wax so many contrary figures from a rule so straight and so firm. When has that been more evident than in France nowadays? Those who have seized it on the left hand, those who have seized it on the right, those who use black to portray it and those who use white, employ religion in such a similar way in their violent and ambitious enterprises, behave according to a pattern so identical in excess and injustice, that they render doubtful and hard to believe the contradictory opinions which they claim to hold concerning the thing on which depend the conduct and principle of our life. Can one see come out of the same school and the same doctrine ways of acting more uniform, more completely identical?

. . .

Let us confess the truth: were one to sift out of the army, even the average legitimate army, those who participate in it solely through the zeal of a religious devotion, and also those who are concerned only with the protection of the laws of their country or the service of the prince, one would not be able to form with them a complete company of soldiers. Whence comes it that there are so few who have maintained a uniform will and effort in our public disturbances and that we see them sometimes advance at a walk, sometimes gallop at top speed, and the same men sometimes harm our cause by their violence and harshness, sometimes by their lack of zeal, their softness, and their slowness, unless it be that they are moved by personal and casual considerations according to the varying nature of which they bestir themselves?

This I see clearly, that we readily give to religion only the services which flatter our passions. There is no hostility so fine as Christian hostility. Our zeal does marvels when it supports our inclination toward hatred, cruelty, ambition, avarice, slander, rebellion. On the contrary, toward kindness, gentleness, temperance, unless by a miracle some rare quirk of character drives it in that direction, it neither runs nor flies.

Our religion is made to root out vices; we use it to cover them, feed them, encourage them.

One must not offer God straw instead of grain (as the popular saying goes). If we believed in him, I do not say through faith, but with a simple belief, indeed (and I say it to our great confusion) if we believed in him and knew him as we might some other matter, as we might know one of our companions, we should love him above all other things for the infinite goodness and beauty which shine in him; at least he would occupy in our affection the same rank as wealth, pleasures, glory, and our friends.

The best of us does not fear to offend him as he fears offending his neighbor, his relative, his master. Is there a mind so simple that, having on the one side the object of one of our vicious pleasures, and on the other, equally clearly known and understood, the state of an immortal glory, it would give the latter in exchange for the former? And yet we often renounce that glory out of pure disdain: for what desire attracts us to blasphemy unless by chance the very desire to offend?

CONVICTIONS ARE WEAK
IF EXTERNAL EVENTS ALTER THEM

The philosopher Antisthenes, as he was being initiated into the Orphic mysteries, was told by the priest that those who devoted themselves to that religion were destined to receive after their death eternal and perfect gifts. "Why, then, don't you die yourself?" he asked the priest. Diogenes, more abruptly according to his manner, and on a somewhat different subject, said to the priest who was exhorting him similarly to join his order so that he might attain the blessings of the next world: "Don't you want me to believe that Agesilaus and Epaminondas, such great men, will be wretched, and that you, who are only a fool, will be blessed because you are a priest?"

If we received with the same authority as a philosophical discourse these great promises of eternal blessedness, we should no longer view death with the horror in which we now hold it.

> No longer would the dying man lament
> His dissolution, but he would rejoice
> To leave the body as the snake is freed
> Of its worn skin, or as the stag grown old
> Lets fall at last its horns now overlong.
> [Lucretius III, 613]

I wish to be dissolved, we should say, and to be with Jesus Christ. The force of Plato's teaching concerning the immortality of the soul encouraged indeed some of his disciples to seek death in order to enjoy more promptly the hopes which he gave them.

All that is a very obvious sign that we receive our religion only in our way, and by our hands, and not otherwise than other religions are received. We happened to be in the region where it was observed; or we esteem its antiquity or the authority of the men who have taught it; or we fear the threats which it directs against unbelievers; or we are drawn by its promises. Those considerations must be employed for our belief, but as secondary supports: they are based on human ties. A different region, other witnesses, similar promises and threats, might impress upon us in the same way a contrary belief. We are Christians for the same reason that we are either Perigordians or Germans.

As for what Plato says, that there are few men so firm in atheism that a pressing danger does not bring them back to the recognition of divine power, such an influence does not touch a true Christian. It is only for mortal and human religions to be received or rejected according to the situation in which we find ourselves. What faith must that be which cowardice and weakness of heart implant and nourish within us? A strange faith which believes what it believes only because it does not have the courage not to believe it! Can a vicious passion such as weakness and terror produce within our soul anything which is well ordered?

Atheists establish, says Plato, by the authority of their judgment, that what is related about hell and future torments is false. But, since the opportunity to test it presents itself when old age or illnesses bring them close to their death, the terror which these inspire fills them then with a new belief through the horror of the condition which is approaching for them. And, because such impressions make hearts fearful, he forbids in his laws any teachings about these menaces, and the belief that from the gods there can come to man any harm unless for his greater good, when the case does present itself, and for a salutary effect. They tell of Bion that, corrupted by the atheistic teachings of Theodorus, he had long been wont to make sport of religious men; but when death came suddenly upon him he gave himself over to the most extreme superstitions, as if the gods absented themselves and came back according to Bion's situation.

Plato and these examples tend to conclude that we are brought back to belief in God either by love or by force. Atheism being, so to speak, a doctrine unnatural and monstrous, difficult also and troublesome to establish in the human mind, however insolent and disordered that mind may be, one has seen a rather large number of persons, out of vanity and out of pride in imagining uncommon opinions which aim at reforming the world, affect the profession of atheism as a pose; these persons, if they are foolish enough, are not strong enough, however, to have established it firmly in their conscience. They will not fail to raise clasped hands toward heaven if you give them a good sword-thrust in the chest. And, when fear or illness will have got the better of that licentious fervor of fickle mood, they will not fail to turn about quite discreetly and conform to public beliefs and practices. A seriously digested dogma is one thing; these superficial impressions which, born of the idleness of an unbalanced mind, go swimming rashly and uncertainly in fantasy are another. Men so wretched and scatterbrained, who try to be worse than they can!

          .   .   .

Let us then consider for the moment man alone, without outside help, armed only with his own weapons, and stripped of grace and divine understanding, which are all his honor, his strength, and the foundation of his being. Let us see what kind of figure he cuts in such a fine array. Let him make me understand by the effort of his reason upon what foundations he has built those great advantages which he thinks he has over all other creatures. What has convinced him that this admirable motion of the vault of heaven, the eternal light of those torches revolving so proudly above his head, the awe-inspiring movements of that infinite sea, were established and have continued for so many centuries for his convenience and in order to serve him? Is it possible to imagine anything so ridiculous as that wretched and puny creature, who is not even master of himself, exposed to offenses from all things, and who yet proclaims himself master and emperor of the universe, concerning which it is not within his power to know the slightest part, let alone govern it? And this privilege that he attributes to himself of being alone in this great creation in having the capacity to recognize its beauty and understand its structure, in being able to give thanks to the architect and to note the balance of income and outlay of the world—who placed the seal upon this privilege accorded him? Let him show us the patent of this fine and great prerogative.

Was it granted in favor of the wise only? It concerns few people, then. Are the foolish and wicked worthy of such an extraordinary favor, and they who are the worst part of creation, should they be given a privileged position above all the rest?

Shall we believe on this score him who says: "For whom then shall we say that the world was made? Doubtless for animate beings who have the use of reason. These are gods and men, to whom surely nothing is superior." [Cicero, *De natura deorum* II, 53] It is impossible ever to ridicule sufficiently the impudence of thus associating gods and men.

But, puny creature that he is, what has man in himself worthy of such a privileged position? Considering the incorruptible life of the heavenly bodies, their beauty, their greatness, their movement continued according to so precise a rule:

> When we lift up our eyes to the celestial vaults
> Of this great universe, and toward the heaven set
> With shining stars, and when we call to mind the course
> Of moon and sun;
>
> [Lucretius V, 1205]

considering, too, the domination and power which those bodies have not only over our lives and the conditions of our fortune,

> For he has made the deeds and lives of men
> Dependent on the stars,
>
> [Manilius III, 58]

but over our very inclinations, our reasonings, our wills which they govern, drive and stir at the mercy of their influences, as our reason teaches us and reveals,

> For reason recognizes that those stars we see
> So distant from us, govern men by hidden laws;

> That movements of the universe entire are ruled
> By periodic causes, and the turns of fate
> Revealed by certain signs;
>
> [Manilius I, 60]

seeing that not a single man, not a king, escapes their influence,
but that monarchies, empires, and this whole world here below
move in accord with the slightest tremor of the celestial movements,

> How great are the effects the slightest motion brings:
> So mighty is that power which governs even kings!
> [Manilius I, 55 and IV, 93]

if our virtue, our vices, our competence and learning, and this very
conclusion which we draw concerning the power of the stars, and
this comparison of them with ourselves, if all that comes, as our
reason judges, by their means and their favor,

> One, mad with love,
> Is doomed to cross the sea and Troy town overthrow;
> Another's fated to draw up a nation's laws;
> Here children slay their parents, and parents slay their
> sons;
> And armed against his brother, one fights in cruel affray.
> This war's not of our doing; fate wills these agitations,
> And makes them hurt themselves, slashing each other's
> limbs.
> And fate wills too that I should thus discourse of fate;
> [Manilius IV, 79 and 118]

if we owe to heaven's distribution this share of reason which we
possess, how can it make us heaven's equal? How can its essence
and its conditions be subject to our learning? Everything which we
see in those bodies awes us. "What was the effort, what were the
instruments, the levers, the machines, the workers who erected so
vast an edifice?" [Cicero, *De natura deorum* I, 8] Why do we consider
them without soul, and life, and reason? Have we recognized in
them some heavy and unfeeling stupidity, we whose only relationship to them is one of obedience? Shall we say that we have seen
in no other creature but man the employment of a reasoning soul?
What then! Have we seen anything similar to the sun? Must we say
that it does not exist because we have never seen anything like it?
And that its movements do not exist because they are without parallel? If what we have not observed does not exist, our learning is

wonderfully restricted: "How narrow are the limits of our mind!" [Cicero, *De natura deorum* I, 31] Is it not a dream of human vanity to make of the moon a celestial earth, to imagine on it mountains and valleys as Anaxagoras did, to set up there human habitations and abodes, and to establish there colonies for our convenience as Plato and Plutarch do, and of our earth to make a light-giving and luminous star? "Among other infirmities of human nature is this blindness of the mind which not only forces it to err, but which makes it love its errors." [Seneca, *De ira* II, 10] "The corruptible body weighs down the soul, and its earthly covering oppresses it even in the exercise of thought." [St. Augustine, *City of God* XII, 15, citing *Book of Wisdom*]

MAN'S SUPERIORITY OVER ANIMALS
A DELUSION BASED ON PRIDE

Presumption is our natural and original malady. The most calamitous and fragile of all creatures is man, and at the same time the proudest. He sees and feels himself placed here in the mire and dung of the world, attached and fixed in the worst, most lifeless, and most corrupt part of the universe, on the meanest floor of the house and the farthest removed from the vault of heaven, with animals of the worst condition of the three; and he goes installing himself in his imagination above the circle of the moon and bringing the heavens beneath his feet. It is by the vanity of this same imagination that he makes himself God's equal, that he ascribes to himself divine attributes, that he winnows himself and separates himself from the mass of other creatures, determines the share allowed the animals, his colleagues and companions, and distributes to them such elements of faculties and powers as seem good to him. How does he know, by the effort of his intelligence, what inwardly and secretly moves animals? By what comparison of them with ourselves does he deduce the stupidity which he attributes to them?

When I play with my cat, who knows whether she is not making me her pastime more than I make her mine? Plato, in depicting the golden age under Saturn, counts among the principal advantages of the man of those days the ability he had to communicate with the animals, for questioning them and learning from them, he knew the real qualities of each; in that way he acquired a quite perfect understanding and wisdom, and in consequence conducted his life far more happily than we can do. Do we need a better proof to judge human presumption concerning animals? That great author gave it as his opinion that so far as the corporal form which nature gave them is concerned, she had regard, in the main, only for the prognostications which one was accustomed to draw from them in his day.

· · ·

But, to return to my subject, we have as part of our lot inconstancy, irresolution, incertitude, mourning, superstition, concern about things to come (even after our life), ambition, avarice, jealousy, envy, appetites which are lawless, frenzied, and uncontrollable, war, falsehood, disloyalty, slander, and curiosity. Certainly we have paid strangely and dearly for that fine reason in which we glory, and that capacity to judge and know, if we have bought them at the price of this infinite number of passions to which we are a constant prey. That is, unless it still pleases us to insist, as Socrates does indeed, upon that notable prerogative over the other animals which we enjoy in that nature, whereas she has prescribed for them certain seasons and limits to sexual pleasure, has given us a free rein at all times and under all circumstances.

> "As wine is rarely good for invalids and is also most often harmful to them, so it is better not to give them any at all than to expose them to a manifest harm in the hope of a problematical advantage; so, perhaps, it would be better for mankind had nature refused us that activity of thought, that penetration, that industry which we call reason and which she has so liberally accorded us, since that activity is healthful to only a small number and fatal to all others."
>
> [Cicero, *De natura deorum* III, 27]

Of what profit can we consider that understanding of so many things to have been to Varro and Aristotle? Did it free them from the annoyances of human life? Were they spared the accidents which beset a common porter? Did they draw from logic some consolation for the gout? Because they knew how that humor settles in the joints, did they suffer any less from it? Were they reconciled with death for knowing that some nations rejoice at it, and with cuckoldry for knowing that in some regions wives are held in common? On the contrary, having held the highest rank for knowledge, one among the Romans and the other among the Greeks, and in the age when learning flourished most, we have not, however, learned that they had any special excellence in their lives; indeed the Greek is rather hard put to it to clear his name of certain note-worthy stains.

Has it been found that pleasure and health are more keenly en-joyed by one who knows astrology and grammar . . . and that shame and poverty are less a burden?

> Illness and weakness you will doubtless thus escape,
> And will be spared both grief and cares; a longer life
> And better fate will then be granted you.
>
> [Juvenal XIV, 156]

I have in my day seen a hundred artisans, a hundred peasants, wiser and happier than university rectors, and whom I should prefer to resemble. Scholarship, so I believe, has a place among the things necessary for life, like honor, nobility, dignity, or at most like beauty, wealth, and such other qualities which really contribute to it, but from afar, and somewhat more through imagination than by their essential value.

We need scarcely more services, rules, and laws of living, in our society, than cranes and ants do in theirs. And yet we see that they behave in a very well-ordered way without erudition. If man were wise, he would attribute to each thing its proper worth according as it was most useful and fitting for his life.

VIRTUE IS BORN OF HUMILITY AND SUBMISSION

Were one to judge us by our actions and excesses, there would be found a greater number of excellent men among the ignorant than among the learned, and I affirm it for every sort of virtue. Old Rome seems to me to have indeed borne men of greater worth, both for peace and for war, than that learned Rome which brought about its own ruin. Though in all other respects they might be equal, at least honesty and innocence would remain on the side of old Rome, for these qualities dwell singularly well with simplicity.

But I leave aside this reasoning, which would draw me farther than I should care to go. I shall merely reaffirm that it is only hu-mility and submission which can produce a worthy man. One must not leave to the judgment of each person the recognition of his duty; it must be prescribed for him, not left for him to choose by the light of his own reason. Otherwise, according to the foolishness and infinite variety of our reasonings and opinions, we should end up by creating for ourselves duties which would result in our eating one another, as Epicurus says. The first law which God ever gave man was a law of pure obedience; it was a command, pure and simple, in which man had nothing to understand or discuss—appropriately so, since obedience is the principal function of a reasonable soul, recognizing a celestial superior and benefactor. From obedience and submission are born all other virtues, as from presumption is born all sin. And, on the other hand, the first temptation which came to human nature from the devil, his first poison, slyly entered our being through the promises which he gave us of understanding and knowledge: "Ye shall be as gods, knowing good and evil." [*Genesis* III, 5] And, in Homer, the sirens, to lure Ulysses and draw him into their dangerous and ruinous snares, offered him knowledge as a gift. The scourge of man is his claim to knowledge. That is why ignorance is so recommended to us by our religion as essential to belief and obedience. "Beware lest any man spoil you through philosophy and vain deceit, after . . . the rudiments of the world." [*Colossians* II, 8]

PRESUMPTION LEADS TO VAIN BOASTING ABOUT MAN'S STATE AND POWERS

There is general agreement among all the philosophers of all schools that the sovereign good consists in tranquility of soul and body. But where do we find it?

> In short, the sage sees none above him save great Jove;
> For he is handsome, honored, rich, and free—indeed,
> The very king of kings; but most of all he knows
> Good health—unless he be afflicted with a cold.
>
> [Horace, *Epistles* I, i, 106]

It seems indeed that nature, to console us for our wretched and puny state, has bestowed on us only presumption. That is what Epictetus says—that man has nothing peculiarly his own except the use he makes of his opinions. We have received as our portion only wind and smoke. The gods possess health as part of their essence, says philosophy, and illness only in imagination; man, on the contrary, possesses his gifts only in fancy, and his woes are part of his essence. We have been right to insist upon the powers of our imagination, for all our blessings are only fanciful. Just hear the boastings of this poor and calamity-stricken animal. "There is nothing," says Cicero [*Tusculan Disputations* V, 36 and I, 26], "so pleasant as the pursuit of letters, those letters, I say, by means of which the infinity of things, the immense greatness of nature, the very skies of this world, and the lands and seas are revealed to us; it is they which have taught us religion, moderation, greatness, and courage, and which have snatched our soul away from darkness to show it all things, the lofty and the low, the first and the last, and what lies in between; it is they which furnish us what is necessary to live well and happily, and guide us to spend our life without displeasure and harm." Does he not seem to be speaking of the condition of the eternal and almighty God?

And so far as practice is concerned, a thousand unimportant women led in their village a life more equable, more pleasant, and more consistent than was his.

> A god he was, indeed a very god, who found,
> O noble Memmius, that rule of life which now
> We call Philosophy, and by his wit and skill
> Gave life a firm foundation, quite secure from storms
> And such great darkness, and who brought it forth at last
> Into such great tranquility and such clear light.
> [Lucretius V, 8]

These are quite magnificent and beautiful words; but a very slight accident reduced the understanding of their author to a worse state than that of the meanest peasant, in spite of the teachings of that guiding god and that divine wisdom. Of similar impudence is this promise of the book of Democritus: "I am going to talk to you about all things" [Cicero, *Academica* II, 23]; and this stupid title which Aristotle bestows on us, calling us "mortal gods"; and the judgment of Chrysippus, that Dion was as virtuous as God. And my Seneca recognized, he says, that God had given him life, but that he himself was responsible for living well; this is in keeping with another dictum: "With reason do we pride ourselves upon our virtue, which would not be the case if we held it as a gift from God, and not through our own efforts." [Cicero, *De natura deorum* III, 36] This is also from Seneca: that the wise man has fortitude comparable to God's, but in the midst of human weakness; and for that reason he surpasses God. There is nothing so ordinary as to encounter remarks of such rashness. There is none of us who takes such offense at seeing himself exalted to the level of God as he does at seeing himself pushed back to the level of the other animals: so much more jealous are we of our own interest than of our creator's.

But we must trample down that foolish vanity, and sharply and boldly overthrow the ridiculous foundations on which these false opinions are built. So long as he thinks he has some freedom of action and some power in himself, man will never recognize what he owes to his master; he will always count his chickens before they are hatched, as they say; he must be stripped of all but his shirt.

Let us see a few noteworthy examples of the effect of this philosophy.

Posidonius, being afflicted with such a painful illness that it made him wring his hands and gnash his teeth, thought that he was defying pain by crying out to it: "It does you no good to rack me, if I do not admit that you are hurting me." He feels the same emotions as my servant, but he boasts because he at least holds his tongue according to the laws of his philosophic school. "It was not proper to be boastful in speech, but to yield in fact." [Cicero, *Tusculan Disputations* II, 13]

Arcesilaus was ill with the gout; Carneades, having come to visit him and going away deeply afflicted, Arcesilaus called him back and, pointing first to his feet and then his chest: "What bothers me there," he said to him, "has not affected me here." He has somewhat better grace, for he recognizes that he is suffering and would like to be rid of his infirmity; but his heart, however, has not been overwhelmed and weakened by it. The other maintains his inflexibility, more verbal, in my opinion, than real. And Dionysius of Heraclea, afflicted with a great burning sensation in his eyes, was induced thereby to abandon these Stoic resolves.

IGNORANCE AIDS MORE THAN KNOWLEDGE IN ENDURING MISFORTUNES

But even though learning should achieve what they say, blunting and reducing the bitterness of the misfortunes which pursue us, what does it do that in a more direct and more obvious way ignorance doesn't do? The philosopher Pyrrho, undergoing at sea the hazard of a great storm, presented to those who were with him, as

an example to imitate, only the security of a pig that was traveling with them and that looked out on the storm without fright.
Philosophy, finding its precepts useless, refers us to the example of
an athlete and a mule-driver, in whom one sees ordinarily much
less fear of death, of pain, and of other troubles, and more steadfastness than learning ever furnished to anyone who wasn't born
to it and prepared for it himself by natural habit. What brings it
about that one makes an incision and cuts the tender members of
a child more readily than ours, unless it is ignorance? And what
about those of a horse? How many have been made ill by the mere
force of imagination? We customarily see people bled, purged, and
doctored in order to cure ills which they feel only in their minds.
When we lack real ills, our learning lends us its own. This color
and complexion indicate that you will have some catarrhal discharge; this hot season threatens you with a feverish disturbance;
this break in the life line of your left hand warns you of some important illness about to come. And finally imagination turns de-
structively upon good health itself. That animation and vigor of
youth cannot remain stable; we must remove some of their blood
and strength lest they turn against you. Compare the life of a man
subjected to such imaginations with that of a peasant letting himself go according to his natural inclination, measuring things only
by the way he feels at the moment, without science, and without
foreseeing woes to come, who has illness only when it actually
strikes him. In contrast, the other one often has the stone in his
mind before he has it in his kidneys; as if it were not soon enough
to suffer illness when it is at hand, he anticipates it in imagination,
and hastens to meet it.

. . .

When we say that the infinite number of centuries, both past and
future, are to God only an instant; that his goodness, wisdom,
power are one with his essence, our words declare it, but our intelligence does not understand it. And yet our presumption wishes to
sift the divine through our sieve. And from that are born all the
fanciful ideas and errors which this world has seized upon, bringing to its balance and weighing therein something so remote from
its measure. "It is a marvel how far the arrogance of the human
heart goes, encouraged by the slightest success." [Pliny, II, 23]
May it please nature one day to open her bosom and to reveal

to us as they are the means and operation of its movements, and to prepare our eyes for that revelation! O God! What errors, what misconceptions we should find in our poor science! I am mistaken if science has grasped a single thing correctly; and I shall leave here ignorant of everything except my ignorance.

THE TEACHINGS OF PHILOSOPHY
ARE MERE POETIC SPECULATIONS

Have I not read in Plato this divine remark, that nature is nothing but an enigmatic poem? As perhaps one might say a veiled and obscure painting, gleaming with an infinite variety of reflections to invite our conjectures. "All those things are enveloped and hidden in thick darkness, and there is nothing in the human mind sharp enough to penetrate to heaven and to probe into the depths of the earth." [Cicero, *Academica* II, 39]

And certainly philosophy is only a sophisticated poetry. Where do those ancient authors draw all their authorities if not from poets? And the first philosophers were poets themselves and treated philosophy in their art. Plato is only a poet writing in a loose, disconnected style. Timon calls him, as an insult, a great forger of miracles.

Just as women use ivory teeth to replace their own that are missing and, instead of their real complexion, make a false one of foreign matter; as they pad their thighs with cloth and felt, and their busts with cotton, and obviously and to everyone's knowledge embellish themselves with a false and borrowed beauty, so too does science (and even our jurisprudence has, they say, legal fictions upon which it founds the truth of its justice).

Our science offers us as an explanation, and as underlying principles of the universe, things that she herself informs us were the product of human imagination. Those epicycles, eccentrics, and concentrics which astrology uses to explain the movement of its stars, it gives them to us as the best it has been able to invent on this subject. Similarly, moreover, philosophy presents to us not what is, or what it believes, but the most pleasant and imposing of its inventions. Plato, speaking of his discussion of the state of our body and that of beasts, declares: "That what we have said is true, we should affirm it if we had on that point the confirmation of an oracle; we can only declare that it has the greatest appearance of truth of what we could say.". . .

I am grateful to the woman of Miletus who, seeing the philosopher Thales occupy himself continually in contemplation of the celestial vault and always keep his eyes turned heavenward, placed something in his way to make him stumble, in order to warn him that it would be time to amuse his thought with things that were in the clouds when he had taken care of those which were at his feet. She surely gave him good advice in advising him to look to himself rather than to heaven. For, as Cicero has Democritus say,

> What lies before his feet, no man regards;
> His eyes explore the vaulted arch of heaven.
> [Cicero, *De divinatione* II, 13]

But our condition makes the knowledge of what we have within our hands as remote from us, and as far above the clouds, as knowledge of the stars. As Socrates says in Plato, to whomever dabbles in philosophy one can reproach what that woman reproached Thales with, that he sees nothing of what is before him. For every philosopher is ignorant of what his neighbor does, yes, and of what he does himself, and of what they both are, whether beasts or men.

OUR OWN BEING IS BEYOND OUR UNDERSTANDING

Those people who consider Sebond's arguments too weak, who are ignorant of nothing, who govern the universe, who know everything,

> What causes rule the sea; what regulates the seasons;
> If stars move at their own free will or by command;
> What veils in darkness the moon's orb, and what reveals
>   it;
> What is the will and power in nature's complex plan
> Which joins in perfect harmony discordant things;
> [Horace, *Epistles* I, xii, 16]

have they not sometimes probed, amid their books, the difficulties which stand in the way of their knowing their own being? We see indeed that the finger moves and that the foot moves; that some parts move by themselves, without our leave, and that our will controls others; that a certain fear makes us flush, and a certain other turn pale; this notion affects our spleen only, and that one our brain; one makes us laugh, and another weep; a certain other chills us and paralyzes all our senses, and stops the movement of our limbs. At a certain sight, our stomach rises; at a certain other, some lower part. But how a spiritual impression produces such an effect in a massive and solid subject, and the nature of the linking and union of these admirable mechanisms, never has man known that. "All these things are impenetrable to human reason and hidden in the majesty of nature," says Pliny [*Natural History* II, 37]; and St. Augustine declares: "The manner in which the spirit is united with the body is completely marvelous, nor can it be understood by man; yet that union is man himself." [*City of God* XXXI, x] Such considerations, however, do not arouse men's doubts, for their opinions are received according to ancient beliefs, with authority and credit, as if they were religion and law. One accepts, as by rote, what is commonly held; one accepts this truth with all its structure and appendages of arguments and proofs, as a firm and solid whole which one no longer shakes, which one no longer judges. On the contrary, each vies with the others in plastering and fortifying this accepted belief with all that his reason can add—and the reason is an adaptable instrument, which can be made to serve any form. Thus the world is full of, and steeped in, inanities and falsehood.

THE MOST LOGICALLY CONSTRUCTED SYSTEMS ARE BASED ON UNCERTAIN PRINCIPLES

The reason that people rarely doubt things is that they never test common ideas; they don't probe their foundations, where the fault and weakness lie; they debate only about subordinate matters; they don't ask if that is true, but if it was understood in this way or in that. They don't ask if Galen said anything worthwhile, but if this is what he said, or something else. Really it was right that this check-rein on the liberty of our judgments, and this tyranny over our beliefs, should extend to the schools and the arts. The god of scholastic learning is Aristotle; it is sacrilegious to debate his laws as it was those of Lycurgus at Sparta. His doctrine serves as magisterial law, though it may by chance be as false as any other. I don't know why I shouldn't accept as readily either the ideas of Plato, or the Atoms of Epicurus, or the Plenum and the Void of Leucippus and Democritus, or the Water of Thales, or the Infinity of Nature of Anaximander, or the Air of Diogenes, or the Numbers and Symmetry of Pythagoras, or the Infinite of Parmenides, or the One of Musaeus, or the Water and Fire of Apollodorus, or the Simi-

lar Parts of Anaxagoras, or the Discord and Harmony of Empedocles, or the Fire of Heraclitus, or any other opinion of that infinite
confusion of ideas and maxims which this fine human reason produces by its certitude and clearsightedness in everything it dabbles
in, as I should accept the opinion of Aristotle, on this subject of
the principles of natural things. He builds these principles out of
three elements: matter, form, and privation. And what is more vain
than to make emptiness itself a cause of the production of things?
Privation is a negative; by what strange whim could he have made
it the cause and origin of things which are? No one would dare disturb that belief, however, except as an exercise in logic. One de-
bates nothing in Aristotle's teaching in order to put it in doubt,
but only to defend the creator of the school against objections from
outside: his authority is the limit beyond which it is not permitted
to push any inquiry.

It is very easy, on accepted premises, to build anything you like,
for, according to the principle and organization of this beginning,
the rest of the pieces of the structure are easily put in place without
any contradiction among them. By following this route, we find our
argument well founded, and our reasoning rolls along easily, for
our masters seize and occupy in our minds in advance as much
ground as they need to conclude afterwards what they will, in the
manner of geometricians, with their concessions demanded beforehand, the consent and approval which we accord them permitting
them to lead us to left or right, and to spin us about at will. Whoever is believed in his presuppositions is our master and our god;
he will take for his foundations a base so broad and so easy that,
upon them, there will be no limit to the structure up which he can
take us. In this practice and manner of conducting learning, we
have taken at face value the statement by Pythagoras that each
expert must be believed in his field. The logician refers to the gram-
marian on the meaning of words; the rhetorician borrows from the
logician the structure of his arguments; the poet borrows rhythms
from the musician; the geometrician borrows proportions from the
arithmetician; the metaphysicians take as a foundation the conjectures of physics. For each field of learning has its presupposed principles by means of which human judgment is held in check from
all sides. If you happen to strike against this barrier in which lies
the principal error, they straightway declare that there is no arguing with those who deny the principles.

Now there can be no universally valid principles for men unless the divinity has revealed them to them; all the rest, the beginning, the middle, and the end, is only dream and smoke. Against those who argue by presupposition, you must, contrary to all reason, presuppose the very axiom which is the subject of debate. For any human presupposition and any declaration has as much authority as any other, unless the reason establishes a difference. Thus one must weigh them all, and first of all the general ones and those which exercise a tyranny over us.

. . .

Now out of the knowledge of this changeable nature of mine, I have by chance engendered within myself some constancy of opinions, and I have scarcely altered my early and natural ones. For, whatever plausibility there may be in new ideas, I do not change readily lest I have occasion to lose in so doing. And, since I am not capable of choosing, I take the choice of others and remain in the position where God placed me. Otherwise, I could not keep myself from rolling constantly. So, by God's grace, I have kept completely, without agitation and disturbance of my conscience, the old beliefs of our religion, in spite of all the sects and divisions which our century has produced. The writings of the ancients (I mean the good writings, substantial and solid) attract me and stir me almost as they wish; the one I am listening to seems to me always the strongest; I find that each in turn is right, even though they contradict one another. One must recognize that facility which great minds have to make whatever they wish seem plausible, and the fact that there is nothing so strange but they undertake to color it sufficiently to fool a simple nature such as mine; that shows obviously the weakness of their proof. The sky and the stars revolved for three thousand years; everyone had believed so until Cleanthes of Samos or, according to Theophrastus, Nicetas of Syracuse took it into his head to maintain that it was the earth which moved around the oblique circle of the Zodiac, spinning on its axis; and, in our day, Copernicus has so well established that doctrine that he uses it in a quite systematic way for all astronomical computations. What shall we draw from that, if not that we should not worry which of the two systems is true? And who knows that a third opinion, a thousand years from now, may not overthrow the two previous ones?

So rolling time affects the status of all things:
What once was held in high esteem, from honor falls;
Now something new prevails, emerging out of scorn—
Each day it's more desired, receives bouquets of praise,
And among men it holds a place of highest honor.

[Lucretius V, 1275]

DISTRUST OF NEW DOCTRINES

Thus when we encounter some new doctrine, we have good reason to distrust it, and to consider that before it was produced its contrary was in vogue; and as that earlier doctrine was overthrown by this one, there can well be born in the future a third discovery which will similarly upset the second one. Before the principles which Aristotle introduced were generally accepted, other principles satisfied the human reason as his satisfy us now. What warrant do his have, what special privilege, that the course of our seeking ends with them, and that to them belongs for all time dominion over our belief? They are no more exempt from being ousted than were the ideas which preceded them. When a new argument is urged upon me, it is up to me to consider that, where I cannot find a satisfactory answer, someone else will; for to believe all the appearances which we cannot explain away is to be a great simpleton. Such willingness to believe would lead the common throng of men (and we are all of the common throng) to have beliefs which spin about like a weathervane; for their soul, being soft and without resistance, would be forced to receive unceasingly new impressions one on top of the other, the latest always effacing the trace of the preceding one. He who feels weak must answer, as they do in the law courts, that he will seek advice on the matter, or rely upon those wiser men under whom he served his apprenticeship. How long has the art of medicine existed? They say that a newcomer, Paracelsus by name, is changing and overthrowing the whole order of ancient rules, and maintains that heretofore medicine has served only to kill men. I believe that he will easily verify that; but as for submitting my life to the test of his new experience, I think that would not be great wisdom.

One must not believe everyone, the saying goes, because everyone can say all manner of things.

Edmund Spenser

21

Amoretti AND *Prothalamion*

Edmund Spenser (*ca.* 1552–1599), one of the best and most representative poets of the late Renaissance, was educated at Cambridge, where he became acquainted with the group of Platonists who were the leading intellectuals at the university. As secretary to Lord Grey, Spenser accompanied him in the English campaigns to subdue Ireland. Spenser was rewarded with a modest estate in Ireland and there wrote much of his later work. Although well known and esteemed, especially for his long poem, *The Faerie Queene,* he never succeeded in gaining much material reward from his patrons.

Spenser's poetry is characteristic of the Renaissance in several respects. Elaborate in rhyme schemes and metrical patterns, it reveals in its imagery and themes a thorough knowledge of classical literature as well as respect for a moral code influenced by such gentlemanly ideals of love and honor as were advanced, for instance, in Castiglione's *Courtier.*

The selections presented here are from poems that reveal Spenser's ingenious skill in ornamenting conventional themes. The *Amoretti* (1595), a sequence of sonnets, show the influence of Renaissance sonneteers (from Petrarch on) who made of love an ethical and aesthetic ideal. The *Prothalamion* (1596) dignifies with its artistic conventions an actual occurrence. By elaborately classicizing the English scene, it refers allegorically to real people—the daughters of the Earl of Worcester, who are pictured sailing up the Thames to meet their bridegrooms at the London home of the Earl of Essex. "Great England's glory," as Spenser calls Essex, was one of the glamorous, unruly, and talented noblemen who gave drama and color to the Elizabethan Age.

Edmund Spenser, "Amoretti" and "Prothalamion," in *The Works of Edmund Spenser* (London: Routledge, 1896), 466–73.

AMORETTI

VIII

More than most fair, full of the living fire
Kindled above unto the Maker near;
No eyes but joys, in which all powers conspire
That to the world naught else be counted dear;
Through your bright beams doth not the blinded guest
Shoot out his darts to base affections wound;
But angels come to lead frail minds to rest
In chaste desires, on heavenly beauty bound.
You frame my thoughts, and fashion me within;
You stop my tongue, and teach my heart to speak;
You calm the storm that passion did begin,
Strong through your cause, but by your virtue weak.
  Dark is the world, where your light shined never;
  Well is he born that may behold you ever.

XXIV

Like as a ship, that through the ocean wide,
By conduct of some star doth make her way,
Whenas a storm hath dimmed her trusty guide,
Out of her course doth wander far astray;
So I, whose star, that wont with her bright ray
Me to direct, with clouds is overcast,
Do wander now, in darkness and dismay,
Through hidden perils round about me placed;
Yet hope I well that, when this storm is past,
My Helicë, the lodestar of my life,
Will shine again, and look on me at last,
With lovely light to clear my cloudy grief:
  Till then I wander careful, comfortless,
  In secret sorrow, and sad pensiveness.

LXX

Fresh Spring, the herald of love's mighty king,
In whose coat-armour richly are displayed

All sorts of flowers the which on earth do spring
In goodly colours gloriously arrayed;
Go to my love, where she is careless laid,
Yet in her winter's bower not well awake;
Tell her the joyous time will not be stayed,
Unless she do him by the forelock take;
Bid her therefore herself soon ready make
To wait on Love amongst his lovely crew;
Where everyone that misseth then her make
Shall be by him amerced with penance due.
    Make haste, therefore, sweet love, whilst it is prime;
    For none can call again the passed time.

LXXIX

Men call you fair, and you do credit it,
For that yourself ye daily such do see:
But the true fair, that is the gentle wit
And virtuous mind, is much more praised of me:
For all the rest, however fair it be,
Shall turn to nought and lose that glorious hue;
But only that is permanent and free
From frail corruption that doth flesh ensue.
That is true beauty; that doth argue you
To be divine, and born of heavenly seed;
Derived from that fair Spirit from whom all true
And perfect beauty did at first proceed:
    He only fair, and what he fair hath made;
    All other fair, like flowers, untimely fade.

PROTHALAMION

Calm was the day, and through the trembling air
Sweet breathing Zephyrus did softly play,
A gentle spirit, that lightly did delay
Hot Titan's beams, which then did glister fair;
When I (whom sullen care,
Through discontent of my long fruitless stay
In princes' court, and expectation vain
Of idle hopes, which still do fly away,

Like empty shadows, did afflict my brain)
Walked forth to ease my pain
Along the shore of silver streaming Thames;
Whose rutty bank, the which his river hems,
Was painted all with variable flowers,
And all the meads adorned with dainty gems
Fit to deck maidens' bowers,
And crown their paramours
Against the bridal day, which is not long:
　　Sweet Thames! run softly, till I end my song.

There, in a meadow, by the river's side,
A flock of nymphs I chanced to espy,
All lovely daughters of the flood thereby,
With goodly greenish locks, all loose untied,
As each had been a bride:
And each one had a little wicker basket,
Made of fine twigs, entrailed curiously,
In which they gathered flowers to fill their flasket,
And with fine fingers cropt full feateously
The tender stalks on high.
Of every sort, which in that meadow grew,
They gathered some; the violet, pallid blue,
The little daisy, that at evening closes,
The virgin lily, and the primrose true,
With store of vermeil roses,
To deck their bridegroom's posies
Against the bridal day, which was not long:
　　Sweet Thames! run softly, till I end my song.

With that I saw two swans of goodly hue
Come softly swimming down along the Lee;
Two fairer birds I yet did never see;
The snow, which doth the top of Pindus strew,
Did never whiter shew,
Nor Jove himself, when he a swan would be
For love of Leda, whiter did appear;
Yet Leda was, they say, as white as he,
Yet not so white as these, nor nothing near;
So purely white they were,
That even the gentle stream, the which them bare,

Seemed foul to them, and bade his billows spare
To wet their silken feathers, lest they might
Soil their fair plumes with water not so fair,
And mar their beauties bright,
That shone as heaven's light,
Against their bridal day, which was not long:
   Sweet Thames! run softly, till I end my song.

Eftsoons the nymphs, which now had flowers their fill,
Ran all in haste to see that silver brood,
As they came floating on the crystal flood;
Whom when they saw, they stood amazed still,
Their wondering eyes to fill;
Them seemed they never saw a sight so fair
Of fowls so lovely, that they sure did deem
Them heavenly born, or to be that same pair
Which through the sky draw Venus' silver team;
For sure they did not seem
To be begot of any earthly seed,
But rather angels, or of angels' breed;
Yet were they bred of summer's heat, they say,
In sweetest season, when each flower and weed
The earth did fresh array;
So fresh they seemed as day,
Even as their bridal day, which was not long:
   Sweet Thames! run softly, till I end my song.

Then forth they all out of their baskets drew
Great store of flowers, the honour of the field,
That to the sense did fragrant odours yield,
All which upon those goodly birds they threw
And all the waves did strew,
That like old Peneus' waters they did seem,
When down along by pleasant Tempe's shore,
Scattered with flowers, through Thessaly they stream,
That they appear, through lilies' plenteous store,
Like a bride's chamber floor.
Two of those nymphs meanwhile, two garlands bound
Of freshest flowers which in that mead they found,
The which presenting all in trim array,

Their snowy foreheads therewithal they crowned,
Whilst one did sing this lay,
Prepared against that day,
Against their bridal day, which was not long:
   Sweet Thames! run softly, till I end my song.

"Ye gentle birds! the world's fair ornament,
And heaven's glory whom this happy hour
Doth lead unto your lover's blissful bower,
Joy may you have, and gentle hearts' content
Of your love's couplement;
And let fair Venus, that is queen of love,
With her heart-quelling son upon you smile,
Whose smile, they say, hath virtue to remove
All love's dislike, and friendship's faulty guile
For ever to assoil;
Let endless peace your steadfast hearts accord,
And blessed plenty wait upon your board;
And let your bed with pleasures chaste abound,
That fruitful issue may to you afford,
Which may your foes confound,
And make your joys redound
Upon your bridal day, which is not long":
   Sweet Thames! run softly, till I end my song.

So ended she; and all the rest around
To her redoubled that her undersong,
Which said their bridal day should not be long;
And gentle Echo from the neighbour ground
Their accents did resound.
So forth those joyous birds did pass along,
Adown the Lee, that to them murmured low,
As he would speak, but that he lacked a tongue,
Yet did by signs his glad affection show,
Making his stream run slow.
And all the fowl which in his flood did dwell
Gan flock about these twain, that did excel
The rest, so far as Cynthia doth shend
The lesser stars. So they, enranged well,
Did on those two attend,

And their best service lend,
Against their wedding day, which was not long:
   Sweet Thames! run softly, till I end my song.

At length they all to merry London came,
To merry London, my most kindly nurse,
That to me gave this life's first native source,
Though from another place I take my name,
An house of ancient fame.
There when they came, whereas those bricky towers
The which on Thames' broad, aged back do ride,
Where now the studious lawyers have their bowers,
There whilom wont the Templar Knights to bide,
Till they decayed through pride;
Next whereunto there stands a stately place,
Where oft I gained gifts and goodly grace
Of that great lord which therein wont to dwell,
Whose want too well now feels my friendless case—
But ah! here fits not well
Old woes, but joys, to tell,
Against the bridal day, which is not long:
   Sweet Thames! run softly, till I end my song.

Yet therein now doth lodge a noble peer,
Great England's glory, and the world's wide wonder,
Whose dreadful name late through all Spain did thunder,
And Hercules' two pillars standing near
Did make to quake and fear.
Fair branch of honor, flower of chivalry,
That fillest England with thy triumph's fame,
Joy have thou of thy noble victory,
And endless happiness of thine own name,
That promiseth the same;
That through thy prowess and victorious arms
Thy country may be freed from foreign harms;
And great Eliza's glorious name may ring
Through all the world, filled with thy wide alarms,
Which some brave muse may sing
To ages following,
Upon the bridal day, which is not long:
   Sweet Thames! run softly, till I end my song.

From those high towers this noble lord issuing,
Like radiant Hesper, when his golden hair
In the ocean billows he hath bathed fair,
Descended to the river's open viewing,
With a great train ensuing.
Above the rest were goodly to be seen
Two gentle knights of lovely face and feature,
Beseeming well the bower of any queen,
With gifts of wit, and ornaments of nature,
Fit for so goodly stature,
That like the twins of Jove they seemed in sight,
Which deck the baldrick of the heavens bright.
They two, forth pacing to the river's side
Received those two fair brides, their love's delight;
Which, at the appointed tide,
Each one did make his bride,
Against their bridal day, which is not long:
  Sweet Thames! run softly, till I end my song.

Martin Luther

<hr>

22

<hr>

Address to the Christian Nobility
of the German Nation

Martin Luther (1483–1546) received training in law and theology at the
University of Erfurt. His career turned suddenly and dramatically toward religion, however, when he undertook a life of strict asceticism as
a monk of the Augustinian order. Luther was later sent to assist at the
new University of Wittenberg, where he lectured on the New Testament.
These theological studies led him to question certain doctrines of the
Church, and, on the matter of indulgences (an explosive issue at that
time), he challenged papal authority with his famous *Ninety-Five Theses*
(1517). Luther's criticism soon broadened to a general attack, stemming
from his belief that the papacy of his day, far from being a God-ordained
institution, was actually a creation of men interested in perpetuating their
own power. Believing that the civil authority had the right and obligation to correct erroneous religious beliefs and practices, Luther appealed
to the German ruling class to expel the "foreign tyranny of the papacy,"
as he termed it. Under the protection of the rulers of the north German
principalities, whose motives were nationalistic and economic as well as
religious, Luther's brand of Protestantism flourished.

The *Address to the Christian Nobility of the German Nation* (1520)
shows Luther at the height of his energies. As the central work in his attack upon the papacy, it contains (in addition to forthright denunciations of Catholic theory and practice) such fundamental points of Lu-
theran doctrine as the priesthood of all believers and the supreme authority of the Scriptures. Its vigorous language, intensely nationalistic
spirit, and fervent denunciations of the papacy appealed to many people.
In their opinion, the *Address,* signaling the complete and irreparable

Martin Luther, *Address to the Christian Nobility of the German Nation Respecting the Reformation of the Christian Estate,* in *Luther's Primary Works,*
ed. Henry Wace and C. A. Buchheim (London: Hodder and Stoughton, 1896),
161–80.

break with Rome, was of vital importance to the success of Lutheranism
—the first major branch of Protestantism to develop during the Reformation.

---

*To His Most Serene and Mighty Imperial Majesty
and to the Christian Nobility
of the German Nation.*

DR. MARTINUS LUTHER

The grace and might of God be with you, Most Serene Majesty,
most gracious, well-beloved gentlemen!

It is not out of mere arrogance and perversity that I, an individual poor man, have taken upon me to address your lordships. The
distress and misery that oppress all the Christian estates, more especially in Germany, have led not only myself, but every one else, to
cry aloud and to ask for help, and have now forced me too to cry
out and to ask if God would give His Spirit to any one to reach
a hand to His wretched people. Councils have often put forward
some remedy, but it has adroitly been frustrated, and the evils have
become worse, through the cunning of certain men. Their malice
and wickedness I will now, by the help of God, expose, so that, being known, they may henceforth cease to be so obstructive and injurious. God has given us a young and noble sovereign, and by this
has roused great hopes in many hearts; now it is right that we too
should do what we can, and make good use of time and grace.

The first thing that we must do is to consider the matter with
great earnestness, and, whatever we attempt, not to trust in our
own strength and wisdom alone, even if the power of all the world
were ours; for God will not endure that a good work should be begun trusting to our own strength and wisdom. He destroys it; it is
all useless, as we read in Psalm xxxiii., "There is no king saved by
the multitude of a host; a mighty man is not delivered by much
strength." And I fear it is for that reason that those beloved princes
the Emperors Frederick, the First and the Second, and many other
German emperors were, in former times, so piteously spurned and
oppressed by the popes, though they were feared by all the world.
Perchance they trusted rather in their own strength than in God;

therefore they could not but fall; and how would the sanguinary tyrant Julius II. have risen so high in our own days but that, I fear, France, Germany, and Venice trusted to themselves? The children of Benjamin slew forty-two thousand Israelites, for this reason: that these trusted to their own strength (Judges xx., etc.).

That such a thing may not happen to us and to our noble Emperor Charles, we must remember that in this matter we wrestle not against flesh and blood, but against the rulers of the darkness of this world (Eph. vi. 12), who may fill the world with war and bloodshed, but cannot themselves be overcome thereby. We must renounce all confidence in our natural strength, and take the matter in hand with humble trust in God; we must seek God's help with earnest prayer, and have nothing before our eyes but the misery and wretchedness of Christendom, irrespective of what punishment the wicked may deserve. If we do not act thus, we may begin the game with great pomp; but when we are well in it, the spirit of evil will make such confusion that the whole world will be immersed in blood, and yet nothing be done. Therefore let us act in the fear of God and prudently. The greater the might of the foe, the greater is the misfortune, if we do not act in the fear of God and with humility. If popes and Romanists have hitherto, with the devil's help, thrown kings into confusion, they may still do so, if we attempt things with our own strength and skill, without God's help.

THE THREE WALLS OF THE ROMANISTS

The Romanists have, with great adroitness, drawn three walls round themselves, with which they have hitherto protected themselves, so that no one could reform them, whereby all Christendom has fallen terribly.

Firstly, if pressed by the temporal power, they have affirmed and maintained that the temporal power has no jurisdiction over them, but, on the contrary, that the spiritual power is above the temporal.

Secondly, if it were proposed to admonish them with the Scriptures, they objected that no one may interpret the Scriptures but the Pope.

Thirdly, if they are threatened with a council, they pretend that no one may call a council but the Pope.

Thus they have secretly stolen our three rods, so that they may be unpunished, and intrenched themselves behind these three walls, to act with all the wickedness and malice, which we now witness. And whenever they have been compelled to call a council, they have made it of no avail by binding the princes beforehand with an oath to leave them as they were, and to give moreover to the Pope full power over the procedure of the council, so that it is all one whether we have many councils or no councils, in addition to which they deceive us with false pretences and tricks. So grievously do they tremble for their skin before a true, free council; and thus they have overawed kings and princes, that these believe they would be offending God, if they were not to obey them in all such knavish, deceitful artifices.

Now may God help us, and give us one of those trumpets that overthrew the walls of Jericho, so that we may blow down these walls of straw and paper, and that we may set free our Christian rods for the chastisement of sin, and expose the craft and deceit of the devil, so that we may amend ourselves by punishment and again obtain God's favour.

THE FIRST WALL
That the Temporal Power Has No Jurisdiction over the Spirituality

Let us, in the first place, attack the first wall.

It has been devised that the Pope, bishops, priests, and monks are called the *spiritual estate,* princes, lords, artificers, and peasants are the *temporal estate.* This is an artful lie and hypocritical device, but let no one be made afraid by it, and that for this reason: that all Christians are truly of the spiritual estate, and there is no difference among them, save of office alone. As St. Paul says (1 Cor. xii.), we are all one body, though each member does its own work, to serve the others. This is because we have one baptism, one Gospel, one faith, and are all Christians alike; for baptism, Gospel, and faith, these alone make spiritual and Christian people.

As for the unction by a pope or a bishop, tonsure, ordination, consecration, and clothes differing from those of laymen—all this may make a hypocrite or an anointed puppet, but never a Christian or a spiritual man. Thus we are all consecrated as priests by baptism, as St. Peter says: "Ye are a royal priesthood, a holy nation" (1 Peter ii. 9); and in the book of Revelations: "and hast made us unto our God (by Thy blood) kings and priests" (Rev. v.

10). For, if we had not a higher consecration in us than pope or bishop can give, no priest could ever be made by the consecration of pope or bishop, nor could he say the mass, or preach, or absolve. Therefore the bishop's consecration is just as if in the name of the whole congregation he took one person out of the community, each member of which has equal power, and commanded him to exercise this power for the rest; in the same way as if ten brothers, co-heirs as king's sons, were to choose one from among them to rule over their inheritance, they would all of them still remain kings and have equal power, although one is ordered to govern.

And to put the matter even more plainly, if a little company of pious Christian laymen were taken prisoners and carried away to a desert, and had not among them a priest consecrated by a bishop, and were there to agree to elect one of them, born in wedlock or not, and were to order him to baptise, to celebrate the mass, to absolve, and to preach, this man would as truly be a priest, as if all the bishops and all the popes had consecrated him. That is why in cases of necessity every man can baptise and absolve, which would not be possible if we were not all priests. This great grace and virtue of baptism and of the Christian estate they have quite destroyed and made us forget by their ecclesiastical law. In this way the Christians used to choose their bishops and priests out of the community; these being afterwards confirmed by other bishops, without the pomp that now prevails. So was it that St. Augustine, Ambrose, Cyprian, were bishops.

Since, then, the temporal power is baptised as we are, and has the same faith and Gospel, we must allow it to be priest and bishop, and account its office an office that is proper and useful to the Christian community. For whatever issues from baptism may boast that it has been consecrated priest, bishop, and pope, although it does not beseem every one to exercise these offices. For, since we are all priests alike, no man may put himself forward or take upon himself, without our consent and election, to do that which we have all alike power to do. For, if a thing is common to all, no man may take it to himself without the wish and command of the community. And if it should happen that a man were appointed to one of these offices and deposed for abuses, he would be just what he was before. Therefore a priest should be nothing in Christendom but a functionary; as long as he holds his office, he has precedence of others; if he is deprived of it, he is a peasant or a citizen like the rest. Therefore a priest is verily no longer a priest after deposition. But now they have invented *characteres indelebiles,* and pretend that a priest after deprivation still differs from a simple layman. They even imagine that a priest can never be anything but a priest—that is, that he can never become a layman. All this is nothing but mere talk and ordinance of human invention.

It follows, then, that between laymen and priests, princes and bishops, or, as they call it, between spiritual and temporal persons, the only real difference is one of office and function, and not of estate; for they are all of the same spiritual estate, true priests, bishops, and popes, though their functions are not the same—just as among priests and monks every man has not the same functions. And this, as I said above, St. Paul says (Rom. xii.; 1 Cor. xii.), and St. Peter (1 Peter ii.): "We, being many, are one body in Christ, and severally members one of another." Christ's body is not double or twofold, one temporal, the other spiritual. He is one Head, and He has one body.

We see, then, that just as those that we call spiritual, or priests, bishops, or popes, do not differ from other Christians in any other or higher degree but in that they are to be concerned with the word of God and the sacraments—that being their work and office —in the same way the temporal authorities hold the sword and the rod in their hands to punish the wicked and to protect the good. A cobbler, a smith, a peasant, every man, has the office and function of his calling, and yet all alike are consecrated priests and bishops, and every man should by his office or function be useful and beneficial to the rest, so that various kinds of work may all be united for the furtherance of body and soul, just as the members of the body all serve one another.

Now see what a Christian doctrine is this: that the temporal authority is not above the clergy, and may not punish it. This is as if one were to say the hand may not help, though the eye is in grievous suffering. Is it not unnatural, not to say unchristian, that one member may not help another, or guard it against harm? Nay, the nobler the member, the more the rest are bound to help it. Therefore I say, Forasmuch as the temporal power has been ordained by God for the punishment of the bad and the protection of the good, therefore we must let it do its duty throughout the whole Christian body, without respect of persons, whether it strike popes, bishops, priests, monks, nuns, or whoever it may be. If it were sufficient reason for fettering the temporal power that it is inferior among the offices of Christianity to the offices of priest or confessor, or to the spiritual estate—if this were so, then we ought to restrain tailors, cobblers, masons, carpenters, cooks, cellarmen, peasants, and all secular workmen, from providing the Pope or bishops, priests and monks, with shoes, clothes, houses, or victuals, or from paying them tithes. But if these laymen are allowed to do their work without restraint, what do the Romanist scribes mean by their laws? They mean that they withdraw themselves from the operation of temporal Christian power, simply in order that they may be free to do evil, and thus fulfil what St. Peter said: "There shall be false teachers among you, . . . and in covetousness shall they with feigned words make merchandise of you" (2 Peter ii. 1, etc.).

Therefore the temporal Christian power must exercise its office without let or hindrance, without considering whom it may strike, whether pope, or bishop, or priest: whoever is guilty, let him suffer for it.

Whatever the ecclesiastical law has said in opposition to this is merely the invention of Romanist arrogance. For this is what St. Paul says to all Christians: "Let every soul" (I presume including the popes) "be subject unto the higher powers; for they bear not the sword in vain: they serve the Lord therewith, for vengeance on evildoers and for praise to them that do well" (Rom. xiii. 1—4). Also St. Peter: "Submit yourselves to every ordinance of man for the Lord's sake, . . . for so is the will of God" (1 Peter ii. 13, 15). He has also foretold that men would come who should despise government (2 Peter ii.), as has come to pass through ecclesiastical law.

Now, I imagine, the first paper wall is overthrown, inasmuch as the temporal power has become a member of the Christian body; although its work relates to the body, yet does it belong to the spiritual estate. Therefore it must do its duty without let or hindrance upon all members of the whole body, to punish or urge, as guilt may deserve, or need may require, without respect of pope, bishops, or priests, let them threaten or excommunicate as they will. That is why a guilty priest is deprived of his priesthood before being given over to the secular arm; whereas this would not be right, if the secular sword had not authority over him already by Divine ordinance.

It is, indeed, past bearing that the spiritual law should esteem so highly the liberty, life, and property of the clergy, as if laymen were not as good spiritual Christians, or not equally members of the Church. Why should your body, life, goods, and honour be free, and not mine, seeing that we are equal as Christians, and have received alike baptism, faith, spirit, and all things? If a priest is killed, the country is laid under an interdict: why not also if a peasant is killed? Whence comes this great difference among equal Christians? Simply from human laws and inventions.

It can have been no good spirit, either, that devised these evasions and made sin to go unpunished. For if, as Christ and the Apostles bid us, it is our duty to oppose the evil one and all his works and words, and to drive him away as well as may be, how then should we remain quiet and be silent when the Pope and his followers are guilty of devilish works and words? Are we for the sake of men to allow the commandments and the truth of God to be defeated, which at our baptism we vowed to support with body and soul? Truly we should have to answer for all souls that would thus be abandoned and led astray.

Therefore it must have been the arch-devil himself who said, as we read in the ecclesiastical law, If the Pope were so perniciously wicked, as to be dragging souls in crowds to the devil, yet he could not be deposed. This is the accursed and devilish foundation on which they build at Rome, and think that the whole world is to be allowed to go to the devil rather than they should be opposed in their knavery. If a man were to escape punishment simply because he is above the rest, then no Christian might punish another, since Christ has commanded each of us to esteem himself the lowest and the humblest (Matt. xviii. 4; Luke ix. 48).

Where there is sin, there remains no avoiding the punishment, as St. Gregory says, We are all equal, but guilt makes one subject to another. Now let us see how they deal with Christendom. They arrogate to themselves immunities without any warrant from the Scriptures, out of their own wickedness, whereas God and the Apostles made them subject to the secular sword; so that we must fear that it is the work of antichrist, or a sign of his near approach.

THE SECOND WALL
That No One May Interpret the Scriptures But the Pope

The second wall is even more tottering and weak: that they alone pretend to be considered masters of the Scriptures; although they learn nothing of them all their life. They assume authority, and juggle before us with impudent words, saying that the Pope cannot err in matters of faith, whether he be evil or good, albeit they cannot prove it by a single letter. That is why the canon law contains so many heretical and unchristian, nay unnatural, laws; but of these we need not speak now. For whereas they imagine the Holy Ghost never leaves them, however unlearned and wicked they may be, they grow bold enough to decree whatever they like. But were this true, where were the need and use of the Holy Scriptures? Let us burn them, and content ourselves with the unlearned gentlemen at Rome, in whom the Holy Ghost dwells, who, however, can dwell in pious souls only. If I had not read it, I could never have believed that the devil should have put forth such follies at Rome and find a following.

But not to fight them with our own words, we will quote the Scriptures. St. Paul says, "If anything be revealed to another that sitteth by, let the first hold his peace" (1 Cor. xiv. 30). What would be the use of this commandment, if we were to believe him alone that teaches or has the highest seat? Christ Himself says, "And they shall be all taught of God" (St. John vi. 45). Thus it may come to pass that the Pope and his followers are wicked and not true Christians, and not being taught by God, have no true understanding, whereas a common man may have true understanding. Why should we then not follow him? Has not the Pope often erred? Who could help Christianity, in case the Pope errs, if we do not rather believe another who has the Scriptures for him?

Therefore it is a wickedly devised fable—and they cannot quote a single letter to confirm it—that it is for the Pope alone to interpret the Scriptures or to confirm the interpretation of them. They have assumed the authority of their own selves. And though they say that this authority was given to St. Peter when the keys were given to him, it is plain enough that the keys were not given to St. Peter alone, but to the whole community. Besides, the keys were not ordained for doctrine or authority, but for sin, to bind or loose; and what they claim besides this from the keys is mere invention. But what Christ said to St. Peter: "I have prayed for thee that thy faith fail not" (St. Luke xxii. 32), cannot relate to the Pope, inasmuch as the greater part of the Popes have been without faith, as they are themselves forced to acknowledge; nor did Christ pray for Peter alone, but for all the Apostles and all Christians, as He says, "Neither pray I for these alone, but for them also which shall believe on Me through their word" (St. John xvii.). Is not this plain enough?

Only consider the matter. They must needs acknowledge that there are pious Christians among us that have the true faith, spirit, understanding, word, and mind of Christ: why then should we reject their word and understanding, and follow a Pope who has neither understanding nor spirit? Surely this were to deny our whole faith and the Christian Church. Moreover, if the article of our faith is right, "I believe in the holy Christian Church," the Pope cannot alone be right; else we must say, 'I believe in the Pope of Rome,' and reduce the Christian Church to one man, which is a devilish and damnable heresy. Besides that, we are all priests, as I have said, and have all one faith, one Gospel, one Sacrament; how then should we not have the power of discerning and judging what is right or wrong in matters of faith? What becomes of St. Paul's words, "But he that is spiritual judgeth all things, yet he himself is judged of no man" (1 Cor. ii. 15), and also, "we having the same spirit of faith"? (2 Cor. iv. 13). Why then should we not perceive as well as an unbelieving Pope what agrees or disagrees with our faith?

By these and many other texts we should gain courage and freedom, and should not let the spirit of liberty (as St. Paul has it) be frightened away by the inventions of the Popes; we should boldly judge what they do and what they leave undone according to our own believing understanding of the Scriptures, and force them to follow the better understanding, and not their own. Did not Abraham in old days have to obey his Sarah, who was in stricter bondage to him than we are to any one on earth? Thus, too, Balaam's ass was wiser than the prophet. If God spoke by an ass against a prophet, why should He not speak by a pious man against the Pope? Besides, St. Paul withstood St. Peter as being in error (Gal. ii.). Therefore it behoves every Christian to aid the faith by understanding and defending it and by condemning all errors.

THE THIRD WALL
That No One May Call a Council But the Pope

The third wall falls of itself, as soon as the first two have fallen; for if the Pope acts contrary to the Scriptures, we are bound to stand by the Scriptures, to punish and to constrain him, according to Christ's commandment, "Moreover, if thy brother shall trespass against thee, go and tell him his fault between thee and him alone; if he shall hear thee, thou hast gained thy brother. But if he will not hear thee, then take with thee one or two more, that in the mouth of two or three witnesses every word may be established. And if he shall neglect to hear them, tell it unto the Church; but if he neglect to hear the Church, let him be unto thee as a heathen man and a publican" (Matt. xviii. 15—17). Here each member is commanded to take care for the other; much more then should we do this, if it is a ruling member of the community that does evil, which by its evil-doing causes great harm and offence to the others. If then I am to accuse him before the Church, I must collect the Church together. Moreover, they can show nothing in the Scriptures giving the Pope sole power to call and confirm councils; they have nothing but their own laws; but these hold good only so long as they are not injurious to Christianity and the laws of God. Therefore, if the Pope deserves punishment, these laws cease to bind us, since Christendom would suffer, if he were not punished by a council. Thus we read (Acts xv.) that the council of the Apostles was not called by St. Peter, but by all the Apostles and the elders. But if the right to call it had lain with St. Peter alone, it would not have been a Christian council, but a heretical *conciliabulum*. Moreover, the most celebrated council of all—that of Nicaea—was neither called nor confirmed by the Bishop of Rome, but by the Emperor Constantine; and after him many other emperors have done the same, and yet the councils called by them were accounted most Christian. But if the Pope alone had the power, they must all have been heretical. Moreover, if I consider the councils that the Pope has called, I do not find that they produced any notable results.

Therefore when need requires, and the Pope is a cause of offence to Christendom, in these cases whoever can best do so, as a faithful member of the whole body, must do what he can to procure a true free council. This no one can do so well as the temporal authorities, especially since they are fellow-Christians, fellow-priests, sharing one spirit and one power in all things, and since they should exercise the office that they have received from God without hindrance, whenever it is necessary and useful that it should be exercised. Would it not be most unnatural, if a fire were to break out in a city, and every one were to keep still and let it burn on and on, whatever might be burnt, simply because they had not the mayor's authority, or because the fire perchance broke out at the mayor's house? Is not every citizen bound in this case to rouse and call in the rest? How much more should this be done in the spiritual city of Christ, if a fire of offence breaks out, either at the Pope's government or wherever it may! The like happens if an enemy attacks a town. The first to rouse up the rest earns glory and thanks. Why then should not he earn glory that descries the coming of our enemies from hell and rouses and summons all Christians?

But as for their boasts of their authority, that no one must oppose it, this is idle talk. No one in Christendom has any authority to do harm, or to forbid others to prevent harm being done. There is no authority in the Church but for reformation. Therefore if the Pope wished to use his power to prevent the calling of a free council, so as to prevent the reformation of the Church, we must not respect him or his power; and if he should begin to excommunicate and fulminate, we must despise this as the doings of a madman, and, trusting in God, excommunicate and repel him as best we may. For this his usurped power is nothing; he does not possess it, and he is at once overthrown by a text from the Scriptures. For St. Paul says to the Corinthians "that God has given us authority for edification, and not for destruction" (2 Cor. x. 8). Who will set this text at nought? It is the power of the devil and of antichrist that prevents what would serve for the reformation of Christendom. Therefore we must not follow it, but oppose it with our body, our goods, and all that we have. And even if a miracle were to happen in favour of the Pope against the temporal power, or if some were to be stricken by a plague, as they sometimes boast has happened, all this is to be held as having been done by the devil in order to injure our faith in God, as was foretold by Christ: "There shall arise false Christs and false prophets, and shall show great signs and wonders, insomuch that, if it were possible, they shall deceive the very elect" (Matt. xxiv. 23); and St. Paul tells the Thessalonians that the coming of antichrist shall be "after the working of Satan with all power and signs and lying wonders" (2 Thess. ii. 9).

Therefore let us hold fast to this: that Christian power can do nothing against Christ, as St. Paul says, "For we can do nothing against Christ, but for Christ" (2 Cor. xiii. 8). But, if it does anything against Christ, it is the power of antichrist and the devil, even if it rained and hailed wonders and plagues. Wonders and plagues prove nothing, especially in these latter evil days, of which false wonders are foretold in all the Scriptures. Therefore we must hold fast to the words of God with an assured faith; then the devil will soon cease his wonders.

And now I hope the false, lying spectre will be laid with which the Romanists have long terrified and stupefied our consciences. And it will be seen that, like all the rest of us, they are subject to the temporal sword; that they have no authority to interpret the Scriptures by force without skill; and that they have no power to prevent a council, or to pledge it in accordance with their pleasure, or to bind it beforehand, and deprive it of its freedom; and that if they do this, they are verily of the fellowship of antichrist and the devil, and have nothing of Christ but the name.

OF THE MATTERS TO BE CONSIDERED
IN THE COUNCILS

Let us now consider the matters which should be treated in the councils, and with which Popes, cardinals, bishops, and all learned men should occupy themselves day and night, if they love Christ and His Church. But if they do not do so, the people at large and the temporal powers must do so, without considering the thunders of their excommunications. For an unjust excommunication is better than ten just absolutions, and an unjust absolution is worse than ten just excommunications. Therefore let us rouse ourselves, fellow-Germans, and fear God more than man, that we be not answerable for all the poor souls that are so miserably lost through the wicked, devilish government of the Romanists, and that the dominion of the devil should not grow day by day, if indeed this hellish government can grow any worse, which, for my part, I can neither conceive nor believe.

It is a distressing and terrible thing to see that the head of Christendom, who boasts of being the vicar of Christ and the successor of St. Peter, lives in a worldly pomp that no king or emperor can equal, so that in him that calls himself most holy and most spiritual there is more worldliness than in the world itself. He wears a triple crown, whereas the mightiest kings only wear one crown. If this resembles the poverty of Christ and St. Peter, it is a new sort of resemblance. They prate of its being heretical to object to this; nay, they will not even hear how unchristian and ungodly it is. But I think that if he should have to pray to God with tears, he would have to lay down his crowns; for God will not endure any arrogance. His office should be nothing else than to weep and pray constantly for Christendom and to be an example of all humility.

However this may be, this pomp is a stumbling-block, and the Pope, for the very salvation of his soul, ought to put it off, for St. Paul says, "Abstain from all appearance of evil" (1 Thess. v. 21), and again, "Provide things honest in the sight of all men (2 Cor. viii. 21). A simple mitre would be enough for the Pope: wisdom and sanctity should raise him above the rest; the crown of pride he should leave to antichrist, as his predecessors did some hundreds of years ago. They say, He is the ruler of the world. This is false; for Christ, whose vicegerent and vicar he claims to be, said to Pilate, "My kingdom is not of this world" (John xviii. 36). But no vicegerent can have a wider dominion than his Lord, nor is he a vicegerent of Christ in His glory, but of Christ crucified, as St. Paul says, "For I determined not to know anything among you save Jesus Christ, and Him crucified" (2 Cor. ii. 2), and "Let this mind be in you, which was also in Christ Jesus, who made Himself of no reputation, and took upon Himself the form of a servant" (Phil. ii. 5, 7). Again, "We preach Christ crucified" (1 Cor. i.). Now they make the Pope a vicegerent of Christ exalted in heaven, and some have let the devil rule them so thoroughly that they have maintained that the Pope is above the angels in heaven and has power over them, which is precisely the true work of the true antichrist.

What is the use in Christendom of the people called "cardinals"? I will tell you. In Italy and Germany there are many rich convents, endowments, fiefs, and benefices, and as the best way of getting these into the hands of Rome, they created cardinals, and gave them the sees, convents, and prelacies, and thus destroyed the service of God. That is why Italy is almost a desert now: the convents are destroyed, the sees consumed, the revenues of the prelacies and of all the churches drawn to Rome; towns are decayed, the country and the people ruined, because there is no more any worship of God or preaching; why? Because the cardinals must have all the wealth. No Turk could have thus desolated Italy and overthrown the worship of God.

Now that Italy is sucked dry, they come to Germany and begin very quietly; but if we look on quietly Germany will soon be brought into the same state as Italy. We have a few cardinals already. What the Romanists mean thereby the drunken Germans are not to see until they have lost everything—bishoprics, convents, benefices, fiefs, even to their last farthing. Antichrist must take the riches of the earth, as it is written (Dan. xi. 8, 39, 43). They begin by taking off the cream of the bishoprics, convents, and fiefs; and as they do not dare to destroy everything as they have done in Italy, they employ such holy cunning to join together ten or twenty prelacies, and take such a portion of each annually that the total amounts to a considerable sum. The priory of Würzburg gives one thousand guilders; those of Bamberg, Mayence, Treves, and others also contribute. In this way they collect one thousand or ten thousand guilders, in order that a cardinal may live at Rome in a state like that of a wealthy monarch.

After we have gained this, we will create thirty or forty cardinals on one day, and give one St. Michael's Mount, near Bamberg, and likewise the see of Würzburg, to which belong some rich benefices, until the churches and the cities are desolated; and then we shall say, We are the vicars of Christ, the shepherds of Christ's flocks; those mad, drunken Germans must submit to it. I advise, however, that there be made fewer cardinals, or that the Pope should have to support them out of his own purse. It would be amply sufficient if there were twelve, and if each of them had an annual income of one thousand guilders.

What has brought us Germans to such a pass that we have to suffer this robbery and this destruction of our property by the Pope? If the kingdom of France has resisted it, why do we Germans suffer ourselves to be fooled and deceived? It would be more endurable if they did nothing but rob us of our property; but they destroy the Church and deprive Christ's flock of their good shepherds, and overthrow the service and word of God. Even if there were no cardinals at all, the Church would not perish, for they do nothing for the good of Christendom; all they do is to traffic in and quarrel about prelacies and bishoprics, which any robber could do as well.

If we took away ninety-nine parts of the Pope's Court and only left one hundredth, it would still be large enough to answer questions on matters of belief. Now there is such a swarm of vermin at Rome, all called papal, that Babylon itself never saw the like. There are more than three thousand papal secretaries alone; but who shall count the other office-bearers, since there are so many offices that we can scarcely count them, and all waiting for German benefices, as wolves wait for a flock of sheep? I think Germany now pays more to the Pope than it formerly paid the emperors; nay, some think more than three hundred thousand guilders are sent from Germany to Rome every year, for nothing whatever; and in return we are scoffed at and put to shame. Do we still wonder why princes, noblemen, cities, foundations, convents, and people grow poor? We should rather wonder that we have anything left to eat.

Now that we have got well into our game, let us pause a while and show that the Germans are not such fools as not to perceive or understand this Romish trickery. I do not here complain that God's commandments and Christian justice are despised at Rome; for the state of things in Christendom, especially at Rome, is too bad for us to complain of such high matters. Nor do I even complain that no account is taken of natural or secular justice and reason. The mischief lies still deeper. I complain that they do not observe their own fabricated canon law, though this is in itself rather mere tyranny, avarice, and worldly pomp, than a law. This we shall now show.

Long ago the emperors and princes of Germany allowed the Pope to claim the *annates* from all German benefices; that is, half of the first year's income from every benefice. The object of this concession was that the Pope should collect a fund with all this money to fight against the Turks and infidels, and to protect Christendom, so that the nobility should not have to bear the burden of the struggle alone, and that the priests should also contribute. The popes have made such use of this good simple piety of the Germans that they have taken this money for more than one hundred years, and have now made of it a regular tax and duty; and not only have they accumulated nothing, but they have founded

out of it many posts and offices at Rome, which are paid by it
yearly, as out of a ground-rent.

Whenever there is any pretence of fighting the Turks, they send
out some commission for collecting money, and often send out indulgences under the same pretext of fighting the Turks. They
think we Germans will always remain such great and inveterate
fools that we will go on giving money to satisfy their unspeakable
greed, though we see plainly that neither *annates,* nor absolution
money, nor any other—not one farthing—goes against the Turks,
but all goes into the bottomless sack. They lie and deceive, form
and make covenants with us, of which they do not mean to keep
one jot. And all this is done in the holy name of Christ and
St. Peter.

This being so, the German nation, the bishops and princes,
should remember that they are Christians, and should defend the
people, who are committed to their government and protection in
temporal and spiritual affairs, from these ravenous wolves in
sheep's clothing, that profess to be shepherds and rulers; and since
the *annates* are so shamefully abused, and the covenants concerning
them not carried out, they should not suffer their lands and people
to be so piteously and unrighteously flayed and ruined; but by
an imperial or a national law they should either retain the *annates*
in the country, or abolish them altogether. For since they do not
keep to the covenants, they have no right to the *annates;* therefore bishops and princes are bound to punish this thievery and
robbery, or prevent it, as justice demands. And herein should they
assist and strengthen the Pope, who is perchance too weak to prevent this scandal by himself, or, if he wishes to protect or support
it, restrain and oppose him as a wolf and tyrant; for he has no
authority to do evil or to protect evil-doers. Even if it were proposed to collect any such treasure for use against the Turks, we
should be wise in future, and remember that the German nation
is more fitted to take charge of it than the Pope, seeing that the
German nation by itself is able to provide men enough, if the
money is forthcoming. This matter of the *annates* is like many other
Romish pretexts.

Moreover, the year has been divided among the Pope and the
ruling bishops and foundations in such wise that the Pope has
taken every other month—six in all—to give away the benefices that
fall in his month; in this way almost all the benefices are drawn

into the hands of Rome, and especially the best livings and dignities. And those that once fall into the hands of Rome never come out again, even if they never again fall vacant in the Pope's month. In this way the foundations come very short of their rights, and it is a downright robbery, the object of which is not to give up anything again. Therefore it is now high time to abolish the Pope's months and to take back again all that has thereby fallen into the hands of Rome. For all the princes and nobles should insist that the stolen property shall be returned, the thieves punished, and that those who abuse their powers shall be deprived of them. If the Pope can make a law on the day after his election by which he takes our benefices and livings to which he has no right, the Emperor Charles should so much the more have a right to issue a law for all Germany on the day after his coronation that in future no livings and benefices are to fall to Rome by virtue of the Pope's month, but that those that have so fallen are to be freed and taken from the Romish robbers. This right he possesses authoritatively by virtue of his temporal sword.

John Calvin

23

The Institutes of the Christian Religion

John Calvin (1509–1564), born and educated in France, was trained both as a churchman and as a lawyer. He was also skilled in classical studies, especially the Greek of the New Testament. Until 1532, indeed, Calvin seemed to have been more concerned with classical scholarship than with theology, but about that time he experienced a religious conversion that led him to reject the Catholic doctrine of justification by faith and works. Rather than try to reconcile his own beliefs with the professions of faith required by a position in the Church, Calvin publicly announced his beliefs, resigned his minor clerical offices, and became a leader of the French religious reformers. Under threat of persecution, he sought refuge in Basel, Switzerland. There he wrote and published *The Institutes of the Christian Religion* in 1536, in Latin, with a French translation appearing in 1540.

On a journey shortly after publication of the *Institutes,* Calvin stopped in Geneva, where many religious exiles had sought refuge, and was persuaded by the Protestant leaders of that city to remain. He became the leading minister of the community and, because of his influence in the pulpit, a powerful force in local politics as well. Calvin's opinion was sought on all matters that came before the city council: questions of law, maintenance of order, trade and manufacture, as well as matters of religious doctrine and church organization. But Calvin's influence soon became international, whereas Luther's tended to remain concentrated only on matters concerning Germany.

The *Institutes* is one of the major works of Christian theology, and its logical presentation of Protestant doctrine—based on a belief in the infallibility of the Bible—was of primary importance in the Reformation. The following selection includes Calvin's discussion of the authority of

From *The Institutes of the Christian Religion* by John Calvin, tr. John Allen. Published 1936, The Presbyterian Board of Christian Education. By permission. [I, 85–87, 314–16, II, 77–82, 170–74, 280–81, 730–31.]

the Scriptures, Chistian liberty, predestination, and the sacraments of the Church. As understood by many of his followers, Calvin's doctrines had a tendency toward perfectionism and demanded rigorous control over private and social behavior.

Before I proceed any further, it is proper to introduce some remarks on the authority of the Scripture, not only to prepare the mind to regard it with due reverence, but also to remove every doubt. For, when it is admitted to be a declaration of the word of God, no man can be so deplorably presumptuous, unless he be also destitute of common sense and of the common feelings of men, as to dare to derogate from the credit due to the speaker. But since we are not favoured with daily oracles from heaven, and since it is only in the Scriptures that the Lord hath been pleased to preserve his truth in perpetual remembrance, it obtains the same complete credit and authority with believers, when they are satisfied of its divine origin, as if they heard the very words pronounced by God himself. The subject, indeed, merits a diffuse discussion, and a most accurate examination. But the reader will pardon me, if I attend rather to what the design of this work admits, than to what the extensive nature of the present subject requires. But there has very generally prevailed a most pernicious error, that the Scriptures have only so much weight as is conceded to them by the suffrages of the Church; as though the eternal and inviolable truth of God depended on the arbitrary will of men. For thus, with great contempt of the Holy Spirit, they inquire, Who can assure us that God is the author of them? Who can with certainty affirm, that they have been preserved safe and uncorrupted to the present age? Who can persuade us that this book ought to be received with reverence, and that expunged from the sacred number, unless all these things were regulated by the decisions of the Church? It depends, therefore, (say they) on the determination of the Church, to decide both what reverence is due to the Scripture, and what books are to be comprised in its canon. Thus sacrilegious men, while they wish to introduce an unlimited tyranny, under the name of the Church, are totally unconcerned with what absurdities they embarrass themselves and others, provided they can extort from the ignorant this one admission, that the Church can do every thing. But, if this be true, what will be the condition of those wretched consciences, which are seeking a solid assurance of eternal life, if all the promises extant concerning it rest only on the judgment of men? Will the reception of such an answer cause their fluctuations to subside, and their terrors to vanish? Again, how will the impious ridicule our faith, and all men call it in question, if it be understood to possess only a precarious authority depending on the favour of men!

But such cavillers are completely refuted even by one word of the Apostle. He testifies that the Church is "built upon the foundation of the apostles and prophets." If the doctrine of the prophets and apostles be the foundation of the Church, it must have been certain, antecedently to the existence of the Church. Nor is there any foundation for this cavil, that though the Church derive its origin from the Scriptures, yet it remains doubtful what writings are to be ascribed to the prophets and apostles, unless it be determined by the Church. For if the Christian Church has been from the beginning founded on the writings of the prophets and the preaching of the apostles, wherever that doctrine is found, the approbation of it has certainly preceded the formation of the Church; since without it the Church itself had never existed. It is a very false notion, therefore, that the power of judging of the Scripture belongs to the Church, so as to make the certainty of it dependent on the Church's will. Wherefore, when the Church receives it, and seals it with her suffrage, she does not authenticate a thing otherwise dubious or controvertible; but, knowing it to be the truth of her God, performs a duty of piety, by treating it with immediate veneration. But, with regard to the question, How shall we be persuaded of its Divine original, unless we have recourse to the decree of the Church? this is just as if any one should inquire, How shall we learn to distinguish light from darkness, white from black, sweet from bitter? For the Scripture exhibits as clear evidence of its truth, as white and black things do of their colour, or sweet and bitter things of their taste.

. . .

I shall be content with citing a single passage, which, however, will resemble a very lucid mirror, in which we may behold at full length the image of our nature. For the Apostle, when he wishes to demolish the arrogance of mankind, does it by these testimonies: "There is none righteous, no, not one; there is none that understandeth, there is none that seeketh after God. They are all gone out of the way, they are together become unprofitable; there is none that doeth good, no, not one. Their throat is an open sepulchre; with their tongues they have used deceit; the poison of asps is under their lips; whose mouth is full of cursing and bitterness; their feet are swift to shed blood; destruction and misery are in their ways; there is no fear of God before their eyes." In this terrible manner he inveighs, not against particular individuals, but against all the posterity of Adam. He does not declaim against the depraved manners of one or another age, but accuses the perpetual corruption of our nature. For his design in that passage is not simply to rebuke men, in order that they may repent, but rather to teach us that all men are overwhelmed with an inevitable calamity, from which they can never emerge unless they are extricated by the mercy of God. As this could not be proved unless it were evinced by the ruin and destruction of our nature, he has adduced these testimonies, which demonstrate our nature to be totally ruined. Let this, then, be admitted, that men are such as they are here described, not only by corrupt habits, but also by a depravity of nature; for otherwise the reasoning of the Apostle could not be supported, "that there is no salvation for man but from the mercy of God; since in himself he is in a ruined and desperate condition." Here I shall not attempt to establish the application of the testimonies, to preclude the appearance of their being improperly introduced. I shall treat them just as if they had been originally uttered by Paul, and not quoted from the Prophets. He divests man first of righteousness, that is, integrity and purity, and then of understanding. Defect of understanding is proved by apostasy from God, the seeking of whom is the first step in the path of wisdom; but this loss must necessarily befall those who have revolted from God. He adds, that all have gone out of the way, and are become altogether corrupt, that there is not one that does good. Then he subjoins the flagitious crimes, with which they, who are once abandoned to iniquity, contaminate all the members of their bodies. Lastly, he declares them to be destitute of the fear of God, the rule by which all our steps ought to be directed. If these are the hereditary characters of mankind, in vain do we seek in our nature for any thing that is good. I grant, indeed, that all these crimes are not exhibited in every individual; yet it cannot be denied that this monster lurks in the hearts of all. For as the body, which already contains within itself the cause and matter of a disease, although it has yet no sensation of pain, cannot be said to enjoy good health, neither can the soul be esteemed healthy, while it is full of such moral maladies; although this similitude will not correspond in every particular; for in the body, however diseased, there remains the vigour of life; but the soul, immersed in this gulf of inquity, is not only the subject of vices, but totally destitute of every thing that is good.

A question, nearly the same as we have already answered, here presents itself to us again. For in all ages there have been some persons, who, from the mere dictates of nature, have devoted their whole lives to the pursuit of virtue. And though many errors might perhaps be discovered in their conduct, yet by their pursuit of virtue they afforded a proof, that there was some degree of purity in their nature. The value attached to virtues of such a description before God, we shall more fully discuss when we come to treat of the merits of works; yet it must be stated also in this place, so far as is necessary for the elucidation of the present subject. These examples, then, seem to teach us that we should not consider human nature to be totally corrupted; since, from its instinctive bias, some men have not only been eminent for noble actions, but have uniformly conducted themselves in a most virtuous manner through the whole course of their lives. But here we ought to remember, that amidst this corruption of nature there is some room for Divine grace, not to purify it, but internally to restrain its operations. For should the Lord permit the minds of all men to give up the reins to every lawless passion, there certainly would not be an individual in the world, whose actions would not evince all the crimes, for which Paul condemns human nature in general, to be most truly applicable to him. For can you except yourself from the number of those whose feet are swift to shed blood, whose hands are polluted with rapine and murder, whose throats are like open sepulchres, whose tongues are deceitful, whose lips are envenomed, whose works are useless, iniquitous, corrupt, and deadly, whose souls are estranged from God, the inmost recesses of whose hearts are full of pravity, whose eyes are insidiously employed, whose minds are elated with insolence—in a word, all whose powers are prepared for the commission of atrocious and innumerable crimes? If every soul be subject to all these monstrous vices, as the Apostle fearlessly pronounces, we clearly see what would be the consequence, if the Lord should suffer the human passions to go all the lengths to which they are inclined. There is no furious beast, that would be agitated with such ungovernable rage; there is no river, though ever so rapid and violent, that would overflow its boundaries with such impetuosity. In his elect, the Lord heals these maladies by a method which we shall hereafter describe. In others, he restrains them, only to prevent their ebullitions so far as he sees to be necessary for the preservation of the universe. Hence some by shame, and some by fear of the laws, are prevented from running into many kinds of pollutions, though they cannot in any great degree dissemble their impurity; others, because they think that a virtuous course of life is advantageous, entertain some languid desires after it, others go further, and display more than common excellence, that by their majesty they may confine the vulgar to their duty. Thus God by his providence restrains the perverseness of our nature from breaking out into external acts, but does not purify it within.

* * *

Christian liberty, according to my judgment, consists of three parts. The first part is, that the consciences of believers, when seeking an assurance of their justification before God, should raise themselves above the law, and forget all the righteousness of the law. For since the law, as we have elsewhere demonstrated, leaves no man righteous, either we must be excluded from all hope of justification, or it is necessary for us to be delivered from it, and that so completely as not to have any dependence on works. For he who imagines, that in order to obtain righteousness he must produce any works, however small, can fix no limit or boundary, but renders himself a debtor to the whole law. Avoiding, therefore, all mention of the law, and dismissing all thought of our own works, in reference to justification, we must embrace the Divine mercy alone, and turning our eyes from ourselves, fix them solely on Christ. For the question is, not how we can be righteous, but how, though unrighteous and unworthy, we can be considered as righteous. And the conscience that desires to attain any certainty respecting this, must give no admission to the law. Nor will this authorize any one to conclude, that the law is of no use to believers, whom it still continues to instruct and exhort, and stimulate to duty, although it has no place in their consciences before the tribunal of God. For these two things, being very different, require to be properly and carefully distinguished by us. The whole life of Christians ought to be an exercise of piety, since they are called to sanctification. It is the office of the law to remind them of their duty, and thereby to excite them to the pursuit of holiness and integrity. But when their consciences are solicitous how God may be propitiated, what answer they shall make, and on what they shall rest their confidence, if called to his tribunal, there must then be no consideration of the requisitions of the law, but Christ alone must be proposed for righteousness, who exceeds all the perfection of the law.　　　·　·　·

The second part of Christian liberty, which is dependent on the first, is, that their consciences do not observe the law, as being under any legal obligation; but that, being liberated from the yoke of the law, they yield a voluntary obedience to the will of God. For being possessed with perpetual terrors, as long as they remain under the dominion of the law, they will never engage with alacrity and promptitude in the service of God, unless they have previously received this liberty. We shall more easily and clearly discover the design of these things from an example. The precept of the law is, "Thou shalt love the Lord thy God with all thine heart, and with all thy soul, and with all thy might." That this command may be fulfilled, our soul must be previously divested of every other perception and thought, our heart must be freed from all desires, and our might must be collected and contracted to this one point. Those who, compared with others, have made a very considerable progress in the way of the Lord, are yet at an immense distance from this perfection. For though they love God with their soul, and with sincere affection of heart, yet they have still much of their heart and soul occupied by carnal desires, which retard their progress towards God. They do indeed press forward with strong exertions, but the flesh partly debilitates their strength, and partly attracts it to itself. What can they do in this case, when they perceive that they are so far from observing the law? They wish, they aspire, they endeavour, but they do nothing with the perfection that is required. If they advert to the law, they see that every work they attempt or meditate is accursed. Nor is there the least reason for any person to deceive himself, by concluding that an action is not necessarily altogether evil, because it is imperfect, and that therefore the good part of it is accepted by God. For the law, requiring perfect love, condemns all imperfection, unless its rigour be mitigated. Let him consider his work, therefore, which he wished to be thought partly good, and he will find that very work to be a transgression of the law, because it is imperfect.

See how all our works, if estimated according to the rigour of the law, are subject to its curse. How, then, could unhappy souls apply themselves with alacrity to any work for which they could expect to receive nothing but a curse? On the contrary, if they are liberated from the severe exaction of the law, or rather from the whole of its rigour, and hear God calling them with paternal gentleness, then with cheerfulness and prompt alacrity they will answer to his call and follow his guidance. In short, they who are bound by the yoke of the law, are like slaves who have certain daily tasks appointed by their masters. They think they have done nothing, and presume not to enter into the presence of their masters without having finished the work prescribed to them. But children, who are treated by their parents in a more liberal manner, hesitate not to present to them their imperfect, and in some respects faulty works, in confidence that their obedience and promptitude of mind will be accepted by them, though they have not performed all that they wished. Such children ought we to be, feeling a certain confidence that our services, however small, rude, and imperfect, will be approved by our most indulgent Father. This he also confirms to us by the Prophet: "I will spare them," saith he, "as a man spareth his own son that serveth him;" where it is evident, from the mention of *service,* that the word *spare* is used to denote indulgence, or an overlooking of faults. And we have great need of this confidence, without which all our endeavours will be vain; for God considers us as serving him in none of our works, but such as are truly done by us to his honour. But how can this be done amidst those terrors, where it is a matter of doubt whether our works offend God or honour him?

This is the reason why the author of the Epistle to the Hebrews refers to faith, and estimates only by faith, all the good works which are recorded of the holy patriarchs. On this liberty there is a remarkable passage in the Epistle to the Romans, where Paul reasons that sin ought not to have dominion over us, because we are not under the law, but under grace. For after he had exhorted believers, "Let not sin, therefore, reign in your mortal body; neither yield ye your members as instruments of unrighteousness; but yield yourselves unto God, as those that are alive from the dead, and your members as instruments of righteousness unto God,"—they might, on the contrary, object that they yet carried about with them the flesh full of inordinate desires, and that sin dwelt in them; but he adds the consolation furnished by their liberty from the law; as though he had said, Although you do not yet experience sin to be destroyed, and righteousness living in you in perfection, yet you have no cause for terror and dejection of mind, as if God were perpetually offended on account of your remaining sin; because by grace you are emancipated from the law, that your works may not be judged according to that rule. But those, who infer that we may commit sin because we are not under the law, may be assured that they have no concern with this liberty, the end of which is to animate us to virtue.

The third part of Christian liberty teaches us, that we are bound by no obligation before God respecting external things, which in themselves are indifferent; but that we may indifferently sometimes use, and at other times omit them. And the knowledge of this liberty also is very necessary for us; for without it we shall have no tranquillity of conscience, nor will there be any end of superstitions. Many in the present age think it a folly to raise any dispute concerning the free use of meats, of days, and of habits, and similar subjects, considering these things as frivolous and nugatory; but they are of greater importance than is generally believed. For when the conscience has once fallen into the snare, it enters a long and inextricable labyrinth, from which it is afterwards difficult to escape; if a man begin to doubt the lawfulness of using flax in sheets, shirts, handkerchiefs, napkins, and table cloths, neither will he be certain respecting hemp, and at last he will doubt of the lawfulness of using tow; for he will consider with himself whether he cannot eat without table cloths or napkins, whether he cannot do without handkerchiefs. If any one imagine delicate food to be unlawful, he will ere long have no tranquillity before God in eating brown bread and common viands, while he remembers that he might support his body with meat of a quality still inferior. If he hesitate respecting good wine, he will afterwards be unable with any peace of conscience to drink the most vapid; and at last he will not presume even to touch purer and sweeter water than others. In short, he will come to think it criminal to step over a twig that lies across his path. For this is the commencement of no trivial controversy; but the dispute is whether the use of certain things be agreeable to God, whose will ought to guide all our resolutions and all our actions. The necessary consequence is, that some are hurried by despair into a vortex of confusion, from which they see no way of escape; and some, despising God, and casting off all fear of him, make a way of ruin for themselves. For all, who are involved in such doubts, which way soever they turn their views, behold something offensive to their consciences presenting itself on every side.

.   .   .

The covenant of life not being equally preached to all, and among those to whom it is preached not always finding the same reception, this diversity discovers the wonderful depth of the Divine judgment. Nor is it to be doubted that this variety also follows, subject to the decision of God's eternal election. If it be evidently the result of the Divine will, that salvation is freely offered to some, and others are prevented from attaining it,—this immediately gives rise to important and difficult questions, which are incapable of any other explication, than by the establishment of pious minds in what ought to be received concerning election and predestination—a question, in the opinion of many, full of perplexity; for they consider nothing more unreasonable, than that, of the common mass of mankind, some should be predestinated to salvation, and others to destruction. But how unreasonably they perplex themselves will afterwards appear from the sequel of our discourse. Besides, the very obscurity which excites such dread, not only displays the utility of this doctrine, but shows it to be productive of the most delightful benefit. We shall never be clearly convinced as we ought to be, that our salvation flows from the fountain of God's free mercy, till we are acquainted with his eternal election, which illustrates the grace of God by this comparison, that he adopts not all promiscuously to the hope of salvation, but gives to some what he refuses to others. Ignorance of this principle evidently detracts from the Divine glory, and diminishes real humility. But according to Paul, what is so necessary to be known, never can be known, unless God, without any regard to works, chooses those whom he has decreed. "At this present time also, there is a remnant according to the election of grace. And if by grace, then it is no more of works; otherwise, grace is no more grace. But if it be of works, then it is no more grace; otherwise, work is no more work." If we need to be recalled to the origin of election, to prove that we obtain salvation from no other source than the mere goodness of God, they who desire to extinguish this principle, do all they can to obscure what ought to be magnificently and loudly celebrated, and to pluck up humility by the roots. In ascribing the salvation of the remnant of the people to the election of grace, Paul clearly testifies, that it is then only known that God saves whom he will of his mere good pleasure, and does not dispense a reward to which there can be no claim.

They who shut the gates to prevent any one from presuming to approach and taste this doctrine, do no less injury to man than to God; for nothing else will be sufficient to produce in us suitable humility, or to impress us with a due sense of our great obligations to God. Nor is there any other basis for solid confidence, even according to the authority of Christ, who, to deliver us from all fear, and render us invincible amidst so many dangers, snares, and deadly conflicts, promises to preserve in safety all whom the Father has committed to his care. Whence we infer, that they who know not themselves to be God's peculiar people will be tortured with continual anxiety; and therefore, that the interest of all believers, as well as their own, is very badly consulted by those who, blind to the three advantages we have remarked, would wholly remove the foundation of our salvation. And hence the Church rises to our view, which otherwise, as Bernard justly observes, could neither be discovered nor recognized among creatures, being in two respects wonderfully concealed in the bosom of a blessed predestination, and in the mass of a miserable damnation. But before I enter on the subject itself, I must address some preliminary observations to two sorts of persons. The discussion of predestination—a subject of itself rather intricate—is made very perplexed, and therefore dangerous, by human curiosity, which no barriers can restrain from wandering into forbidden labyrinths, and soaring beyond its sphere, as if determined to leave none of the Divine secrets unscrutinized or unexplored. As we see multitudes every where guilty of this arrogance and presumption, and among them some who are not censurable in other respects, it is proper to admonish them of the bounds of their duty on this subject. First, then, let them remember that when they inquire into predestination, they penetrate the inmost recesses of Divine wisdom, where the careless and confident intruder will obtain no satisfaction to his curiosity, but will enter a labyrinth from which he will find no way to depart. For it is unreasonable that man should scrutinize with impunity those things which the Lord has determined to be hidden in himself; and investigate, even from eternity, that sublimity of wisdom which God would have us to adore and not comprehend, to promote our admiration of his glory. The secrets of his will which he determined to reveal to us, he discovers in his word; and these are all that he foresaw would concern us or conduce to our advantage.

"We are come into the way of faith," says Augustine; "let us constantly pursue it. It conducts into the king's palace, in which are hidden all the treasures of wisdom and knowledge. For the Lord Christ himself envied not his great and most select disciples when he said, 'I have many things to say unto you, but ye cannot bear them now.' We must walk, we must improve, we must grow, that our hearts may be able to understand those things of which we are at present incapable. If the last day finds us improving, we shall then learn what we never could learn in the present state." If we only consider that the word of the Lord is the only way to lead us to an investigation of all that ought to be believed concerning him, and the only light to enlighten us to behold all that ought to be seen of him, this consideration will easily restrain and preserve us from all presumption. For we shall know that when we have exceeded the limits of the word, we shall get into a devious and darksome course, in which errors, slips, and falls will often be inevitable. Let us, then, in the first place, bear in mind, that to desire any other knowledge of predestination than what is unfolded in the word of God, indicates as great folly, as a wish to walk through unpassable roads, or to see in the dark. Nor let us be ashamed to be ignorant of some things relative to a subject in which there is a kind of learned ignorance. Rather let us abstain with cheerfulness from the pursuit of that knowledge, the affectation of which is foolish, dangerous, and even fatal. But if we are stimulated by the wantonness of intellect, we must oppose it with a reflection calculated to repress it, that as "it is not good to eat much honey, so for men to search their own glory, is not glory." For there is sufficient to deter us from that presumption, which can only precipitate us into ruin.

Others, desirous of remedying this evil, will have all mention of predestination to be as it were buried; they teach men to avoid every question concerning it as they would a precipice. Though their moderation is to be commended, in judging that mysteries ought to be handled with such great sobriety, yet, as they descend too low, they have little influence on the mind of man, which refuses to submit to unreasonable restraints. To observe, therefore, the legitimate boundary on this side also, we must recur to the word of the Lord, which affords a certain rule for the understanding. For the Scripture is the school of the Holy Spirit, in which, as nothing necessary and useful to be known is omitted, so nothing is taught which it is not beneficial to know. Whatever, therefore, is declared in the Scripture concerning predestination, we must be cautious not to withhold from believers, lest we appear either to defraud them of the favour of their God, or to reprove and censure the Holy Spirit for publishing what it would be useful by any means to suppress. Let us, I say, permit the Christian man to open his heart and his ears to all the discourses addressed to him by God, only with this moderation, that as soon as the Lord closes his sacred mouth, he shall also desist from further inquiry. This will be the best barrier of sobriety, if in learning we not only follow the leadings of God, but as soon as he ceases to teach, we give up our desire of learning. Nor is the danger they dread, sufficient to divert our attention from the oracles of God. It is a celebrated observation of Solomon, that "it is the glory of God to conceal a thing." But, as both piety and common sense suggest that this is not to be understood generally of every thing, we must seek for the proper distinction, lest we content ourselves with brutish ignorance under the pretext of modesty and sobriety. Now, this distinction is clearly expressed in a few words by Moses. "The secret things," he says, "belong unto the Lord our God; but those things which are revealed belong unto us, and to our children for ever, that we may do all the words of this law." For we see how he enforces on the people attention to the doctrine of the law only by the celestial decree, because it pleased God to promulgate it; and restrains the same people within those limits with this single reason, that it is not lawful for mortals to intrude into the secrets of God.

. . .

From what has been said, I conceive it must now be evident what judgment we ought to form respecting the Church, which is visible to our eyes, and falls under our knowledge. For we have remarked that the word *Church* is used in the sacred Scriptures in two senses. Sometimes, when they mention the Church, they intend that which is really such in the sight of God, into which none are received but those who by adoption and grace are the children of God, and by the sanctification of the Spirit are the true members of Christ. And then it comprehends not only the saints at any one time resident on earth, but all the elect who have lived from the beginning of the world. But the word *Church* is frequently used in the Scriptures to designate the whole multitude, dispersed all over the world, who profess to worship one God and Jesus Christ, who are initiated into his faith by baptism, who testify their unity in true doctrine and charity by a participation of the sacred supper, who consent to the word of the Lord, and preserve the ministry which Christ has instituted for the purpose of preaching it. In this Church are included many hypocrites, who have nothing of Christ but the name and appearance; many persons ambitious, avaricious, envious, slanderous, and dissolute in their lives, who are tolerated for a time, either because they cannot be convicted by a legitimate process, or because discipline is not always maintained with sufficient vigour. As it is necessary, therefore, to believe that Church, which is invisible to us, and known to God alone, so this Church, which is visible to men, we are commanded to honour, and to maintain communion with it.

As far, therefore, as was important for us to know it, the Lord has described it by certain marks and characters. It is the peculiar prerogative of God himself to "know them that are his," as we have already stated from Paul. And to guard against human presumption ever going to such an extreme, the experience of every day teaches us how very far his secret judgments transcend all our apprehensions. For those who seemed the most abandoned, and were generally considered past all hope, are recalled by his goodness into the right way; while some, who seemed to stand better than others, fall into perdition. "According to the secret predestination of God," therefore as Augustine observes, "there are many sheep without the pale of the Church, and many wolves within." For he knows and seals those who know not either him or themselves. Of those who externally bear his seal, his eyes alone can discern who are unfeignedly holy, and will persevere to the end; which is the completion of salvation. On the other hand, as he saw it to be in some measure requisite that we should know who ought to be considered as his children, he has in this respect accommodated himself to our capacity. And as it was not necessary that on this point we should have an assurance of faith, he has substituted in its place a judgment of charity, according to which we ought to acknowledge as members of the Church all those who by a confession of faith, an exemplary life, and a participation of the sacraments, profess the same God and Christ with ourselves. But the knowledge of the body itself being more necessary to our salvation, he has distinguished it by more clear and certain characters.

Hence the visible Church rises conspicuous to our view. For wherever we find the word of God purely preached and heard, and the sacraments administered according to the institution of Christ, there, it is not to be doubted, is a Church of God; for his promise can never deceive—"where two or three are gathered together in my name, there am I in the midst of them."

. . .

The readers may now see, collected into a brief summary, almost every thing that I have thought important to be known respecting these two sacraments; the use of which has been enjoined on the Christian Church from the commencement of the New Testament until the end of time; that is to say, baptism, to be a kind of entrance into the Church, and an initiatory profession of faith; and the Lord's supper, to be a continual nourishment, with which Christ spiritually feeds his family of believers. Wherefore, as there is but "one God, one Christ, one faith," one Church, the body of Christ, so there is only "one baptism" and that is never repeated; but the supper is frequently distributed, that those who have once been admitted into the Church, may understand that they are continually nourished by Christ. Beside these two, as no other sacrament has been instituted by God, so no other ought to be acknowledged by the Church of believers. For that it is not left to the will of man to institute new sacraments, will be easily understood if we remember what has already been very plainly stated—that sacraments are appointed by God for the purpose of instructing us respecting some promise of his, and assuring us of his good-will towards us; and if we also consider, that no one has been the coun-sellor of God, capable of affording us any certainty respecting his will, or furnishing us any assurance of his disposition towards us, what he chooses to give or to deny us. Hence it follows, that no one can institute a sign to be a testimony respecting any determina-tion or promise of his; he alone can furnish us a testimony respect-ing himself by giving a sign. I will express myself in terms more concise, and perhaps more homely, but more explicit—that there can be no sacrament unaccompanied with a promise of salvation. All mankind, collected in one assembly, can promise us nothing respecting our salvation. Therefore they can never institute or establish a sacrament.

Let the Christian Church, therefore, be content with these two, and not only neither admit nor acknowledge any other at present, but neither desire nor expect any other to the end of the world.

St. Ignatius of Loyola

24

The Spiritual Exercises

St. Ignatius of Loyola (1491–1556) was a soldier up to the age of thirty when, recovering from a severe wound, he experienced a spiritual turmoil that resulted in his abandoning the profession of arms and turning to the Church. His military training is evident, however, in the fact that he called himself the knight of Christ and that his followers used military discipline and terminology.

On his return from a pilgrimage to Jerusalem, Loyola undertook studies at Barcelona; later, while at the University of Paris, he gathered together a small group of fellow students who bound themselves by vows of poverty, chastity, and obedience, and offered their services to the pope for whatever missions he might wish to send them on. Meanwhile, the group continued to teach, offer spiritual counsel, and tend the sick and needy. Ordained a priest in 1537, Loyola persisted in his efforts on behalf of the association, which he named (in military terms) the Company of Jesus; later it became known as the Society of Jesus. He gained formal recognition of the order from the pope in 1540. The Jesuits, "the shock troops of the papacy," as they have been called, were instrumental in checking the further spread of Protestantism in the sixteenth century. The Jesuits' reliance on rigorous education as a way of preventing the growth of heresy encouraged a more systematic and widespread education for the clergy and laity than the Church had hitherto provided.

After 1540 Loyola was principally concerned with drawing up the *Constitutions* (in which he prescribed the duties of his followers in their missionary and educational work on behalf of the papacy) and *The Spiritual Exercises,* which he completed in 1548. The latter work reflects the spirit of Catholic Christianity and embodies the aims of the sixteenth-century Catholic Reformation. It reaffirms religious discipline for both the clergy and the laity and reasserts the role of the Church as the guardian

The Spiritual Exercises of St. Ignatius of Loyola, trans. Charles Seager (London: Dolman, 1847), 1–4, 15–17, 25–26, 173–85. (This is an adaptation.)

of man's spiritual welfare. The *Exercises* are so arranged that the reader can follow a regular pattern of devotion and spiritual instruction. The following selection illustrates this pattern and includes guides for the individual to attain harmony of thought and action with the Church.

ANNOTATIONS

The first annotation is that the term Spiritual Exercises means any method of examining one's own conscience—of meditating, contemplating, praying mentally and vocally, and, finally, of performing any other spiritual operation that will be described hereafter. Just as walking, traveling, and running are bodily exercises, preparing the soul to remove ill-ordered affections, and after their removal seeking and finding the will of God with respect to the ordering of one's own life and the salvation of one's soul, are Spiritual Exercises.

The second annotation is that he who gives another the order and method of meditating or contemplating should set forth faithfully the facts of the meditation or contemplation, going briefly through the chief points only and adding merely a very brief exposition, so that he who is about to meditate, having first understood the foundation of the historical truth, may afterwards go over the ground and reason by himself. The effect of this will be that when he finds anything which may furnish more elucidation or understanding (whether this be effected by his own reasoning or by divine illumination of the mind), he will experience a more delightful taste and more abundant fruit than if the matter itself had been set forth in greater detail by another. It is not the abundance of the knowledge, but the inner feeling which satisfies the soul.

The third annotation is that, whereas in all of the following Spiritual Exercises we use acts of the intellect when we reason, but of the will when we are affected, we must notice that . . . while we converse vocally or mentally with the Lord God or His Saints a greater reverence is required of us than when we use the intellect to attain understanding.

The fourth annotation is that the following Exercises are divided into four weeks: in the first week the consideration may be of sins; in the second, concerning the life of our Lord Jesus Christ up to His entrance into Jerusalem on Palm Sunday; in the third, concerning His Passion; in the fourth, concerning His Resurrection and Ascension. Then the three methods of prayer are added. Yet these weeks are not to be understood as if each should contain seven or eight days. It happens that some are slower, others more ready in attaining what they seek (for instance, in the first week contrition, grief, and tears for their sins), and that some are more or less agitated and tried by various spirits. It is, therefore, sometimes expedient that any week should be cut down or extended according to the nature of the subject matter. The Exercises customarily take up the space of thirty days or thereabouts.

The fifth annotation is that he who receives the Exercises is wonderfully assisted if, coming to them with a liberal mind, he offers his whole desire and will to his Creator, so that he may serve Him according to His will.

The sixth is that he who gives the Exercises, if he perceives that the one who receives them undergoes no spiritual commotions of the mind, such as sadness, nor any agitations of different spirits, ought carefully to inquire whether he performs the Exercises themselves at the prescribed times and in what way.

. . .

The seventh annotation is that he who has the care of the exercising of another, if he sees him affected by desolation or temptation, ought to take care not to show himself hard or austere, but rather mild and gentle. He should strengthen his mind to act vigorously in the future and, having laid open to him the wiles of our enemy, prepare him for the consolation to follow.

. . .

CERTAIN SPIRITUAL EXERCISES BY WHICH A MAN MAY BE ABLE TO CONQUER HIMSELF AND, WITH DECISIONS FREE FROM HARMFUL DESIRES, PLAN HIS LIFE

In the first place, in order that exercises of this kind benefit him who gives and him who receives, it must be presupposed that every pious Christian prefers to put a good interpretation on another's opinion or proposition than to condemn it. But if he can in no way defend it, let him inquire the speaker's meaning and, if he thinks erroneously, correct him kindly. If this does not suffice, all suitable means should be tried to render his meaning sound and safe from error.

Man was created that he might praise and reverence the Lord his God, and, serving Him, at length be saved. But the other things which are placed on the earth were created for man's sake, that they might assist him in pursuing the end of his creation; whence it follows that they are to be used or abstained from in proportion as they profit or hinder him in pursuing that end.

* * *

DAILY AND PARTICULAR EXAMINATION

The first time of examining is morning when a man ought, as soon as he rises from sleep, to decide to guard against some particular sin or fault which he desires to overcome.

The second is the afternoon in which he must ask of God the grace to be able to remember how often he has fallen into that particular sin or fault and to beware of it in the future. Then let him perform the first reexamination, asking account of his soul concerning the sin or fault already spoken of and, running through the parts of the day from the hour in which he rose down to the present, see how many times he has committed it.

* * *

The third time will be the evening in which, after the hour of supper, another review will have to be made by running through in like manner the several hours which have elapsed from the former examination to the present and in the same way remembering and enumerating the times he has been in fault.

* * *

A METHOD OF GENERAL EXAMINATION IN FIVE POINTS

The first point is to thank the Lord our God for the benefits we have received.

The second, to entreat grace for the knowledge and expulsion of our sins.

The third, to ask account of our soul concerning the sins committed during the present day, searching through the several hours from the time when we rose. Thoughts should come first, then words and deeds, in the same order laid down in the particular examination.

The fourth, to ask pardon concerning our faults.

The fifth, to propose amendment with the grace of God—and after all the above to say the Lord's Prayer.

THE USE OF GENERAL CONFESSION AND OF COMMUNION

From a general confession voluntarily made many advantages are gained, especially these three:

The first: although he who confesses at least once every year is not obliged to make a general confession, yet the person who does so gains much more merit on account of the greater sorrow he experiences for his sins and for the wickedness of his past life.

The second: having seen by means of the Spiritual Exercises much more clearly than before the nature and wickedness of sin, he will gain greater advantage and merit.

The third: it is reasonable to expect that he who has thus rightly confessed and is thus rightly disposed will be much better prepared for the reception of the Eucharist, which aids in the highest degree both the expulsion of sin and the preservation and increase of grace received.

This general confession will be best placed after the exercises of the first week.

SOME RULES TO BE OBSERVED
IN ORDER THAT WE MAY THINK
WITH THE ORTHODOX CHURCH

The first: removing all judgment of one's own, one must always keep one's mind prepared and ready to obey the true Spouse of Christ, our Holy Mother, which is the Orthodox, Catholic, and Hierarchical Church.

The second: it is proper to commend confession of sins to the priest and the receiving of the Eucharist at least once a year. It is more commendable to receive the same Sacrament every eighth day or at least once in each month.

. . .

The third: one should commend to Christ's faithful people the frequent and devout hearing of the holy rite or sacrifice of the Mass; also the saying of the Church hymns, the psalms, and long prayers, either within the Churches or outside; also to approve the hours marked out for the Divine Office, for prayers of whatever kind, and for the Canonical Hours.

The fourth: to praise vows . . . of chastity, poverty, and perpetual obedience, and other works of perfection and supererogation. Here it must be noted in passing that . . . a vow relates to those things which lead more closely to the perfection of Christian life. Concerning other things which lead away from perfection, for example . . . matrimony, a vow is never never to be made.

. . .

The sixth: to praise relics, the veneration and invocation of Saints, also the stations and pious pilgrimages, indulgences, jubilees, the candles lighted in the Churches, and other such aids to our piety and devotion.

The seventh: to praise abstinence and fasts, such as Lent, Ember Days, Vigils, Fridays, Saturdays, and others undertaken for the sake of devotion; also voluntary afflictions of one's self, which we call penances, not merely internal, but external.

The eighth: to praise the construction of Churches and their adornment; also images . . . to be venerated . . . for the sake of what they represent.

The ninth: to uphold all the precepts of the Church and not impugn them in any manner; but, on the contrary, to defend them promptly, with reasons drawn from all sources against those who do impugn them.

The tenth: we ought to be more ready to approve and praise the statutes, recommendations, and the lives of our superiors than to reprove them; because, although sometimes they may not be worthy of praise, to speak against them either in public preaching or in speaking before the common people would cause murmuring and scandals rather than good. Consequently, the people would be angry with their superiors, either spiritual or temporal. Therefore, as it is mischievous to speak ill to the people concerning superiors who are absent, so it may be useful to speak concerning their evil lives to those persons who can remedy them.

The eleventh: to put the highest value on sacred teaching, both the positive and the Scholastic, as they are commonly called. For as it was the object of the ancient holy Doctors, Jerome, Augustine, Gregory, and the like, to stir up men's minds to embrace the love and worship of God, so it is characteristic of Blessed Thomas, Bonaventure, the Master of the Sentences, and other more modern Divines, to lay down and define more exactly the things necessary for salvation, and, according to what was fitting for their own times and for posterity, helpful in the confutation of heresies. Moreover, the Doctors of this kind, being later in date, are not merely endowed with the understanding of the Sacred Scripture, and assisted by the writings of the old authors, but also with the influx of the Divine Light, and use, happily for the help of our salvation, the decisions of Councils, the decrees, and various constitutions of Holy Church.

The twelfth: we must avoid the comparison of men still living on the earth, however worthy of praise, with the Saints, saying this man is more learned than St. Augustine, that man is another St. Francis, he is equal to St. Paul in holiness, or in some virtue he is not inferior, and so on.

The thirteenth: finally, so as to be altogether of the same mind and in conformity with the Church herself, if she shall have defined anything to be black which to our eyes appears to be white, we ought in like manner to pronounce it to be black. For we must undoubtingly believe that the Spirit of our Lord Jesus Christ, and the Spirit of the Orthodox Church, His Spouse, by which Spirit we are governed and directed to salvation, is the same; and that the God who of old delivered the precepts of the Decalogue is the same who now instructs and governs the Hierarchical Church.

The fourteenth: it must also be borne in mind that although it be most true that no one is saved except he who is predestinated, we must speak with circumspection concerning this matter lest, perchance stretching too far the grace of predestination of God, we should seem to wish to shut out the force of free will and the merits of good works, or on the other hand, attributing to the latter more than belongs to them.

•   •   •

The fifteenth: for the like reason we should not speak on the subject of predestination frequently, and if it occur occasionally, we ought so to temper what we say as to give the people no occasion of erroneously saying: If my salvation or damnation is already determined regardless of whether I do ill or well, it cannot happen differently. It happens, consequently, that many neglect good works and other helps of salvation.

The sixteenth: it also happens not infrequently that from immoderate preaching and praise of faith without distinction or explanation being added, the people . . . become indifferent to good works which precede faith or follow it.

. . .

The seventeenth: nor must we push to such a point the preaching and inculcating of the grace of God that there may creep into the minds of the hearers the deadly error of denying the faculty of our free will. Concerning grace itself, therefore, it is allowable, indeed, to speak fully, God inspiring us, but no more than redounds to His more abundant glory, lest in our dangerous times both the use of free will and efficacy of good works be taken away.

The eighteenth: although it is in the highest degree praiseworthy and useful to serve God from pure love, yet the fear of the Divine Majesty is greatly to be commended. And not that fear only which we call filial, which is the most pious and holy, but also the other which is called servile, as being . . . very often necessary . . . because it helps much towards rising from mortal sin. After a person has emerged from this, he easily arrives at the filial fear which is altogether acceptable and agreeable to our Lord God because it is inseparably joined with Divine love.